THE
BOOMER'S
GUIDE
TO HIKING
IN MAINE

THE BOOMER'S GUIDE TO HIKING IN MAINE

FROM WOODSY RAMBLES
TO DOZENS OF PEAKS

PETER AND SUELLEN DIACONOFF

iUniverse, Inc.
Bloomington

The Boomer's Guide to Hiking in Maine
From Woodsy Rambles to Dozens of Peaks

iUniverse books may be ordered through booksellers or by contacting:

iUniverse
1663 Liberty Drive
Bloomington, IN 47403
www.iuniverse.com
1-800-Authors (1-800-288-4677)

ISBN: 978-1-4620-3557-1 (sc)
ISBN: 978-1-4620-3558-8 (ebk)

Printed in the United States of America

iUniverse rev. date: 09/29/2011

For our friend Milt Wright, fount of knowledge about all things Maine, including, first and foremost, Maine trails.

List of Illustrations

Cover: Lower Wright Trail
Easy hiking, or pup in a pocket, Mt. Blue ix
A Bigelow classic: Saddleback on the AT.................................. xvii
Katahdin in early morning light from Daicey Pond......................4
Moose crossing, a frequent sign on Maine highways....................8
Hikers at Puzzle overlook in Grafton Notch.............................11
Cozy sleeping at Carlo Col Shelter..14
Mooselookmeguntic Lake at Height of Land 16
Azalea, Asticou Garden 26
On the nearly bare top of Jockey Cap..34
A wildflower treasure..37
Ferns in the afternoon sunlight 40
Bridge and stream at Vaughan Woods 46
Onto Belgrade lakes and village from French Mountain.............52
Lower Dunn Falls 59
Jamies Pond and canoeists..64
"Your Move," Maine's most famous outhouse,
    Piazza/Saddleback trail 71
Mountain flower...82
The Featherbed on South Ridge of Cadillac, Acadia...................86
Loon at Great Pond, Acadia...96
"Where's the trail?" After a big rain on Hogback......................102
Typical Maine creek...106
"How do I even start hiking?" First challenge of the
    Mahoosuc Notch 112
Frolicking dogs at Northern Headwaters 115
Sabbath Day Pond lean-to on a snowy Christmas Day...............120
A famous Maine State Scenic Byway: Grafton Notch.................128
Nesowadnehunk Stream, Little and Big Niagara Falls,
    Baxter State Park...135
Winter at Schoodic Peninsula 137

Acadia and St. Sauveur Loop, Acadia 144
Fall trail on the way to Bald and Speckled Mountains 148
Kayaker along the shoreline at Great Pond, Acadia 152
Moose antlers for sale by the side of the road 157
Views onto pond and ocean,
      Bowl and Champlain Trail, Acadia.....................................163
A typical Maine trail 171
Stratton Pond outlet crossing in the Bigelows 177
Lone Mountain trail sign...183
Climbing to the top of Rumford Whitecap 188
Success Mountain overlook with a view to New Hampshire 192
From Doubletop a view of Katahdin 200
Descending Sargent and Penobscot 201
AT trail sign and cautionary language, entry to
      Hundred-Mile Wilderness...205
On top of the world at Goose Eye in the Mahoosucs 212
Waterfall at Gulf Hagas...217
From Little Jackson to Lake Webb 222
Rock cairn at the South Summit of Puzzle Mountain...................226
From Speck Pond toward the Mahoosuc Notch 229
Moose bones on the White Cap trail,
      Hundred-Mile Wilderness...235
View onto Onawa Lake from Barren Ledges 242
Climbing Katahdin on the Hunt Spur 243
"Is this hiking or rock climbing?" Hunt Spur, Katahdin.............244
From West to Avery in the Bigelow range 248
Lower Deer Hill area, Evans Notch...251
The Authors at Katahdin summit 265

Easy hiking, or pup in a pocket, Mt. Blue

Contents

Preface xv
Introduction 1

What's Great About Hiking in Maine 1
Youngsters, Geeezers, and Maine Trails 2
Notes to New Hikers and Some Old Hands 6
The Joys of GPS 12
A Couple More Words By Way of Suggestion 14
The Terrain Ahead, or What to Expect from This Book 16
The Mental Rewards of Hiking 18

Section I, Boomer Rating One:
   Starting Out—Woodsy Rambles 21
Overview
Featured Hikes
   Acadia Gardens, Northeast Harbor 23
   B-52 Crash Site on Elephant Mountain, outside Greenville 27
   The Gott Pasture Preserve Loop, Wayne 30
   Jockey Cap, Fryeburg 32
   Monument Hill, Leeds 35
   "The Mountain," Belgrade Lakes 39
   Parker Pond Headland Preserve Fayette 41
   Porter Preserve, Barters Island, Boothbay 43
   Vaughan Woods, Hallowell and Farmingdale 45

Section II, Boomer Rating Two:
   Knocking Off a Few Under Five Miles 49
Overview
Featured Hikes
   A Belgrade Lakes Threesome 51
   Bog Brook Trail, Waldo County 55

Dunn Notch and Falls, Andover 57
Fernald's Neck Preserve, Camden area 60
Jamies Pond, Hallowell/Manchester 63
Oven's Mouth Preserve Trails,
    Boothbay Regional Land Trust 66
Piazza Rock, Bigelows 69
Spruce Mountain to Pleasant Mountain Road,
    Georges Highland Path 73

Section III, Boomer Rating Three:
    Upping the Ante 77
Overview
Featured Hikes
Bald Rock Mountain, Lincolnville 80
Cadillac South Ridge Trail, Acadia, East Side 83
Cranberry Pond, Bigelows 87
Frye Mountain, Georges Highland Path 91
Great Pond Trail to Great Notch,
    Western Mountains, Acadia 94
Hogback Mountain, Georges Highland Path 98
Lower Lone Mountain, Phillips/Madrid 103
Lower Wright Trail to the North-South Junction,
    Mahoosuc Range 107
Mahoosuc Notch Trail, Mahoosuc Range 110
Northern Headwaters Trail, Waldo County 113
Sabbath Day Pond, Rangeley 117
Schoodic Mountain, East Franklin 121
Surplus Pond, Andover 124
Table Rock, Grafton Notch State Park 127
Valley Trail to Beech Mountain, Acadia, West Side 130
Others
Borestone, Elliotsville 133
Little Harbor Brook/Amphitheater Trail, Acadia 133
Little and Big Niagara Falls, Baxter State Park 134
Little Wilson Falls, Monson 135
Schoodic Peninsula, Acadia 136
Sentinel Mountain, Baxter State Park 137

    Thuya Gardens to Jordan Pond House, Acadia......................138

Section IV, Boomer Rating Four:
    Earning Your Spurs!...140
Overview
Featured Hikes
    Acadia and St. Sauveur Loop, Acadia, West Side.................143
    Bald and Speckled Mountains, Oxford County 147
    Bernard Mountain by Great Pond Trail, Acadia, West Side..150
    Big Moose Mountain, near Greenville..................................155
    Blueberry Mountain, Weld...159
    The Bowl and Champlain Mountain, Acadia, East Side.......162
    Burnt Mountain, Sugarloaf area...166
    Caribou Mountain, Evans Notch...169
    Eyebrow Trail, Grafton Notch State Park 173
    Horns Pond Trail, Bigelows...176
    Lone Mountain, Phillips/Madrid..181
    Rumford Whitecap Mountain, Rumford Center....................185
    Success Mountain, Grafton Notch/Mahoosuc Range 190
    Tumbledown Mountain, Weld...194
    Others
    Bemis Mountain and Bemis Stream Trails............................197
    Chairback 198
    Doubletop, Baxter State Park...198
    North Crocker...199
    Sargent and Penobscot, Acadia 199

Section V, Boomer Rating Five:
    Super Strenuous, Super Rewards.....................................203
Overview
Featured Hikes
    Baldpate Peaks, Grafton Notch State Park...........................206
    Carlo-Goose Eye Loop, Mahoosucs.....................................210
    Gulf Hagas Trail, Katahdin Ironworks/
        Brownville Junction..214
    Little Jackson Mountain, Weld...221
    Puzzle Mountain, South Summit, Grafton Notch 224

Speck Pond Trail, Mahoosucs 228
White Cap Mountain, Katahdin Ironworks,
    Hundred-Mile Wilderness..231
Wright-Goose Eye Loop, Mahoosucs 236
Others
Barren Mountain, Hundred-Mile Wilderness........................241
Fire Wardens Trail, Bigelows 242
Katahdin, by the Hunt Trail, Baxter State Park.....................243
Old Speck, Grafton Notch. 245
Saddleback, Rangeley 246
Sugarloaf, Carrabassett Valley 246
West and Avery, Bigelows...247

Bonus
    Good Places for Snowshoe Jaunts 250

Appendices...252
Map Recommendations...253
A Lighthearted Glossary..256
Hike Locator..260

About the Authors...264

Preface

Why a hiking book for Boomers? Because you are a unique and dynamic demographic in the United States, some 79 million strong, and because one size *doesn't* fit all. Which is why this couple of Boomers—*post*-Boomers, if truth be told—have written this book expressly for you.

As you will discover, our approach combines humor, practical advice, and a frank assessment of the physical challenges you'll meet on the trail. Whether it's ambling down a forest path, clambering over jumbles of rocks, fording streams, or ascending rungs and ladders, we give you the real skinny, so that you'll know exactly what to expect once you hit the trail.

Unlike other hiking books that don't specifically have you in mind, we've organized this one according to Boomer Ratings, from One to Five, corresponding to the level of challenge involved and the physical output required. You'll find dozens of choices, whether for lazy days when a woodsy ramble fits the bill, or longer hikes of the middling variety, or still others that take on some of Maine's tough trails. With over fifty Featured Hikes and nearly twenty others, there is something for everyone, regardless of your physical prowess. We'd wager that even the armchair hiker will enjoy perusing this book for its special features, including a potpourri of amusing anecdotes, many concerning critters from moose to mice, plus the segments on trail lore, Maine history and figures from the past, and a generous sprinkling of helpful advice about alleviating cranky knees and unhappy feet.

The opening pages of the book set the stage, telling you what's great about hiking in Maine, offering some rumination on "youngsters, geezers, and Maine trails," and presenting a lot of useful information for both novice and experienced hikers. From the beginning, our objective is to engage you in way that is informal and lighthearted

Peter and Suellen Diaconoff

before getting down to brass tacks and describing for you each individual hike. If you want to check out our hiking credentials, turn to The Authors section at the end of the book.

We look forward to meeting you on the trail!

Suellen and Peter

A Bigelow classic: Saddleback on the AT

Introduction

What's Great About Hiking in Maine

After nearly an hour of climbing through the woods on what seemed like a relentless ladder straight up a rock mountain of boulders, we emerged in an alpine environment and were at once awestruck by the beauty of the magical landscape far below: acre after acre of forest in autumnal splendor, set off by a long, gleaming ribbon of lake. As the late-afternoon clouds moved over the forested panorama, the light changed from golden to pink to lavender, as though the scene were part of an artist's palette. Alone on the mountaintop, except for a couple of sentinel Canadian Jays looking for a handout, and with the magnificent view spread out some 3000 feet below, we agreed that this was the glory of hiking in Maine, more than worth all the sweat it had taken, even on a cool fall day, to reach the summit. What a view! What a scenic state!

Of course it's no secret in the broader hiking community that Maine is considered one of the premier hiking states in the nation. With its 6000 lakes, 32,000 miles of rivers, 5000 miles of coastline, and 17 million acres of forestland, the state has a trail for every level of walker or hiker and for every season of the year. While many trails deliver precisely the combination of challenge and reward described above, there are also plenty of rambles with less daunting challenges that still offer lots of beauty and pleasure. It's our intention to bring to you that full spectrum.

You can, for instance, meander along forest pathways and through the nineteenth-century elegance of Vaughan Woods, near Augusta, to admire the imposing stone bridges built to last for generations; or take a gentle stroll alongside glistening Great Pond on the "quiet side" of Acadia National Park, perhaps even catching the glimpse of a loon; or set forth on the short but stiff climb up rock ledge, near beautiful Height of Land, to access the fairytale woods leading to Sabbath Day Pond.

If you're committed to more challenge, you can opt for a whole range of trails and reap even more impressive rewards by hiking the steep but highly scenic trail up to the bald summit of Rumford Whitecap, through its "islands" of wind-sculpted dwarf trees surrounded by patches of blueberries. Or you could head for the real backcountry wilderness of another White Cap, this one on the Appalachian Trail, where you'll hike up a rough creek bed to the sprawling top that looks out, from one side of the summit, onto layer after layer of mountains, including Maine's fabled mile-high mountain, Katahdin, the terminus for the 2175-mile Appalachian Trail.

In fact, this state has it all. Whether you're a Boomer, a post-Boomer, or a twenty-something, there is a hike for everyone. We know, because we've not only hit the trails throughout the "Pine Tree State" but have hiked and backpacked throughout the U.S. as well as in Canada, Europe, and North Africa.

Still, truthfulness compels us to confide that we didn't *begin* hiking in earnest until we reached the "advanced" ages of 56 and 63 respectively. Well over a decade later, hiking remains our passion. Which means that we're here to tell you that it's never too late to *start* hiking, nor are you ever too old to *continue* hiking.

Youngsters, Geeezers, and Maine Trails

All of us middle-aged and Boomer-plus hikers have had the experience on the trail of meeting the young and excessively fleet of foot. For instance, we recall a young man, equipped with only a water bottle in hand, who passed us on the Goose Eye trail not once but twice on a single day, having already negotiated the infamous Mahoosuc Notch, toward which he was heading for a second time—now from the opposite direction, since it had been "so much fun on the first go-through."

And then there was a young couple in Acadia National Park who were eagerly picking off hikes full of scary ladders and dramatic drop-offs, having completed both the Beehive and the Precipice Trail that morning, and who asked *us*, of all people, if we knew of any other similar trails.

Or the Maine sisters who trekked the entire AT, from Katahdin to Springer Mountain in Georgia, and then turned around and repeated it—all barefoot!

So, the youngsters are pretty amazing, to be sure.

Who's a Baby Boomer?

According to the U.S. Census Bureau:

- Baby Boomers are those born between 1946 and 1964.
- On January 1, 2011, there were 79 million Baby Boomers.
- The heart of the Baby Boom generation falls in the age category 45 to 54 years of age.
- Starting in January 2011, more than 10,000 Baby Boomers a day will turn 65.

Like we said, there are a *bunch* of us!

At the same time, if you're a Boomer or post-Boomer, you certainly will not be without your peer group on the trails of Maine. Perhaps it is the traditional rigors of living in this northern outpost that leads to an unusually high percentage of hardy, older types. Like 89-year old Bruce who still bushwhacks on Lone Mountain, or 83-year old Al, amazingly game for the steep haul of more than 2300 feet up Puzzle Mountain in western Maine. And our hiking mentor, Milt, who for nearly six decades made a point of climbing Katahdin every summer, often by the tough Cathedral Trail, and frequently choosing to "trip the light fantastic" across the Knife Edge, that alarmingly steep and narrow spine that crosses the sky with precipitous drops on either side.

And, of course, there are all those thru-hikers on the AT, many of whom are middle-aged, upper-middle-aged, or even hoarier yet, who, day after day, stalwartly rack up the miles, walking through state after state, in blazing heat and pouring rain. By the time they hit Maine, they're on the last leg of the journey, seasoned to the rigors of the trail, and like "Wyoming" (his AT trail moniker), have become akin to the "old man of the mountain," ready, even, to defend the original trail builders for charting the route *straight up* every single mountain, rather than by those "sissy" switchbacks found on trails in the American West.

Katahdin in early morning light from Daicey Pond

We also remember with admiration the two craggy codgers from Tennessee whom we encountered on a steep and forbidding stretch of the AT Horns Pond Trail. As we wearily sought a way to haul ourselves up yet another boulder face, one of them cheerily bent down to lend a strong hand, commenting, "Back where we come from, we don't call this hiking, but rock climbing." Then, spry as an old rooster, he descended the face, all the while trading jocular barbs with his hiking companion.

The point, then, is that there are a lot of older hikers out in the woods. And, in fact, we would argue, there are real pluses to being an older hiker. To begin with, you're not expected to break any records or keep up with the 20-somethings, or even with the 40-somethings. In fact, you have carte blanche to be slow or take a lot of "breathers," and you'll probably still win plaudits, or, at least, reluctant admiration from younger trailblazers. After all, you're doing something they don't expect people your age to be engaging in.

Speed-hiking is not, of course, our goal, and we doubt that it's yours. We do, however, clock ourselves, and if in the past, we could pretty well count on two miles an hour or faster, even with an altitude gain of 1000+ feet, now we don't make those kinds of assumptions. On level, groomed surface, we can make three miles an hour, but on many Maine trails, with their roots and rocks and all manner of impediments, plus altitude gain, we're more likely to be a lot slower. On really steep sections, like the boulder "ladder" up to the West Peak of Baldpate, we may make not much more than a mile an hour.

Spectacular Boomers
- In 1998, at the age of 79, Earl V. Shaffer completed his third thru-hike on the 2175-mile AT. Fifty years earlier, he had been the first to report a thru-hike of the entire AT Trail from Georgia to Maine, a feat he repeated in 1965 in reverse direction.
- In 2004, Lee Barry completed his second thru-hike at the age of 81.
- The oldest female thru-hiker, Emma Gatewood, better known as "Grandma Gatewood," mother of 11 children and grandmother of 23, was 67 when she first hiked the Trail in 1955. Two years later, she completed her second thru-hike and became the first person to complete the Trail three times when she finished a section-hike at age 76.

We also know that the same hike may require differing amounts of time on different occasions, depending on weather and various conditions. For us, the Saddleback trail (11.6 round-trip miles, 2900-foot altitude gain) is a case in point. The first time we did it, we spent an ungodly ten hours and were completely bushed. The next year we did it in seven and-a-half hours. And *four years later*, in seven and three-quarters hours. The question is why did it take so long when we were five years younger? Was it particularly hot, were the bugs out, did we not bring enough food, did we fritter away time in the beginning, or were our biorhythms "off"? It could be any of these factors, but the point is that *age* was not the primary culprit.

Naturally, everyone's physical challenges are different, so of course you will listen to your own body. But age, in and of itself, is not the determining factor about whether and how long into your upper years you hike. You may change your goals and expectations a little, but as long as you can still drive to the trailhead, you're likely to be able to find a trail that both challenges and rewards your efforts.

Notes to New Hikers and Some Old Hands

Given that our aim is to make this book useful especially to the Boomer crowd, who may or may not have a few cranky joints or other minor ailments, we're going to offer a few ideas about things that have worked for us. Of course, if you're an old hand at hiking, you have permission to skip this part.

To begin with, we highly recommend hiking poles. Properly extended, they transfer the intensity of impact from your knees to your arms, and anyone who has even the tiniest bit of trouble with their knees will profit enormously. In fact, we cannot imagine hiking without poles and actually feel "lost" without them. Not only do they ease the blow to your knee joints, especially on the downhill sections, when your legs are already a little mushy from the work of getting to the summit, but they also enhance balance and let you test the quality of a step or movement *before* you launch off to discover that the stone is unstable enough to pitch you into the creek or that the log is rotted through. More times than we can say, our hiking poles have kept us upright, preventing a fall, or, at least, a wet pair of britches.

If you've got a couple of arthritic joints like we do, it's also very helpful to take one capsule of ibuprofen before beginning a hike and then another one following it. Too much ibuprofen may be hard on your stomach, of course, but if you're not hiking every day, these two pills can really work wonders, reducing pain and swollen joints.

Keeping Young

A *New Yorker* cartoon quips that "70 is the new 50," while others comment that "60 is the new 40." However that may be, there are lots of us who ask why pay a monthly premium to belong to a gym, when we can get our exercise and stay fit, *for free*, in the woods?

Weight-bearing joints, of course, are affected not only by the amount of weight you are carrying on your body but by the possibly more amenable-to-reduction weight you've got in your backpack. Let's consider the latter, because there is a trade-off between being prepared and weighing yourself down unnecessarily.

In the last few years and well within the decade in which we have been hiking, there has been a real boom in hiking light. Jokes abound about backpackers on multi-day excursions cutting down weight by sawing their toothbrush in half, and, as readers of *Backpacker* know, there is a running debate as to the benefits of hiking in tennis shoes or low-hikers, whether to carry a backpack or just a fanny pack, or maybe even just a water bottle.

Day-hikers don't need to go extremes, but we know from experience that you do need to be prepared for anything in the mountains. We've been caught without adequate batteries for our headlamps on a trail after dark; without raingear on a 12+ mile hike in sleet and freezing rain; without extra food and snacks when our energy has been seriously depleted; short of water on a hot day; minus an adequate map to lead us out of the forest by an alternative path.—Not all at once, of course!

But because we want to underscore the point, we'll risk appearing dimwitted and admit to careless oversights that greatly increased our chances of getting hurt or dehydrated or hypothermic. Let our mea culpa be a warning to heed!

Mercifully, despite our carelessness, the mountain gods let us off, and now we go prepared, regardless of how sunny the day starts out, how few hours we intend to spend on the trail, how many times we've done the trail before, or how un-thirsty we are upon launching a hike. We also carry a GPS and a cell phone, although we know perfectly well in terms of the latter that you cannot rely on getting an adequate signal everywhere, nor should you count on your cell phone to get you out of a pickle. Every hiker is responsible for keeping him or herself safe and "unlost." At the very least, a rescue mission could cost you a bundle and should definitely be saved for real emergencies.

Moose crossing, a frequent sign on Maine highways

In addition to raingear—always, always, always—and back-up batteries for headlamps and GPS, and an emergency safety kit with bandages, ointments and a primer on essential first-aid, each of us also carries an emergency foil sleeping sack, should one of us become injured or we come upon another hiker who needs to spend the night in the forest. Before we started carrying this emergency blanket, we did once encounter a party with an older woman who, incredibly enough, had recently undergone heart surgery, and who had still decided to make one of the hardest climbs in Maine, to Mt. Katahdin. Apparently she and her family had underestimated both the terrain and the demands of an all-day hike on her, so that, on the return trip, still three miles from base camp and in the fading light of late afternoon, she was too exhausted to continue. Had we had our emergency sacks, we could at least have been Good Samaritans.

And how else do we go prepared now? Let's start with what we wear and then make a trip through both our pockets and our two daypacks.

In regard to hiking clothes, we take a conservative approach. We both wear long pants, which protect the legs against scrapes, mud, sunburn, and insect bites. We prefer shirts that wick away moisture and dry quickly when you remove a sweaty backpack for lunch or a rest stop. We've had varying luck with shirts treated with Buzz-Off (a built-in insect repellent) but always back it up with Ben's (a bottled insect repellent); and we try to remember the sunblock lotion to protect against the risk of skin cancer from the sun's rays. We value pants and shirts that offer spacious pockets, especially the baffle kind on shirts that close with a Velcro strip, or zipped cargo pockets on pants, so that valuables don't get lost.

The distaff member of our couple uses one front shirt pocket for gum and hard candies and the other for camera filters, map, pen, and notepad. Into one pants pocket go sweatband and handkerchief, and in the other, tissues and plastic baggies for leave-no-trace potty stops. She carries a plastic water bottle with iced tea in a side holster, slings a camera around her neck, and has a telephoto lens in the other side holster, looking and feeling something like a "six-shooter hiker."

As the principal navigator, the male half of our couple carries the GPS unit, compass, and binoculars so that we stay found and capable of seeing over long distances. He wears a canteen around his neck, keeps a filled 48-oz. water canister in his pack, and often carries a water-filtering system, as well.

In his shirt pocket are plastic-sandwich bags of Gorp for instant energy (our own combo of M & M's, peanuts, hard mints, and dried fruit). At the bottom of his pack is an emergency space blanket, which actually has wilderness survival tips printed on it, in case we have "to build a shelter with fallen timber," treat each other for hypothermia, construct "a solar still to collect water" (!), or administer emergency first aid. The least fear-inspiring of the tips relates to countering a panic attack in an emergency by recalling the four letters of the word, S-T-O-P: stop, think, observe, and plan. Good advice.

Happy Feet

Since feet are key to a successful hike, you really do want to keep them happy.

- Start with well-fitted boots, even if it takes months to find a suitable pair.
- You might consider using Super-Feet™ inner soles, specially molded for your feet.
- Count on a break-in period of 50 miles of hiking. If the boots aren't broken in by then, return them to the store. One store that is particularly good about returns is L.L. Bean in Freeport, Maine.
- If you have sweaty feet or are bothered by blisters:
  - o Stop immediately when you feel a hot-spot developing. It may only be wrinkle in your sock, but more likely it's an incipient blister.
  - o We've found the product Second-Skin to be excellent, working both on hot-spots and actually helping to cure an open blister. Use the scissors on your tiny penknife to fit the bandage. Extra adhesive is not a bad idea, either.
  - o Take a footbath in a cool creek during lunch or on a break.
  - o Change your socks at lunch.
  - o During breaks, remove your boots and massage and wriggle your toes and feet.
  - o Some people use sock liners, but for folks with sweaty feet, they may only add to the problem. Give them a try and decide for yourself.

A further inventory of his pack reveals: 20 feet of nylon rope, several feet of cord, a Leatherman all-purpose tool or Swiss army knife, headlamp, whistle, lighter, mini-flashlight, and extra batteries.

Hikers at Puzzle overlook in Grafton Notch

Also, a first-aid kit with arm splint, gauze and absorbent cotton, adhesive bandages, antiseptic towel and ointment, moleskin, and even a 3" x 5" 60-page first-aid manual, in case we want to compare what it says with the Wilderness Survival tips. It would be a good idea, every year, to take a look at the contents of this first-aid kit to ascertain whether anything has either dried up or gotten too degraded to be useful.

And what else is in his pack? Rain jacket, insect repellent, a ballpoint pen and notebook, cell phone, wallet, car keys, and lunch. Oh yes, and this might seem eccentric, but it is actually very useful: a bicyclist's rear vision mirror that clips onto the temple of his sunglasses, so that he can see how far behind his partner is lagging and/or prevent being surprised by a stealth hiker quietly gaining on him.

Her daypack includes lunch, an extra pair of socks (if the first pair gets wet or too sweaty) and handkerchief, sock liners (to be used against blisters), two shoelaces (a broken shoe lace could be a real problem, plus enough shoelaces tied together might allow you to rappel down a mountainside, no?), a Gore-Tex rain slicker, glove liners (hardly weigh a thing and have saved her from frozen hands more than once), headlamp, and spare batteries.

She also carries a large empty trash bag. It's an emergency cover for her camera if it rains, but it gets most utility as a seat cover to protect her hiking pants from log pitch or from turning green when sitting on moss. Plus, of course, it can serve its intended purpose as a container for trash, if something really big needs to be carried out. (A bear, perhaps?)

A further peek in her pack also reveals extra ibuprofen and aspirin in empty film containers, as well as miscellaneous camera equipment, a package of lamb's wool for padding squished toes, matches (for that fire she hopes not to have to start), lip balm, a few anti-diarrhea pills, a small flashlight, a little bottle of hand sanitizer, a small flattened roll of toilet paper, a net face-cover for when the black flies are really horrible, Second-Skin blister pads, penknife (with scissors), Ben's insect repellent, sunscreen, a whistle, and a few hidden-away five dollar bills, in case she needs to bribe someone to get her off the mountain.

That sounds like a lot of stuff, but every last thing has been essential at one point or another. And it really doesn't weigh all that much. Each to his or her own, however.

Needless to say, if you keep your daypack packed, you're always ready to go, after just filling up the water bottles and throwing in a lunch. Otherwise, if you have to repack each time, you're bound to forget some key item.

The Joys of GPS

The hikes presented in this guidebook are trail hikes, not bushwhacks. However, even on established routes, wrong turns can be taken, landmarks misunderstood, your directional sense become confused—in short, you can get lost. Extraneous factors, such as sudden changes in the weather or shortness of remaining daylight, can increase the likelihood of mistakes. With that in mind, we strongly urge you always to hike with at least the basic tools of way-finding assistance—compass and map—and know how to use them. If you do only that, you will greatly reduce your chances of getting lost.

On Maps

√   Everyone wants a map that is both accurate and legible, and we also really like those that give clear-to-read contour lines and divide the trail into segments for which the mileage is calculated. If you're already pooped, it's useful to know how many vertical feet remain, or how close you are to the summit.

√   In the preliminary information to each hike in this book, we indicate our recommended map.

√   An entire list of the maps we use for hiking in Maine is found in the appendices at the end of this volume.

But there is another, higher-tech "helper" that could lend some extra insurance. It's the handy electronic gadget known as a GPS (Global Positioning System) receiver, often referred to simply as a "GPS." The system itself is based on a grid designed to identify any location on earth, as well as earth-orbiting satellites, which, by sharing signals with your GPS receiver, permit you to know the coordinates of your position with accuracy to a few meters or yards. You can also "mark" locations, known as waypoints, along the route, thus making it possible to find your way back to these waypoints—for instance, a parked vehicle or a campsite. If you carry the appropriate map based on the same grid system for which the GPS receiver is set, you can pinpoint your location on the map, in effect making it impossible to be truly "lost." Plus, in case of need and in areas where cell phone contact is possible, you can report your location by the GPS coordinates, whether or not you have a map.

GPS receivers can be bought at affordable prices, and books or CDs describing their use, as well as general compass and map usage, can be found in outfitting catalogs such as those of L.L. Bean and others. Do note that a GPS is not the same thing as the much more expensive PLB (Personal Locator Beacon; see Glossary), which you probably don't need.

Cozy sleeping at Carlo Col Shelter

A Couple More Words By Way of Suggestion

One of the best things we did when we started hiking was to keep a log. At first, it was just to name the hike, the number of miles, and how long it took, as well as a few notations of agreement or disagreement in reaction to descriptions by the hiking guide we had used. But later on, we found real pleasure—to say nothing of usefulness in recording more details: our reactions to the trail, the weather, the extent to which insects were or were not an aggravation, sometimes physical ailments (usually battered feet, a "crick" in the side, or occasionally a minor fall if an errant branch had caught us unaware), and sometimes, too, a few words about unusual people we talked to on the trail.

In fact, the trail is a great place for brief encounters, and because most of the trails we frequent are not really popular, these fleeting meetings become more imprinted on the memory. We've always found it fun to meet AT thru-hikers, who, by and large, are an admirable lot: independent, resourceful, tough, and disciplined.

Of course, there are a few who are real characters, too, like "Peanut Pete"—his trail moniker—who was so worried that he was physically vanishing as a result of the daily exertions required to be a thru-hiker that, without the slightest provocation, he would raise his shirt to reveal his ribs, asserting to his embarrassed interlocutor that to forefend against his own physical disappearance he was consuming a half jar of peanut butter a day. Little surprise, then, that his reputation amongst AT hikers had spread up and down the trail, and literally every hiker we met on the Chairback trail that day had either already encountered him or knew about him. His fame was such that three weeks later, when we were hiking the Wright-Goose Eye trail, we met a young, blonde AT thru-hiker who knew of and was trying to avoid him!

Other hikers are less colorful, but many are really interesting people doing unusual things. Like the couple in their 50s from North Carolina, whom we met on Little Bigelow Mountain, who were heading toward Katahdin to finish the AT, having done what few parents can claim: hiked to the graduation of their youngest child—since, as they explained, Dartmouth College is just off the AT. It amused us to think that they must have been the only parents that year to show up for the graduation ceremony carrying backpacks and hiking sticks.

Another time, we met a solo thru-hiker on the Bemis trail, a middle-aged nurse, who told us that every night she strung a hammock between two trees in the woods rather than bunch up in a crowded lean-to with possibly boisterous youngsters. Later, in discussing her intrepid spirit in hitting the trail alone, we also reflected that given the frequency with which tiny, four-legged forest creatures are known to run over sleeping bags at night in the lean-tos, she had the right idea about that hammock . . . .

For us, this post-hike writing has provided a lot of pleasure in reading back over the pages, laughing and recalling both the people we met and our own feats and follies. It's a kind of a combined hiking and personal history that will still cause a chuckle when we *do* have to be confined to our rocking chairs. One word to the wise, however, especially if you keep a hiking log over a long span of years: don't fudge on hiking times. Because if you shave off time to make you look more brilliant now, think about how you're going to feel when you make the comparison five years later!

Mooselookmeguntic Lake at Height of Land

The Terrain Ahead, or What to Expect from This Book

Since we've pounded trails throughout the state, you can expect to find hikes from the western mountains, to Central Maine, to the coastal areas, to the Monson and Moosehead area, and Baxter State Park. Rarely do we include a hike that exceeds ten miles, and most are well below, though, of course, even a shorter hike over rough terrain may become an all-day affair. Nor do we offer any technical climbs or really scary ones—no Knife Edges or Precipice trails for us; we're too acrophobic for that.

But just because we are targeting people in the Boomer category doesn't mean that we've eliminated hikes that a lot of people, regardless of age, would consider tough. After all, we reason, if we've done these hikes, in our fifth, sixth, and seventh decades, we think that you can, too. If we're willing to crawl up a rock face on all fours, we think that you may be, too. If we're not daunted by the need to pull ourselves up by tree roots and to scoot on our bottoms down a steep drop to the trail below, we assume that you won't find it beneath your dignity, either. At least we hope not. You're out in the woods, after all!

But we do put such hikes in a special category—Boomer Ratings Four or Five—and give a realistic assessment of the difficulties, so that you'll be forewarned. Just as important, and this is key, we give you our "take" on the special nature of the rewards for your efforts—whether it's that splendid sense of isolation on a mountain top with unbeatable views, or the peacefulness of a quiet, cathedral-like forest, or the discovery of the unexpected, like the tombstones of pioneers, in a clearing off the side of the trail.

And, since we have grouped the hikes by difficulty, you still have a sizeable choice of outings in the first three Boomer Ratings, which don't require you to make like a mountain goat in any way. How about the fairly level trail of Lower Lone Mountain with its picturesque creeks and miniature tinkling waterfalls? Or beautiful Parker Pond Headland Preserve, whose needled path wanders through groves of ancient hemlocks? Or the exceptional Valley Trail in Acadia, built along a route that beautifully uses nature's bounty of rock and ledge? Or then again, the Northern Headwaters Trail, which takes you back into the days of early Maine farming history, when you come upon half-hidden root cellars and remnants of old, still-standing stonewalls? The spectrum of hikes in Maine is enormous. And the choice is yours!

Since this book is arranged by a rating based on the quality of physical challenge, rather than geographic location, we start each section with an *Overview* to the Boomer Rating in question, telling you how we determined the ranking—primarily based on quality of the footpath, mileage, and vertical gain—and give a brief introduction of the variety of hikes within this rating.

The real "meat" of the book is found in the *Featured Hikes* of each section. For each of these hikes, described in full, we give you all the practical information (driving directions, total round-trip distance, vertical rise, and any other miscellaneous information, like the availability of water and privies) that is useful to know. In addition, each hike is prefaced by a rubric we call *The challenge and the payoff* with our brief assessment of the physical output required and the reward obtained. Occasionally we intersperse tips on dealing with "kvetchy" knees or joints, blisters and bunions, rain and muck, or nasty insects. And we often tell you about encounters, human and otherwise, that we had on the trail, in order to give you the flavor of our experience and, hopefully, amuse or beguile you into wanting to create or recall your own.

Throughout the book, we include numerous textboxes in which we dish out interesting facts or tidbits from Maine history, samples of hiking lore or statistics about trail building and maintenance, anecdotes about encounters with wildlife, and so forth. The objective of this feature is to provide curious, useful, or entertaining information about the great Maine outdoors, and to give either you or the armchair hiker some conversational gambits for the hiker's "cocktail circuit."

Finally, Boomer Ratings Three, Four, and Five end with a section, called *Other Hikes*, which likewise belong in the same Boomer Rating, and for which we include briefer descriptions.

At the end of the book are three Appendices, including one on *Map Recommendations*, a lighthearted but also useful *Glossary for the New Hiker*, and a *Hike Locator* to identify which hikes are in the same area.

The Mental Rewards of Hiking

It's often been said that while hiking wearies the physical body, it renews the spirit. But it also can do something else. Veteran long-distance hiker Colin Fletcher, author of *The Man Who Walked Through Time*, once alluded to the idea that hiking can activate both sides of the brain; the cognitive left side of the brain works out the mileage, directions, and judgment issues, while the right-hand side—the intuitive, creative side—is stimulated by the sights and sounds and feel of nature: that carpet of wildflowers on a trailside bank, the delightful music of the burbling brook rippling over mossy stones, the sensual imprint of the sun on your back, or the ethereal vision of light rays filtered through a grand forest.

All of which means that hiking is a kind of three-for-one deal, simultaneously nourishing mind, body, and spirit. And available for free in the great outdoors.

Now, let's hit the trails!

A caveat

√   While we have hiked and re-hiked many of the routes in this book in recent years, errors may have crept in, so it's lucky there are two of us to share the blame for silly mistakes or poor handwriting.

√   But human error aside, we also know that trails, to say nothing of conditions on the trail, often change rapidly, so that certain markers—a forked tree, a dwelling, even signposts—may be absent when you go. The situation is particularly fluid with Land Trusts where trails may be in development mode.

√   Trails can also be re-routed for various reasons, such as change in ownership, or to reduce environmental impact, or because of an earth slide or damaging ice storm.

√   So, please be aware that while we've described what we found, things on the trail can change rapidly, due to nature or man.

Overview
Boomer Rating One:
Starting Out—Woodsy Rambles

Okay, so you're hooked on wanting to enjoy the outdoors, but either don't have much time or maybe are just getting back into shape after a hiatus from hiking. We've got just what you're looking for in our Boomer Rating One suggestions, because these rambles require neither many miles nor, for the most part, any real altitude challenge. All of our recommendations are less than two miles round-trip, and many are shorter, though some of them could be extended. Their footpaths will have some up and down, or a single steep section, but we deem them all to be fully "doable" by most folks. Still, we would take along a single hiking stick, but that's primarily because we take a hiking stick even when we take a walk around the neighborhood.

Most of our selections are like "Sunday walks in the woods," offering all the pleasures that such a title suggests. Plus, for a very modest amount of energy, you'll have the opportunity to see the state and explore several regions from the coast to the western mountains, and the broader Capitol area, all the while learning some history and getting outdoors.

As we have continued to discover, Maine has many hidden gems that even longtime residents may not know about. For example, it wasn't until we had lived in the state for nearly two decades that our friend Milt took us to one of these hidden treasures—beautiful Vaughan Woods with its picturesque stone bridges and waterfalls, evoking an earlier age of elegance.

Garden areas, also, will make for especially nice walks, from the small and very worthwhile Thuya Gardens in Northeast Harbor on Mount Desert Island, to the nearby, peaceful Asticou Azalea Garden.

For woodlands serenity, you could take the short and well laid out path near a pond at Gott Pasture in Wayne, or the short but steep path up French Mountain in Belgrade Lakes, or the lovely Parker Pond trail in Fayette. On the coast, at Boothbay Harbor, visit the Porter Preserve, where you can choose from among a variety of fine walks on a sixteen-acre preserve.

If you're up for a little huffing and puffing, take the short and charming walk to the summit of Jockey Cap, in western Maine, on the outskirts of Fryeburg. You'll be amazed at what a simple one-quarter mile trail can lead to: splendid 360-degree views including famous peaks in both New Hampshire and Maine.

Should you want a more dramatic trip, visit the hallowed ground of the B-52 crash at Elephant Mountain, outside Greenville, where, spread throughout the forest, you will see the fuselage and pieces of the plane, and get shivers as you find yourself recreating the scene of that fateful winter day more than four decades ago.

What is wonderful about Maine is that while there are many fine strolls that have been around for a long, long time, every year seems to bring more new possibilities, particularly on Maine's nearly one hundred Land Trusts. So, do check the Web to discover what may be near you. And in the meantime, we offer a handful of delightful recommendations to get you started. To the outdoors!

Acadia Gardens: Thuya Garden at Asticou Terraces and Asticou Azalea Garden
(Northeast Harbor)

Everyone loves a garden, and you couldn't ask for two better ones than these gems on Mount Desert Island, bound to delight and charm with their serene beauty.

Driving directions (DeLorme 16, 3-C): Coming from Ellsworth on ME-3, get on ME-198/102 after leaving Thompson Island. Continue for about 5 miles, and at Somesville, take a left on ME-198/3 in the direction of Northeast Harbor for 5.5 miles, then make a left turn for ME-3 (ME-198 goes to Northeast Harbor, which is not your destination). Asticou Azalea Garden is on the east side of this corner, with parking on the west side. For Thuya, after making the left turn to follow ME-3, you will very shortly pass the Asticou Inn. Just past the Inn, on the right side of the road there is a small parking lot for eight to ten cars. If you want to drive up to Thuya, continue past the parking area and take the first sharp left onto Thuya Drive, a single-lane road.

Total round-trip distance: roughly 0.3 mile for Thuya; 0.25 mile for Asticou Azalea Garden.

Vertical rise: 160 ft. for Thuya; none for Asticou Azalea Garden.

Miscellaneous: Both gardens are owned and maintained by the Mount Desert Land and Garden Preserve and a committee of volunteers, so visitors are asked to make a donation at both spots. There is a restroom at Thuya behind the lodge.

Map: Acadia NP, East Side, I-10.

Description of Thuya Garden. When you leave your car on ME-3, cross the road on the pedestrian walkway, and immediately begin climbing the broad rock stairway that steeply wends its way up the terraces of the cliffside. On one landing, you will see a carved granite dedication to Joseph Henry Curtis, the landscape architect from Boston, who was a long-time summer resident of Northeast

Harbor and whose rustic lodge next to the garden can be visited before or after seeing the garden.

> **The challenge and the payoff.** The climb up the steep stone steps of the terraces, and continuing on the raked pebble pathway to Thuya Garden, may leave you a bit breathless, but look upon this as great exercise taken not in a gym but on a path graced by bowery beauty. Only if you're with your aged and infirm aunt should you wimp out and drive to the top (see Driving directions). After your initial short hike to the top, the terraced gardens present no challenge. As for Asticou Azalea Garden, you park your car in a small nearby lot and then proceed along pleasantly meandering pathways past pools and, in the late spring, flowering trees and bushes.

During your climb up the pathway, you come upon occasional log or stone benches, strategically placed in case you need to catch your breath. At other spots, there are vistas back down to the boat harbor, including one from an overlook with a covered structure in an Asian-like style. Ferns and wildflowers grace the forested pathway and lichens and mosses drape themselves on the rocks and tree trunks.

> **On Thuya**
> The name Thuya comes from the Latin name for the area's abundant white cedars, *Thuya Occidentalis*. Many of the original planted cedars were brought from the personal estate of Beatrix Jones Ferrand (1872-1959), one of America's foremost landscape designers. Worried that after her demise her garden would not be properly maintained, Beatrix had the garden "de-constructed" in order to put the plants into properly responsible hands. This was how Charles Savage was able to acquire not only azaleas, rhododendrons, and the great Alberta spruce located in the garden, but also the cedars.

As you reach the top, the path turns to a terraced and pebble pathway (design-raked daily by the gardeners), and soon you come to the Curtis Lodge on the left. Just beyond is the beautifully carved wooden gate through which you enter the gardens. Originally designed by Curtis, the gardens were greatly expanded by Charles K. Savage, with financial support from John D. Rockefeller, Jr. Laid out in levels on a plot of lawn, the garden is based on a classic "T" axis, with mixed borders of old-fashioned annual and perennial country flowers—goatsbeard and stocks, zinnias, dahlias, and plume poppies, monkshood and snapdragons. There are also day lilies, delphiniums, heliotropes, and various kinds of carpet bedding, plus a small built pond that reflects both flowers and a giant concrete vase.

What makes the garden so pleasing is that there is nothing pretentious or overly manicured about it. Instead, the visitor is invited to meditate on the quiet beauty of the place, perhaps from the cushioned settees in a pavilion at one end of the garden. When you are ready, return to the Lodge, whose interior of dark wood and turn-of-the-century artifacts offers a rustic elegance that carries you to another age. Do take a moment to admire the outstanding horticultural library.

If you are interested in exploring beyond the garden, you can access a forest trail through an exit at the back of the garden. For a description, see *Other Hikes* in Boomer Rating Three.

Sculpting the Land
Hats off to early landscape architects who faced special challenges in designing gardens that could thrive on the rocky coast of Maine and in the harsh winter climate. In fact, from the 1860s to the 1940s, at least thirteen professional landscape designers worked on about 150 private estates in Mount Desert Island, putting Maine at the forefront nationally in formal landscape architecture.

Description of Asticou Azalea Gardens. About 0.5 mile from Thuya Garden is a second beauty spot, this one modeled on the serenity of a Japanese garden. Built in 1956-1957, this little park bears the vision and talents of Charles Savage. The gardens are laid out in a fluid design, allowing you to stroll on paths past stone bridges and a stream that leads to a pool where ducks placidly swim. Along the way, you'll see ancient stone lanterns peeking out from among the plantings and more than twenty varieties of azaleas.

This is a garden for all seasons. For the explosion of color for which the garden is famous, visit during prime color season, from mid-May to mid-June. Later, in the summer, the mood changes, with soothing and peaceful greens dominating, while in the fall, color will return in all its autumnal glory. In the winter, under a light blanket of snow, a walk in the garden becomes a very peaceful experience.

Azalea, Asticou Garden

B-52 Crash Site on Elephant Mountain

On Elephant Mountain outside Greenville, take a dramatic walk through the woods to the site of a plane crash that occurred in the dead of winter, 1963, and represents a bit of Cold War history.

Driving directions (DeLorme 41, D-3, C-4): There are two ways to reach the site. By the first, after leaving the center of Greenville, you turn right on Scammon Road, following it east for 10 or 11 miles, as marked by the yellow B-52 site markers. For the second approach, which involves less driving on the gravel road—only 6.9 miles—take the Lily Bay Road 6.5 miles north from Greenville, turning right when you see the first yellow sign for the B-52 crash site. By either approach, follow the yellow signs, turning, when there is a choice, always in the direction pointed by a sign showing the nose of a bomber plane. Park along the road, and enter the woods marked by the yellow B-52 site sign and by another larger sign with its dedication to peace.

Total round-trip distance: about 0.25 mile or more, depending upon how much exploring you do.

Vertical rise: a few feet.

Beginning altitude: 1701 feet.

Miscellaneous: No restroom or water.

Map: DeLorme (see above).

The challenge and the payoff. The single small challenge of this outing is the drive on the remote road to the site of the crash (see Driving directions). At the same time, this very remoteness lends drama to the story of the B-52 crash into the side of Elephant Mountain, which killed all but two of its nine-man crew. As you walk up the path and see parts of the plane still strewn throughout the forest, you will find yourself recreating the human tragedy and be drawn to agreeing with the unofficial caretaker of the crash site that this is, indeed, sacred ground.

Description. At the point of entry to the footpath, a Strategic Air Command sign reads, "Peace is Our Profession." As you begin walking up the footpath to view the primary site of the wreckage, you soon see twisted pieces of aluminum from the plane scattered on either side of the trail and off other short trails leading back in the woods. Immediately, you are struck by the horror of a plane crash in a remote and forested landscape.

Even worse, the crash occurred in the dead of winter, January 14, 1963, involving a nine-man crew on board a B-52 on a training mission in the early development of low-level radar avoidance. As the ill-fated warplane came over the area, only one hundred feet above the ground, the outside temperature registered minus 14 degrees Fahrenheit, with winds gusting to 40 knots, and snow on the ground five feet deep. When the plane began to encounter violent turbulence, the pilot, Lieutenant Colonel Dante E. Bulli, attempted to fly above it. But at about 3 PM, a heavy crosswind ripped the vertical stabilizer from the plane, with a loud report. Unable to level the airplane, Bulli ordered ejection.

Only three of the nine men had time to eject. One was killed when he hit a tree while parachuting to the ground a mile away, and two were to spend the night in the frozen woods. Bulli sustained a broken ankle after landing thirty feet above ground in a tree, and Captain Gerald Adler landed on the snow-covered ground, fracturing his skull and breaking three ribs. That night the temperatures dipped to minus 28 degrees. Bulli wrapped himself in a sleeping bag from his survival kit, and Adler used his parachute for protection, since his survival kit could not be retrieved.

The next day, snowplows from Greenville were sent to clear the ten-mile access road of snow drifts up to fifteen feet, which enabled rescuers to get within one-and-a-half miles of the site and ultimately to evacuate the men. In all, some eighty rescuers participated, and the two men were saved, although each was to endure months of hospitalization.

Today, at the top of a low knoll, you'll see the largest intact piece of the plane, the tailgunner's section, and a large black slate marker with small American flags. Beyond are wheels, pieces of the wings, and landing gear, even including one piece of wreckage stamped

28

with the sign "OGAMA repaired; inspected, 23 May 1962." It seems an ironic comment.

For years the crash site remained out of reach of salvage crews. According to one account of a hiker from May 1963, Air Force personnel still guarded the wreckage, and the entire area continued to smell of jet fuel. In subsequent years, as, first, underbrush and then trees grew back, the salvage task became even more difficult. In the 1990s, however, new logging roads were built, and skidders were able to drag the heavy jet engines to be hauled away by trucks. Realizing that they were about to lose a piece of history, residents from Greenville organized to preserve the site, which continues to draw approximately 2500 visitors a year—not bad for a such a remote area, and certainly worth your exploration and homage.

More on the Region

√ Since the early 1980s, members of the Moosehead Riders Snowmobile Club have been the keepers of the site. Every January they gather with military representatives for a commemorative ceremony. At the thirtieth memorial anniversary service, in 1993, one of the two survivors, Captain Gerald J. Adler, then 74, returned to the mountain for the first time since he had been evacuated by helicopter three decades earlier.

√ The current owner of the land is the Plum Creek Timber Company, which has made improvements to the site and declared it off-limits to any future salvage efforts.

The Gott Pasture Preserve Loop (Wayne)

For a sweet, little walk through the woods at almost any time of year, head for this peaceful preserve where you'll be drawn into gentle communion with nature.

Driving directions (DeLorme 12, B & C-2): From Route 133 in Wayne Village, turn south on Old Winthrop Road (0.7 mile) past Gingerbread Farm Perennials; go right on Morrison Heights Road, with views onto Androscoggin Lake on the right, for 1.4 miles; bear left on Hardscrabble Road, which becomes a dirt road, for 1.3 miles. Look for a Kennebec Land Trust sign on the left after passing George's Road.
Round-trip distance: 1.25 mile loop.
Vertical rise: approximately 165 feet.
Miscellaneous: No restroom or water at trailhead. At the trailhead, by the sign, there is space to park one or two cars.
Map: DeLorme (see above), then follow the blue blazes.

> **The challenge and the payoff.** This is a short hike of mostly reward, as you walk down through a pleasant forest, past remnants of old stone fences, to Wilson Pond, with a view out to a couple small islands, then along by the shore, before climbing back into the forest to return to your car.

Description of the hike. The trail starts to the right of where you parked your car, down stones placed as steps. Follow the blue slashes as you descend the pine-needle path, passing through pleasant woods and by remnants of an old stone fence. The trail, often lined with ferns, is well maintained, even including a couple of bog bridges to protect plants. In no more than fifteen minutes, you will be down at the water's edge. Then the trail pulls back into the woods and goes down again to the lake, once or twice, for pleasant views onto the chain of islands in the water. At one place there are logs arranged so that you can sit and enjoy the quiet lake and the opposite shore, with its moored boats belonging to cabin owners whose homes you do not see.

History, Past and Present
√ Back in the nineteenth century, this property was a hardscrabble family farm owned by John Stevens and Abigail Richards Stevens. For more than a century, however, the land has largely been allowed to revert to its original state in nature—a great "bennie" for nature lovers in Central Maine.
√ Another family, the Ladds, donated the 75-acre parcel to the Kennebec Land Trust in 2003. As for the origin of the name, Gott Pasture, it presumably belongs to some other person or persons whose identity remains a mystery—to us, at least.

The loop continues along the shore and by coves with grasses and boulders sitting in the water. In all, there are about 1100 feet of undeveloped shoreline. On the return trip you'll be climbing uphill in a moderately steep fashion. By one of the stone fences, the trail rejoins the path you took down to the lake. If you didn't linger by the lake—but why not?—you will complete the entire hike in under a half-hour. But make it an hour, and enjoy the serenity and beauty of this area, which has scarcely been touched for a hundred years.

Jockey Cap

Hidden away in the northern part of Fryeburg, this geological anomaly offers surprisingly fine views onto many of the highest peaks in the White Mountains of New Hampshire, as well as of Evans Notch in Maine.

Driving directions (DeLorme 4, A-1): The trail to Jockey Cap is found on the north side of US-302, one mile east of the intersection of 302 and ME-113. The trailhead is located between the Jockey Cap Store and Motel at a picket fence and archway over which are emblazoned the words, Jockey Cap Trail.
Total round-trip distance: 0.5 mile.
Vertical rise: 200 ft.
Highest point: 626 ft. at the summit of Jockey Cap.
Miscellaneous: Water and restrooms available at the store or in town.
Map: DeLorme (see above).

The challenge and the payoff. After following a pleasant pine needle-covered path in the woods, you'll make a short, steep ascent to the ledge summit, where you'll enjoy a panoramic perspective onto many mountains that you'll be able to identify with the help of a bronze locator disk on a pedestal. For once, there won't be any question about what you're seeing! Though this hike is short, the use of a hiking pole may be helpful through the forest and steep section.

Description of the hike. This is a kind of mini-hike, yet very characteristic of Maine, with a beautiful forest, steep climbing, and rocks, leading to an excellent viewpoint. First, you climb through a pleasant woods on a pine-needle path, and then negotiate rocky patches as the trail gets much steeper.

From the gateway, the short route is well marked. After passing through the gate, turn right, where you have the option of taking the right or left fork. We took the left, passing a huge boulder and cave, to come up the left side of the Cap. In a few minutes and after a bit of perspiring, you're at the top.

From a distance, there is no question about the name of this feature, since the top, composed of a granite dome, really does look like a cap. There you will find a monument, dedicated to Admiral Robert E. Peary identifying features of the 360-degree view: Mt. Washington, South Baldface, Royce, Chocorua, Mt. Tripyramid, Black Cap, Evans Notch, Speckled, and other mountains.

Maine's Link to North Pole

Admiral Peary (1856-1920), the famous polar explorer who led the first successful expedition to the North Pole in 1909, lived in Fryeburg in 1878-1879, after earlier attending Portland High School and graduating from Bowdoin College. Not too far away from Jockey Cap is twin-peaked Peary Mountain (958 ft.), likely named for him, and offering a 2.5 mile round-trip hike.

Recently, the Fryeburg Historical Society uncovered some very interesting documents concerning a former ski tow at Jockey Cap, the first rope tow built in the state, dating from 1936. Skiers from Portland arrived at the Fryeburg station on board a snow train, and farmers offered them a ride to Jockey Cap on hayracks. Outdoor enthusiasts had the choice of either the ski slopes or a toboggan chute. And amazingly enough, there were even opportunities to hit the slopes on Friday and Saturday nights, since the ski tow was lighted.

Today, neither skiing nor tobogganing is possible, since the area has been reforested, but folks who love the sporting life still show up. Now you are apt to share the trail with rock climbers, clanking with gear, as they prepare to partake of some pretty good bouldering.

On the nearly bare top of Jockey Cap

Monument Hill (Leeds)

Discover how history and nature are in complement on a walk in the woods to a Civil War monument evoking the town's early history, and, from the hilltop, enjoy views of nearby farmland, plus in the distance, the Mahoosucs of western Maine and far-off mountains in New Hampshire.

Driving directions (DeLorme 12, C-1): Going north on ME-106, just short of Leeds, turn west on Merrill Road, taking it about 0.5 mile until turning right (north) on North Road. Continue about 0.5 mile until, on the right, you see a sign for the Monument Hill Trail. Park off the road.
Total round-trip mileage: 1.0 mile.
Vertical rise: 200 ft.
Highest point: 656 ft.
Miscellaneous: No water or restroom for this short hike.
Map: DeLorme (see above).

> **The challenge and the payoff**. You'll be climbing only 200 feet in one-half mile, which means that most everyone, including small children, can do it. And if you're up there on the highest spot in the town of Leeds on a clear day, you'll be rewarded with nice views of the Presidentials in New Hampshire and of Maine's western mountains. But it may be the history of the place that you'll find most intriguing.

Description of the hike. Begin walking on the clearly marked trail, and within 200 feet you will come to a fork, where, if you're in a hurry, choose the option on the right, which gets you to the partially wooded summit in ten or fifteen minutes. On the top, you come, first, to a large shade tree with its roots poking out above ground through ledge and rock. Here is where you get the best views. Behind this area is the Civil War "peace monument," a tall obelisk, and another freestanding stone monument, both erected by the Howard brothers, who were distinguished citizens and peace activists who had fought in the Civil War. Take a moment to read some of the names of town citizens who were killed in action. Today, Cub Scouts conduct patriotic celebrations at this spot.

On your way down, consider that it is quite possible that you are walking on a route that is more than two hundred years old. Given that this hill is the highest point in Leeds, one can reasonably imagine that well before the erection of the monument in 1895, early settlers would have climbed the mountain. According to Brian McCauley (*The Names of Maine*, 2004), Leeds was first settled in 1779 by two brothers, Thomas and Roger Stinchfield, veterans of the French and Indian War, who, by livelihood, were trappers, which means that they would most certainly have tramped through this forested land. They are the ones who are credited with naming the town after Leeds, England, where their father was born.

As for later Civil War history, it is not surprising that a peace monument was erected, for it is dedicated to the memory of the 161 men from Leeds who fought in the war and whose very number gave Leeds the distinction of being the town in Maine to have sent to battle for the Union the largest per capita number of men. Three of these men—brothers Major General Oliver Otis Howard, Reverend Roland Bailey Howard, and Brigadier General Charles H. Howard—are remarkable for their commitment to public service and to the cause of free men.

Oliver Otis Howard, born in Leeds in 1830, was a staunch opponent of slavery. Educated at Bowdoin and at West Point, he fought in the battles of Bull Run, Fair Oaks (where he lost an arm), Antietam, Fredericksburg, Chancellorsville, and Gettysburg. After the war, he became a commissioner of the Freedman's Bureau, tasked with providing food and medical facilities to former slaves. In 1867, he helped to establish Howard University and served as its president from 1869-1874. The oldest of the three brothers, he was the last to die, in 1909.

The Reverend Rowland Bailey Howard (1834-1891), also a graduate of Bowdoin, was with his brother during the Civil War, and later became Secretary of the American Peace Society. The freestanding monument on top of Monument Hill is a memorial to him, in recognition of his proposal that a peace monument be erected.

The youngest brother, Charles Henry Howard (1838-1908), was the third to graduate from Bowdoin. He also attended Bangor Theological Seminary. During the Civil War, he served on his brother's staff and subsequently became a brevet Brigadier General in his own right. He, too, worked with the Freedman's Bureau, in addition to becoming editor of several newspapers, and assisted his brother in founding colleges and in the settling of Native Americans in the West.

A wildflower treasure

You'll probably agree that this is quite a distinguished group of men to come from such a tiny town. No wonder that civic-minded townspeople organized the first Historic Leeds Day in September 2007. For there is a lot of interesting history here—from the early Native American tribes who portaged through an area now known as Indian Carry, to late eighteenth-century inhabitants who farmed the land in earnest and lived in what was then Massachusetts and known as Littleborough. Among the many early sites listed on the historic route of Leeds are Foss Corner Church, built in 1836, on the corner of Routes 219 and 106. Today, it uses the pews, pulpit, and organ from the nineteenth-century church. On one side of the church is a cemetery, while on the other is the 1786 Foss homestead, which operated for a period as a stagecoach stop known as the Temperance Hotel.—So, no drinks there, after your trip through the woods!

Did You Know?
- √   Maine was admitted to the Union as the 23rd state on March 15, 1820.
- √   It is the only state in the U.S. whose name has one syllable.
- √   It's also the only state that shares its border with only one other state.
- √   Augusta is the most eastern capital city in the United States. With a total area of 33,215 square miles, Maine covers nearly as many square miles as the other five New England states combined.

"The Mountain" (Belgrade Lakes)

Despite its generic name, "The Mountain" offers a very fine short hike of two loops—one through a forest dotted with glaciated boulders, the other to a partial lookout over Long Pond—for a pleasant hour of easy walking

Driving directions (DeLorme 20, E-4): One mile north of Belgrade Lakes Village, on ME-27, turn east onto Mountain Drive driving 0.3 mile to a parking area. An informational board indicates that the Great Pond Loop (green arrow) will be 0.4 mile from the parking area, while the Long Pond Loop (white arrow) will be 0.5 mile from it.
Total round-trip distance: 1.6 miles.
Vertical rise: 200 ft.
Highest point: 665 ft. at the summit of "The Mountain."
Miscellaneous: No water or restrooms.
Map: The Belgrade Regional Conservation Alliance (BRCA) map, available from the BRCA or at the Village Store in Belgrade Lakes.

The challenge and the payoff. Very little challenge—one hiking pole suffices—and a very pleasant walk, especially on the quieter Great Pond Loop side as you descend into a pretty boulder field in the forest. When you have scant time but want to get out into nature even briefly, this is a great little "hikette."

Description: Both loops are off the main trail, which begins up a broad path and former logging road, climbing gently. We started out with the Long Pond Loop (white arrow), taking a very nice path through tall trees, then by and over great slabs of granite, before coming to an overlook above Route 27. A clever, sloping wooden bench provides a seat at a viewpoint on the ledge, just short of the precipitous drop warned by several posted signs. (In icy conditions, or if small children accompany you, definitely heed the warning.) The view here is somewhat obstructed by trees, though you will see the northern portion of Long Pond and up to French Mountain, from which, at 716 feet, there is a striking V-shaped view onto Belgrade Lakes. Road noise rising from Route 27 breaks into the calm, however, so continue your hike up the trail behind you.

Sidebar Savvy. Many Mainers think that the 1981 Oscar-winning film *On Golden Pond* was filmed in the Belgrade Lakes region, but, in fact, though the scenery may be similar, the actual locale was Squam Lake in New Hampshire. Yet even if Belgrade Village is not the site of the film, it could have been, because what Hollywood scouts wanted was "the perfect New England lake," and that's what Belgrade Village offers.

When you exit the woods to the main trail, you will turn right no more than thirty yards later to pick up the green arrow loop, going south now. After arriving at a summit with a pile of rocks, you descend into the forest on a picturesque trail that winds its way downward past many moss-covered boulders. The photographer may want to be equipped with a tripod to shoot a time-exposure in the low light of this part of a very pretty woods. When you exit this loop, you will rejoin the main trail for a last half-mile back to your car.

Ferns in the afternoon sunlight

Parker Pond Headland Preserve (Fayette)

Find peace and quiet in a lovely woods on this short loop hike, which dips down to a fine, clear pond, wends its way past tall hemlocks, and has a ledge viewpoint to an island.

Driving directions (DeLorme 12, A-2 & B-2): From Route 17 in Kent's Hill, take Rt. 41 north 3.6 miles to the Chimney in West Mt. Vernon. Then take Sandy River Road 2.5 miles to Fellows Cove Road, going to its end where there is a parking area with room for several cars.

Total round-trip distance: 1.5 miles approximately.

Miscellaneous: 1) This would also be a great place to snowshoe. 2) The Parker Pond Association comprises both shorefront owners and "friends of the Pond," who work together to preserve the beauty of the area and to protect the natural resources of the Pond, particularly from the threat of invasive milfoil, which can take over a lake and strangle other aquatic life.

Map: DeLorme (see above).

The challenge and the payoff. This is an easy little walk through a very appealing woods, but because you are not walking on level pavement, it couldn't hurt to have along one hiking stick, "just in case," especially if your knees are at all tetchy.

Description of the hike. What stands out about this short hike is the forest of beautiful hemlocks and the pleasant way that the trail wends its way through the forest, down to the pond, then out to a granite cliff overlooking a single island in the water.

From the parking area, you make an easy descent through woods, toward the pond, which is accessed by a short side trail marked by three blazes. From there you pull back into the woods, making a left turn to continue the loop, this time toward an area of ledge with a good view out to the pond. As you leave the ledge, you come down through stands of ferns that in high summer are beautifully green. Continue the loop until you are back at the parking area.

Sidebar Savvy

Parker Pond Preserve is one of the nearly three dozen constituent parts of the Kennebec Land Trust, which in turn is one of nearly ninety land trusts throughout Maine. These land trusts are a great resource at the doorstep of Maine residents for occasions when you don't have time to make it out to one of the more distant hiking areas for which the state is better known.—Which just goes to show that good things can also come in small packages.

This hundred-acre peninsula with 5000 feet of pristine rocky shoreline on Parker Pond has a boat-launching site at the northeast end, but the day we were there, nothing broke the quiet beauty. We imagine that on snowshoes, on a winter's day, it would be just as lovely.

Porter Preserve (Barters Island, Boothbay)

Located in a forested area on the tip of an island, this short loop hike will offer pleasant views of the Sheepscot River plus stone walls and other reminders of people who lived and farmed the land in the eighteenth and nineteenth centuries.

Driving directions (DeLorme 7, C-2): From Boothbay Harbor travel north on ME-27. Take a left at the monument in Boothbay Center onto Corey Lane, and continue for 0.3 mile. (**NB:** While these directions are easy to follow, not all the roads are named in DeLorme. However, once you locate Barters Island on the map, you'll be able to visualize the route.) Bear right at the fork onto Barters Island Road and drive 2.2 miles, crossing two bridges. Take a left on Kimballtown Road, continuing for 0.5 mile, and turn left at the fork onto a dirt road. Porter Preserve is 0.1 mile up the dirt road on the right. There is a small parking area on your right just beyond the cemetery.

Total round-trip distance: 0.86 mile.

Vertical rise: Not much.

Miscellaneous: No water or restroom. Park so that you do not block the road, since property owners need access. Binoculars would be an asset on this walk for spotting harbor seals and to get a better view of the islands in the river.

Map: Brochure at trailhead.

> **The challenge and the payoff.** Easy walking of the sightseeing variety, with much of interest to note along the way, so do pick up the brochure, "Porter Discovery Trail Tour by Numbers" at the trailhead.

Description of the hike. If you availed yourself of the brochure at the trailhead and are interested in making an educational walk, leave the parking lot and walk counter-clockwise from "station" to "station," noting the names of trees, and testing yourself on your knowledge and retention. You'll learn how long it takes a sapling to become an adult and how many thousand saplings die so that one-hundred trees per acre can be harvested. You'll find out what rock tripe is and how rock polypody adjusts to drought and wetness. And you'll discover how and why stone walls were used, how earlier families lived and what crops they grew, where they located their freshwater well, and at what point their houses fell into decay.

You'll also learn about the great variety of birds that make Barters Island either home or a temporary resting ground during migration, and you'll find out how on a clear day at low tide, it is possible to spot harbor seals sunbathing on a ledge in the Sheepscot River.

A Maine History of Firsts
√   It is said that the first ship built by English colonists in the Americas was launched on the Kennebec River in 1607.
√   The new nation's first sawmill was established near York in 1623.
√   The first naval battle of the Revolutionary War was fought off Machias in 1775.

As you make the loop, there will be pretty views of salt marsh grasses that fringe the cove and provide habitat for marine organisms. You'll even be given a lesson about the forests that one finds on the Maine coast. For one thing, in past centuries, the forest was not so thick, and the trees were much taller. Later settlers harvested the wood for everything from construction of wooden ships to firewood to the shaping of wooden tools of every kind. Then, some hundred years ago, farming ended on the island, and subsequently red spruce (which occupies most of the forest today), was seeded so that trees could take back over.

Vaughan Woods (Hallowell and Farmingdale)

Step back in time as you descend a former carriage road bordered by a beautiful forest and come to a picturesque brook with stone bridges and waterfalls for a lovely walk through a landscape that is highly photogenic in all seasons, becoming under snow a veritable winter wonderland.

Driving directions (DeLorme 12, C-5): From Water Street in Hallowell, turn west onto Winthrop Street. Take the third left onto Middle Street, heading south for 0.7 mile. Where Middle Street intersects with Litchfield Road, there is a small parking area. To access the trail, step through the stone fence and enter the wooded area that opens onto a field above the Vaughan Homestead off to the left. Cross the field, then reenter the woods.
Total round-trip distance: About 2 miles for the main loop trail; one-third mile to the dam.
Vertical rise: Some rise and fall.
Miscellaneous: No restroom. Since the Vaughan Woods spans the line between Hallowell and Farmingdale, it can also be accessed from the latter town, next to the tennis courts behind Hall-Dale High School. This access trail connects to the main loop trail.
Map: DeLorme (see above).

The challenge and the payoff. The walk downhill on the main path to the brook poses little challenge, and the loop trail through the woods adds on only a little more. Still, we always prefer to have along at least one hiking stick. The Vaughan Woods is as wonderful as it is unexpected, a resource for walkers or joggers in the drier months and for those who snowshoe and ski in the winter. For all, it is a real beauty spot.

Description. After you have left your car and walked across the grassy field accented by some magnificent oaks, you enter the relaxing cool of the forest on a broad carriage path bedded with wood chips. You're into a nineteenth century of the imagination. Streams feeding Vaughan Brook pass under the trail from the wooded hillside by means of gracefully arched culverts, constructed of massive granite slabs quarried long ago. There are wonderful old trees and ferns, and, on the left, the forest drops sharply down.

As you descend the trail path, you'll hear the brook before you see it. Then you are invited to cross over a charming curved footbridge of cut granite, from which there are views of the picturesque brook and its gentle cascades of descending water. Upstream there is a larger stone bridge, and from behind it, a granite dam, through whose many joints flows the water that keeps the brook running. Once, after heavy rains, we were amazed by the dramatic churning water as it roared down the stream. Re-crossing the Vaughan Brook via the larger bridge, you can now access the dam and even climb onto it for an excellent view of the large backup pool it impounds.

Bridge and stream at Vaughan Woods

There are a number of ancillary trails, including walking paths that intersect the brook from the south, giving access to farm fields, and ultimately stretching to the right-of-way of Interstate 95. To return to your car, continue the loop back to the carriage path.

What makes this walk through the forest graced by brook and old stone bridges so pleasant is that you will also be dipping into early American history as you retrace the steps of the Vaughan family, whose roots go back to colonial days and whose geographic reach extends from Europe to Jamaica to Maine. Read more of their history recounted below.

The Vaughan Family
- Father, Samuel Vaughan (1720-1802), was a London merchant and Jamaican sugar plantation owner. He married Sarah Hallowell (1727-1809) of Boston in 1747.
- Benjamin, the eldest of their ten children, was born in Jamaica in 1751. He obtained degrees in both law and medicine before becoming a merchant and marrying Sarah Manning (1754-1834) in London. With knowledge of both sides of the Atlantic, Benjamin helped to negotiate peace between England and the American colonies. Later in 1794, he left England for political reasons, settling in Hallowell, where he became an "agriculturist."
- At the trailhead, a sign relates that in 1807 the well-known French botanist André Michaux visited the Vaughans and explored the Woods.
- Benjamin died in 1835 at the ripe old age of 84, thereby exceeding even today's life expectancy rates.
- History buffs might want to travel to the Massachusetts Historical Society in Boston to consult the forty-one cartons of records and correspondence of the Vaughan family, spanning the years 1768 to 1950. They might also try to get hold of the following accounts: Emma Huntington Nason, *Old Hallowell on the Kennebec* (Augusta, Maine, 1909) and Mary Vaughan Marvin, *Benjamin Vaughan* (Hallowell, Maine, 1979).

Overview
Boomer Rating Two
Knocking Off a Few Under Five Miles

Ready for slightly more challenge? Then consider a Boomer Rating Two hike, which could be just the ticket.

We give this rating to a number of different kinds of trails located throughout the state—on the coast, in Central Maine, in the western mountains, and even one short segment of the Appalachian Trail in the Rangeley/Stratton region.

What they typically have in common is that each of them makes for a pleasant ramble through the woods, whether the destination is to an unusual feature, such as Piazza Rock or Balance Rock at Fernald's Neck, or to a series of splendid waterfalls at Dunn Falls.

Several of the hikes will give you contact with a piece of old Maine history, as with Jamies Pond, while another, Bog Brook, will take you through a quiet woodland with marsh views. At Oven's Mouth there is a shoreline stroll on one side of the peninsula, while on the other a fine walk through the woods. And of course there are hikes to scenic overlooks, with views from Spruce Mountain onto Maine farmland and lakes or from French Mountain onto a famous summer town.

As a rule, a Boomer Rating Two means that the hike is under five miles round-trip with relatively low altitude gain and a generally good footpath—although not always, since both the Dunn Falls trail and Piazza Rock have short sections of rugged climb and descent. So your hiking poles will definitely come in handy.

Some of these hikes may also be appropriate for a snowshoe jaunt—for example, Jamies Pond, Round Top and Sanders Hill in the Belgrade area; Spruce Mountain to Pleasant Mountain Road (Georges Highland Path); and Fernald's Neck. Several also offer the possibility of extending your outing by taking a spur trail or making an additional loop, as with Fernald's Neck and Jamies Pond as well as Oven's Mouth.

A notable feature of several of the hikes is that they are associated with land trusts—Kennebec Land Trust, Sheepscot Wellspring Land Alliance, and the Boothbay Region Land Trust—three examples of how concerned citizens in Maine are protecting and preserving natural resources while working in concert with landowners and their economic interests.

With dozens of land trusts in existence, we highly recommend that you check the Internet to see which ones are located near you. Hiking trails seem to be popping up everywhere, and many of them offer an opportunity to hike either in new areas or without having to drive great distances from your home.

To get you started, here is a chart of our featured Boomer Rating Two hikes with their total round-trip mileage and vertical gain—the two key elements that determine the challenge of the hike.

Hike	Round-trip miles	Vertical gain
Bog Brook	From 1 mile loop to longer	Modest
Dunn Notch and Falls	2.2 miles	Approx. 180 ft.
Fernald's Neck Preserve	1.6 miles for Balance Rock; up to 4 or 5 miles with additional loops	Small for Balance Rock; some rock and ledge
French Mountain	0.8 mile	200 ft.
Jamies Pond	Connecting loops from one-half mile to 2-3 miles	Quite modest
Oven's Mouth - east peninsula - west peninsula	1.6 miles of trails (east) 3.7 miles of trails (west)	Modest 150 ft.
Piazza Rock	3.0 miles	360 ft.
Round-Top (Belgrade)	3.9 miles	400 ft.
Sanders Hill (Belgrade)	2.8 miles	320 ft.
Spruce Mountain	4.6 miles	400 ft.

A Belgrade Lakes Threesome

From a single road in the Belgrade Lakes area, you can access any one of three woodsy hikes with pretty views of famous Maine ponds or combine all three for a full day in the outdoors.

Driving directions (DeLorme 20, E-3): Coming north on ME-27, about 4 miles north of Belgrade Lake Village and past Rome Corner, turn left onto Watson Pond Road. After 0.7 mile heading south, you come to the trailhead for French Mountain on the left (east). Park on the paved apron on the same side as the trailhead. The trailhead for Sanders Hill is 0.6 mile further south, with a small parking area on the west side of Watson Pond Road. The trailhead for Round Top is located at the corner of Wildflower Estate and Watson Pond Road, 4 miles south of where you first turned onto Watson Pond Road from ME-27.

Total round-trip distance: 0.8 mile for French; 2.8 miles for Sanders; and 3.9 miles for Round Top.

Vertical rise: 200 ft. for French; 320 ft. for Sanders; and 400 ft. for Round Top.

Highest point: 716 ft. for French; 854 ft. for Sanders; and 1133 ft. for Round Top.

Miscellaneous: No water or restroom at the trailheads.

Map: The BRCA (Belgrade Regional Conservation Alliance) Map and Guide to The Kennebec Highlands and Nearby Areas is available at Day's Country Store in Belgrade Lakes Village and at the BRCA office in Belgrade Lakes Village (above the post office). The map is both necessary and a good way to support the BRCA.

The challenge and the payoff. Each of the threesome has its own modest challenge, with some altitude gain and sometimes the necessity for route-finding, since this area of the Kennebec Highlands is criss-crossed by miles of unimproved trails and old logging roads. The lake views from French and Round Top mountains are especially nice. All of the trails are also good for snowshoeing.

Description of the hikes

French Mountain. This is probably the most popular trail of the threesome, since it is a short climb up through the forest to a great overlook onto Long Pond. Because you reach your destination in ten or fifteen minutes, we'd call it a "hikette," but for the visitor to the region, French Mountain gives a fine bird's-eye view of the Belgrade Lakes area for very little time and just a bit of effort.

After entering the forest, you pass a sign set out by the BRCA, and the trail begins immediately to climb. At the end of seven or eight minutes, you mount a flight of stone steps placed in logs and step onto ledge, which continues up to the lookout point. From this rocky precipice, you have an excellent view of the northern end of Long Pond and the surrounding region, including Great Pond, The Mountain, and Belgrade Lake Village. You can rest a moment on the split log bench before taking the same trail down to your car, for a total jaunt of less than a mile and about one-half hour, including the time to enjoy the view from the top.

Onto Belgrade lakes and village from French Mountain

Sanders Hill. Since this is a loop trail, it can be hiked in either direction. If your time is short, we recommend starting up the trail in a counter-clockwise direction and heading for Sanders Hill, at a distance of one mile. This way, you will access a very nice area with trees and ledge and the best views of the entire hike. It's also a great spot for a picnic lunch. And, in our opinion, the first half of the trail is more enjoyable than the second half.

Begin the hike from the trail that leaves the north side of the parking area. It passes the south end of Watson Pond and winds westerly, crossing an inflow for the Pond, then follows a former logging road before climbing moderately. As the trail turns sharply north to head for the summit, it follows the ridgeline and gives views to the east of Watson Pond and French Mountain. Then it cuts through and over some large granite slabs at 0.9 mile, coming through a sparsely wooded area before arriving at the summit of Sanders Hill. Here you descend and turn south onto the broad, gravel Kennebec Highlands Trail, following it for 0.75 mile, almost to a bridge over upper Beaver Creek. Just short of the bridge, turn left (east) back into the woods along the brook and then along a logging road, which, in about 0.75 mile, will take you back to your car.

Round Top. The longest of the hiking trails off Watson Pond Road, this loop hike makes for a pleasant outing of under three miles, though we must admit that when we were there early one spring, we found the signage inadequate and ended up exiting to Watson Pond Road by a not very nice logging route that dropped us far from our car. So make sure to have a map and avoid our mistake!

From the parking area, you'll start the hike, moving in a westerly direction, and soon cross a large slab of granite. After a mile you will see the Kennebec Highlands Trail coming in from the right (west). Ignore it and continue going westward. At this point the trail climbs more steadily. You will have some modest views as you approach the summit. At 1.7 miles from the trailhead, you will see a spur trail of 0.3 mile that leads to overlooks onto surrounding ponds. Make sure to take this spur trail for the best views of the hike. Return to the main trail, and you will soon come to an overlook with views of Long Pond, Belgrade Lake Village, and Great Pond.

From the summit, the trail descends fairly steeply, between and over large rocks, for about 0.3 mile, before joining the gravel

Kennebec Highlands Trail, which you take by turning sharply to the south and which should, after 0.75 mile, lead you back to the main trail. It was soon after that we had trouble, at a three-way junction marked by snowmobile trail signs, where you are supposed to bear right. About 100 yards past the junction, and just before a Y-intersection of snowmobile trails, there is supposed to be a rock cairn on the left (east) side of the logging trail. Here you turn left and are back on the Round Top Trail, just under a mile from your car.

Bog Brook Trail (Waldo County)

An excellent walk in a pretty forest, which you can easily extend beyond the initial one-mile loop for a longer hike traversing a very fine woods, attractive glades and wetlands, and with the opportunity to see some striking birds.

Driving directions (DeLorme 14, A-1 and 22, E-1): From ME 3, turn north on ME 220. Continue for 3.4 miles and turn left on Burnham Hill Road. At a Y-corner, continue right on Halldale Road. Again on the right, some 80 yards beyond the Y-corner, you will see the yellow-gold SWLA trail sign for the Bog Brook Trail. Park well off the road.

Total round-trip mileage: We describe a one-mile loop, but the full trail is a 2.5 mile loop.

Vertical rise: Negligible.

Highest point: 800 ft.

Miscellaneous: No restroom or water at the trailhead.

Map: Sheepscot Wellspring Land Alliance Trail Guide, usually available at the information sign post a few steps down from the road.

The challenge and the payoff. Hardly any challenge to speak of—perhaps at times an eroded path, but that is all. Your reward is the unexpected pleasure of a very pleasant area, for those unfamiliar with the upper Sheepscot River watershed.

Description of the hike. You walk down a few steps from Halldale Road and enter a nice woods with trees flanked by beds of ferns. Especially in sunny weather, you will like this shaded path, which grows narrow before opening onto pretty Bog Brook on the left, whose bottom and stones appear black when water is low. As you descend through hemlocks and pines to the marsh, you will first hear the croaking of frogs announcing the watered landscape.

According to the trail guide of the Sheepscot Wellspring Land Alliance, there are some pretty unusual birds living in these bogs

and marshes at various times of the year, including the Great Blue
Heron, the Black-Crowned Night, Green-Backed Heron, Killdeer,
Greater and Lesser Yellowlegs, Solitary and Spotted Sandpiper, and
American Woodcock. Who says that Maine isn't exotic?

From the marsh, the well-marked blue blaze trail pulls back into
the woods and climbs steeply for a few yards before continuing its
easy meander. At an intersection, you can turn north (left) to extend
the hike or terminate it by turning right onto the Halldale Spur. At
first, we turned left and continued on for about ten minutes, along a
nice path but, with rain threatening, decided to head back and exit
by the Halldale Spur with its great stands of hemlocks. The distance
between where we exited and our car was only 0.2 mile.

Just a few yards beyond where you entered the woods for the
Bog Brook Trail, there are excellent views from the road onto the
marsh—much better, in fact, than what you get from the trail. We
lingered to enjoy the peacefulness and take some photographs,
including one of a sign warning that trapping was forbidden in this
area. That was the first time it had occurred to us that even in the
twenty-first century there might be trappers in Central Maine.

More Hiking Opportunities in the Region
The recently developed Sheepscot Headwaters Trail Network
offers five different hiking opportunities off Halldale Road,
whose trailheads are all well marked by yellow-gold trailposts.
They include:
1) The Northern Headwaters Trail (blue), 3.5 mile loop.
2) The Bog Brook Trail (blue), 2.5 mile loop.
3) The Big Pines Trail (red), connecting with the Bog
   Brook Trail for a short, mostly level 1.0 mile (the
   trail begins opposite the nineteenth-century Whitten
   Cemetery, on the west side of Halldale Road).
4) The Halldale Spur (yellow), 0.25 mile, connecting
   with the Bog Brook Trail.
5) The Whitten Hill Trail (orange), approximately 0.5
   mile trail connecting the Northern Headwaters Trail
   to the Bog Brook Trail.
Note, too, that the Sheepscot Wellspring Land Alliance
(SWLA) trail system is joined to the Georges River Land
Trust by the Hogback Connector Trail, in a partnership that
provides eighteen miles of connected trails

Dunn Notch and Falls (Andover)

Short and sweet, if also sometimes rough, this hike takes you to a spectacular series of waterfalls and cascades, which make a final twin drop to a delightful pond. Especially in the fall, when there are few people on the trail, this destination is a real treat.

Driving directions (DeLorme 18, D-2): From the village of Andover, take East Hill Road, also known as East B Hill Road (and on the DeLorme map as Upton Road), for 8 miles to the AT crossing, marked by a sign, on the right. A bit beyond the sign is a parking area. The beginning of the Dunn Notch Trail is on the opposite side of the road, back a number of yards.
Total round-trip distance: 2.2 miles.
Vertical rise: Approximately 180 ft.
Miscellaneous: No restroom or water source at the trailhead. Note that the parking area also serves the Surplus Pond hike, Boomer Rating Three.
NB: The Notch and Falls are approachable either by the Cascade Trail, which requires several rock crossings of the stream, or by the AT. We describe the latter.
Maps: AMC White Mtns. NH & Maine, Map 6 A14.

> **The challenge and the payoff.** This is a little hike with a big reward, but you will deal with a rugged trail in places and a fair amount of steepness. However, the waterfalls are splendid, the woods are very nice, and, as we've said, the hike is short. Just bring your hiking poles to save your knees on the steep sections.

Description of the hike. After descending from the road on some crumbling steps and continuing steeply down the slope over roots, followed by an easy crossing of the brook, you will see an AT sign indicating that the East Peak of Baldpate is 6.2 miles further and Highway 26 is ten miles away. Fortunately, you're not going so far.

Continuing after the stream crossing, first you ascend sharply, then descend, only to again climb, and as you do so, the forest floor will be far below you to the left. The footpath is often typically "Maine," which, as you know, means on the rugged side.

It takes about forty-five minutes to arrive at the Notch, which requires a steep descent through the woods. Once there, you'll be high above a stream, which circles around a ledge that juts out over the water. To the right of the ledge, AT thru-hikers will descend the dirt bank to cross to the other side. You, however, will stay above and follow the side trail to the right for the Upper Falls, which are only 0.2 mile further.

Did You Know?
According to health and fitness experts, hiking over uneven terrain forces the body to use the stabilizing muscles of the abdominals and back, which improves balance and strengthens the core. At home, you can target those core muscles by working the "abs" and back with double leg stretches.

In little more than five minutes, you'll be at the Lower Falls and its picturesque pond, into which, on a nice day, a double set of falls are reflected. For a closer look, make your way down to a beach-like area in front of the falls. By going to the far left side of the "beach," you will be able to look up through the trees to the second series of waterfalls. There are two main vertical drops, one of seventeen yards and the second of twenty-six yards. For a closer view of the Upper Falls, make the short, steep, and somewhat awkward climb up rock slabs to arrive at several good vantage points. Some people may throw caution to the wind and cross the wet ledge to the other side, but being more cautious, we remain on the safe side and just take plenty of pictures.

The 1.1 miles return trip will be quick, though steep, and, once again, you'll be grateful to have your hiking poles to lighten the load on your joints during descents.

We can attest that autumn is a wonderful time to take this short hike with its big view punch, but summer would also be fine, and you may even see some folks cooling off in the pond at the Lower Falls. The last time that we were there, however, in mid-week in mid-September, we had the whole glorious experience to ourselves.

For a further option—if your knees aren't too creaky at the end of the hike—consider extending your outing by also doing the Surplus Pond trail (see Boomer Rating Three) once you get back to East B Hill Road.

Lower Dunn Falls

Fernald's Neck Preserve (Camden area)

On a large peninsula jutting into Megunticook Lake, Fernald's Neck provides a variety of opportunities for pleasant walking, including a visit to Balance Rock, a striking glacial erratic, perched on its end, deposited some 13,000 years ago.

Driving directions (DeLorme 14, C-3): From Camden, take Route 52 north about 4 miles to Youngtown Corner. Just past the corner, turn left onto Fernald's Neck Road. Follow the road, which changes to dirt, bearing left at the fork as shown by a small Nature Conservancy sign. Park in the hayfield where there is room for about fifteen vehicles. No parking on the access road.

Total round-trip distance: 0.8 mile for Balance Rock; 1.7 miles for Orange Loop; 1.3 miles to Mountain View; or more than 5 miles if you take all the trails.

Vertical rise: minimal, but lots of up and down on Blue Loop.

Miscellaneous: No restroom. The preserve is owned by The Nature Conservancy and open for day use only; the gate is locked at 7:30 PM.

Map: Study the color-coded maps posted at the trailhead and along the way.

> **The challenge and the payoff**. The yellow trail to Balance Rock is well-trodden, whereas parts of the upper Blue Loop are somewhat rougher. Naturally you'll want to be cautious on the cliffs. Make sure to pick up a map showing the interconnections between all the trails: entrance trail, blue loop, orange loop, yellow trail, and red trail. Especially on a day when the Preserve has few visitors, the quiet and natural beauty of the land, with its woods and bog and typical Maine views onto the lake, will entice you to while away a couple hours.

Description of the hike. Cross the field and enter the woods where there is a Conservancy sign that marks the path to the preserve. As you walk, you will note that fallen trees are left to lie in the forest to decompose and add their nutrients to the soil. Within minutes from the starting point, you come to two arrows, an orange one to the left, and a blue one to the right. By turning left on the orange loop and left again on a yellow trail, you will access, first, a small beach with a view to Maiden Cliff, looming over Megunticook Lake, and then, a few minutes beyond the beach, Balance Rock, which is less than 0.5 miles from your car.

Some Dramatic History

In 1864, a young girl by the name of Elenora French fell to her death 800 feet off the cliff, which was later named in her memory. A cross marking the spot from which she plunged can be seen from the beach at Fernald's Neck. But do we know why she plunged? Was it an accident or did she jump or was it something more sinister?

Balance Rock is set in a clearing on a slight rise, left by glaciers some 13,000 years ago. If you're there at the right moment, the sun will throw a spotlight on it, inviting you to make a dramatic photograph. To get the best effect and to convey the sense of the boulder's size, place yourself or someone else in the picture along with the boulder. It really is impressive.

From Balance Rock, you need to return to where the yellow trail intersects the orange trail. If you turn left, you can take the Orange Loop, with its side trail to Mountain View, or access the Blue Loop, which passes by the Great Bog and through a tall tree forest, before coming to an outcrop above the lake. Here you have views onto the opposite shoreline, with the occasional home and, in the summer, speedboats racing through the water and making sharp turns, to the thrill of the water skier attached behind.

Since the trails interconnect, you can cut off the top section of the Blue Loop either by means of a yellow trail or an orange trail, both of which meet the blue trail in different spots. Your object is to re-access the Entrance Trail from the blue or orange trails to return to the parking area.

Since you may well become enamored of the area, be sure to have some snacks and water in your backpack, and bring the hiking sticks for the rougher areas alongside the lake.

If you're looking for an all-day outing in the area of Camden, you can easily combine Fernald's Neck and Balance Rock either with the very, very steep but short hike up Mt. Battie, accessed from within town, or with the Bald Rock hike in Lincolnville (see *Featured Hikes*, Boomer Rating Three).

Sidebar Savvy

The Nature Conservancy protects some eleven million acres in all fifty states of the United States and works with partner organizations to preserve and protect fifty million acres in Canada, Latin America, the Caribbean, and the Pacific. That's a lot of protection to provide, and places like Fernald's Neck Preserve make us grateful for it.

Jamies Pond (Hallowell/Manchester)

A shaded forest trail meanders through stately hardwoods left undisturbed for the best part of a century, providing an ideal refuge from heat in the summer and a serene destination for the skier or snowshoe-hiker in the winter.

Driving directions (DeLorme 12, C-4): From Hallowell, take the Outlet Road to where it forks with Jamies Pond Road; from Manchester, use the Collins Road or Meadow Hill Road to Jamies Pond Road. There is a parking area off Collins Road and another off Jamies Pond Road, which is where the hike described below begins.
Total round-trip distance: From 1 mile for the Lower Pond Trail to 1.4 miles for the Hemlock Trail and 1 mile for the Vernal Pond Trail, plus a side-trail to a nineteenth-century dam, or more if you put them all together.
Vertical rise: Negligible.
Miscellaneous: No restroom or running water at trailhead.
Map: Try to obtain the Trail Guide to Jamies Pond Wildlife Management Area from the Hallowell Conservation Commission (207-623-4021) or the Manchester Conservation Commission (207-622-1894).

The challenge and the payoff. There is not much challenge, aside, perhaps, from trying to follow the paper map. On the ground, wherever trails intersect, there are information posts (trail finders) depicting the route and citing its features. Just wander along. The pleasure is in being in a pretty spot and one that hosts numerous birds including ducks, herons, hawks, loons, osprey, woodpeckers, and a wide variety of songbirds.

Description of the hike. Leave the parking area and look for the trail to the right, or northeast end, of the pond. We took the Lower Pond Trail, which winds around the northern shore of the pond before coming out at a little beach with large rocks on which to perch. This

63

was a scenic spot, almost the pond's length and opposite from where we had parked. As we sat there enjoying the peaceful Maine scene, a couple in a canoe glided by to ask what we had been studying so intently in the water. It was a purple wildflower called pickerel weed, which the nature-lover in us found to be a good subject to photograph.

When it comes time to return to your car, you can do so by a different route, perhaps climbing up the Hemlock Trail to a ridge and then continuing a ridge walk over the Vernal Pool Trail with its stands of pine and large boulders.

Just before the end of the outing, you can also take a short side trail for about a hundred yards, going back in the dark forest to an unfinished dam, clearly of nineteenth-century construction, perhaps seventy feet in length and fifteen feet high. It's moss-covered now and partially obscured by forest growth, an apparent anomaly in the woods until one remembers that many such dams intended for lumber and sawmill activity were built in the late 1800s. This one, however, appears never to have been used. Which is a bit sad considering the intensive labor provided by those who hauled the giant blocks of quarried granite to the spot.

If you're hiking during quiet times, you might see wildlife such as moose, deer, fox, squirrels, skunks, otter, beaver, raccoons, porcupines, and fishers, which explains why today the Department of Inland Fisheries and Wildlife maintains these 840 acres as a wildlife management area.

Jamies Pond and canoeists

Pilgrims and Fisheries

During your hike, take time to recall that some of our Pilgrim forebears probably trod the same ground that you are tramping. Indeed, in the 1620s the owners of this land were the Pilgrims of none other than Plymouth Plantation.

Later, the land passed into the hands of a group of Boston businessmen known as the Proprietors of the Kennebec Purchase, and later still, in the 1700s, it was deeded to the Vaughan family of Hallowell (See the Vaughan Woods hike in Boomer Rating One).

Today, the state department of fisheries and wildlife is in charge. So, from Pilgrims to Fisheries and Wildlife—how times change!

Oven's Mouth Preserve Trails
(Boothbay Regional Land Trust)

Very nice trails, with both an easy part and a moderately more demanding section on two peninsulas, in a lovely area of scenic shoreline bordered by swift tidal water, quiet coves, and salt marshes, plus a great forest.

Driving directions (DeLorme 7, C-2): From the monument in Boothbay Center, travel north on Route 27 for 1.7 miles, then turn left on Adams Pond Road. At a fork, keep to the right for Dover Road. Continue 2.2 miles, bearing right at the junction onto the Dover Road Extension. Go to the end of the road, where, on the left, there is parking for several vehicles.

Total round-trip distance: 1.6 miles for the loop on the east peninsula; 5.3 miles if you add the 3.7 miles of trail on the west peninsula.

Vertical rise: 154 ft.

Highest point: 313 ft.

Miscellaneous: No water or restrooms at the trailhead. Note that there is another entrance for Oven's Mouth West, off Dover Cross Road. At the junction referred to above, bear left and drive 0.15 mile for a parking area on the right.

The challenge and the payoff. The two peninsulas present different types of hiking, with the east peninsula offering easy "hoofing" through wooded land coming out to water, and the west peninsula making more demands in terms of a rougher footpath that climbs and descends, occasionally steeply. The gentle beauty of the shoreline is calming, while the hike through the forest on the west is invigorating, so that put together, you get the best of a half-day out in nature.

Description of the hike. The shore loop on the east peninsula is for the most part a very "civilized" walk. It is also educational, if you pick up the "Self Guided Tour of Oven's Mouth East" at the trailhead. On the loop, you'll pass by numbered "stations" indicated by wooden stakes, and the brochure will give you a lot of interesting facts about the natural and human history of the area. For instance, you will learn about the role of the eastern white pine in Maine history and the fact that in early Colonial days, it was a hanging offense to cut the white pine, since the British Navy had first dibs on the best trees. You'll also pass by the site of a former ice dam (see text below for the importance of the ice industry to early Maine), whose remnants are visible at low tide, and a stone house foundation for a house thought to have been built in 1790 on the same site as a pre-Revolutionary log house. Whether you walk to learn, or walk to hike the area, you'll certainly find it pleasant.

For the purposes of hiking, we suggest leaving the parking area by going counter-clockwise on the yellow-blazed trail. When you come to the bridge across the salt marsh at the site of the ice dam, cross the bridge and start the west peninsula loop in counter-clockwise direction, then return to the bridge and complete the remaining portion of the east loop trail.

If you're lucky, you may see a blue heron, osprey, or even an egret, eagle, or otter. And if you're there at the right time, especially on the east side, you'll have the opportunity to identify well over a dozen varieties of wildflowers, even more species of trees and shrubs (watch out for the poison ivy), as well as ferns and mosses and lichens.

When you cross the bridge over to the west peninsula, turn right. The white blazes take you along the shoreline, with 2.3 miles of trail, while both the yellow and blue blazes correspond to trails in the woods. You can, for instance, begin on the Shore Trail (white) going north; then enter the woods at the northern tip of the peninsula, now going south; re-access the Shore Trail for views of the salt marsh; and use the Yellow Trail to reconnect through the woods to the Blue Blaze Trail, now going north, back to the bridge. Make sure to carry a map, available either at the trailhead or on-line at www.bbrlt.org.

On the west peninsula, you have a greater sense of privacy and will feel more as though you are hiking, since the terrain rises and falls through the woods, even rather sharply descending about 150 feet as you make the return for the bridge and the stone dam (the latter was built in 1879 to impound fresh water for an ice pond). The final leg of the loop, on the west peninsula, goes along the salt marsh and by the original eighteenth-century homestead, now marked only by its foundation.

In all, the Boothbay Region Land Trust includes twenty-five miles of hiking trails at more than ten locations, ranging in length from one-half mile to the longer ones here at Oven's Mouth. This is our favorite for its beauty and variety.

More on Maine History

- The name, Oven's Mouth, is attributed to early English explorers who decided that the physical appearance of the peninsulas resembled a Dutch oven, narrow where joined, then broadening to a wide "mouth," or bay.
- At Station 8 of the hike, The Ice Dam, you'll learn that ice trade was an important early industry in nineteenth-century Maine. Natural ice (as opposed to manufactured ice, which came much later) was the source of refrigeration in the 1800s, and Maine played an important role in harvesting ice from frozen ponds and rivers (especially the Kennebec and Penobscot rivers). It was shipped by schooner to Boston and New York, where, it might further be destined for tables in Charleston, South Carolina, Savannah, or New Orleans, and even Martinique and Cuba. The "Ice King," Frederic Tudor of Boston, made a fortune shipping ice cut from the frozen freshwater sources of New England to places as far away as Europe and India.
- According to the *Ice Trade Journal*, the harvest of Maine and Hudson River ice for the years 1878 to 1900 shows yearly quantities ranging from 2,226,000 tons in 1880 to 5,626,430 tons in 1899.
- Ice production was very labor-intensive, performed entirely with hand axes and saws. Though the icebox was developed in 1861, four years later two-thirds of homes in Boston still had their ice delivered daily.

Piazza Rock (Bigelows)

This hike is for a day when you don't have time to do the entire wonderful and demanding Saddleback Trail, but would still like to get out into the scenic Rangeley area for a pleasant walk through the woods to an unusual geological feature.

Driving directions (DeLorme 19, A-1): Driving north on ME-4, along the Sandy River, about 5 miles past Madrid, you will come to the point where the Appalachian Trail crosses the highway. There is a parking lot to the left, on the west side of ME-4. Cross the highway for the trailhead, marked by a sign visible from the road.
Total round-trip distance: 3.6 miles.
Vertical rise: 375 ft.
Miscellaneous: No water or privy at the trailhead. Both are available at the Piazza Rock lean-to, which is 1.8 miles out on the trail. Naturally, don't fail to purify the water you get from the brook.
Map: AMC Maine, Map 2 Rangeley/Stratton Region, D-1.

> **The challenge and the payoff.** The hike begins by climbing a crest for a couple hundred feet, then flattens out or climbs only very gently. The 0.1-mile spur trail to Piazza Rock is steep and eroded, and, if you want to explore the top of the cantilevered slice, you may have trouble shimmying up the wedged rocks that form Piazza Rock. But since you don't get any really special views from up there—although it is neat—you may conclude that you can appreciate this unusual rock just as well from below.

Description of the hike. You begin by walking on a broad grassy road, then use a small bridge to cross over the stream, which is tightly channeled on one side through rock. The climb up the crest is steep, but you are aided by log steps at one point. Once you have crested the hillside, the trail flattens out and offers a number of bog bridges. You will cross a road, then a tote road, and, 1.5 miles from ME-4, come to a trail register. Sign in, because by doing so, you provide important information to the Maine Appalachian Trail Club about how many people use various segments of the trail. At this point, you are 0.3 mile from Piazza Rock and the Piazza Rock shelter (and 4.2 miles from Saddleback Mountain, which may be your destination for another day; see Other Hikes, Boomer Rating Five).

After your initial climb up the crest, you'll find the trail to be very pleasant, especially during the fall when the leaves are changing color, but really at all times, because it's very well-traveled and relatively level.

After signing in at the trail register, you arrive at the side trail to Piazza Rock in little more than ten minutes. On the left of the trail, you'll see a sign for the 200-yard side trail, just before the AT Caretakers tent platform site and a stream crossing. Take the side trail and begin the steep climb up an eroded trail to round a couple boulders and arrive at the opening in front of the Rock. Expect to be struck by how a flat-topped overhanging rock is tucked amongst the forest trees and seems very much to be defying gravity. This huge slab of rock is cantilevered out from the cliff and actually supports mature trees.

You'll have to limber up the "monkey" in you to wedge your way up the rock and gain the top, where you may come across an AT Ridgerunner if you're hiking in the summer. These are the folks who oversee the trail and expound upon the leave-no-trace outdoor ethic, and once they've got you on top of Piazza Rock, you become their captive audience. Which is just fine, because what they have to say is simple but also important: carry out everything you bring in, don't get off the trail, don't pick the flowers, and don't take rocks as souvenirs. But do enjoy the trail and its natural bounties! And why not make a contribution to the Appalachian Trail Conservancy, we might suggest?

When you've had a good look around, descend from the left side of the boulder (or right side, now that you're up there). In other words, don't come down through the rock slabs you earlier used to wedge yourself up. Come to think of it, you could also have come up the left side, which would have been far easier.

You'll return to your car by the same trail, and will probably be promising yourself to come back another day, perhaps with a different destination the next time—all the way to Saddleback summit.

"Your Move," Maine's most famous outhouse,
Piazza/Saddleback trail

The Appalachian Trail

The trail you take out to Piazza Rock is part of the Appalachian Trail. It's shown on Map 6 of the official seven map series for the 281-mile length of the AT in Maine. These maps are extremely useful not only to the thru-hiker, but for you, too. On one side there is a contour map and trail profile, which give you an excellent visual of just how steep the trail is. On the other side, you've got general information, road access, trail descriptions and side trails, and mileages.

The section of the AT in Maine including Piazza Rock is 45.3 miles in length and takes the average AT thru-hiker three to five days to cover. Going south, the cumulative elevation gain will be 12,200 feet; in the opposite direction, 11,200 feet. Along this section, there are six lean-tos or campsites where the AT thru-hiker can overnight. In order to minimize impact on the forest, thru-hikers are discouraged from spending the night elsewhere in the woods. Fires are permitted only in approved fireplaces located at the campsite and prohibited elsewhere. And no trash is to be left—no tin cans nor anything, such as aluminium foil, that can't burn.

Since 1936, more than 9000 hike completions of the entire 2175-mile AT, from Maine to Georgia, have been recorded. More than 200 people have done it twice. In 2005, there were 546 completions, up from 488 in 2004. Only 25 percent of those who start manage to finish. So hats off to all those guys and gals who succeed!

Spruce Mountain to Pleasant Mountain Road
(Georges Highland Path)

On the way up, there are a couple of nice views, first to Grassy Pond, and then from Spruce Overlook onto Mirror Lake and beyond, but perhaps the real draw is that even on a summer weekend, you're likely to have the forest path to yourself.

Driving directions (DeLorme 14, D-2 & 3): On ME-17, south of South Hope and north of West Rockport, you'll find the parking area with room for six or eight cars on the east side of the road, along with an official information board maintained by the Georges River Land Trust and the trailhead for Ragged and Bald mountains. The trail to Spruce Mountain, described below, starts on the other side of ME-17. Be careful of fast-moving traffic as you cross the highway.

Total round-trip distance: 4.6 miles for Pleasant Mountain Road.

Vertical rise: Approximately 400 ft.

Highest point: 835 ft.

Miscellaneous: No water or restroom at the trailhead.

Map: Georges River Land Trust: Watershed & Highland Path, Ragged Mountain Section, which is sometimes available at the trailhead. Note that this hike does not take you to Ragged Mountain, but in the opposite direction, across the road from the parking area.

> **The challenge and the payoff.** In the first half-mile, count on a moderately steep ascent and some ledge to negotiate. Against these largely insubstantial negatives—this is Maine, after all—and despite the fact that the hike doesn't have a view payoff after the Spruce Mountain Overlook, the woods are very pleasant. Plus, there is the added benefit that you will have very little, if any, company in the woods. Solitude makes communion with nature that much easier!

Description of the hike. The trail begins across the road from the parking lot on ME-17. On this side, on the right, you will see a trail sign saying that you'll arrive at the Spruce Mountain Overlook in 0.6 mile. The hike we describe continues on to Mt. Pleasant Road and is a relatively easy 2.3 miles.

Within a couple of minutes, you cross a small seasonal brook, and very soon thereafter, the trail climbs fairly steeply up a ridge. In 0.2 mile, you will come to the Northern Outlook ledge with its view of Grassy Pond to the northwest, and then, 0.4 mile beyond, to Spruce Mountain, with a nice view over Mirror Lake and further out to Penobscot Bay and coastal islands. Your hiking poles (or strong leg muscles) will help you climb up and down the ledge at the Northern Outlook.

Once you leave the overlook on Spruce Mountain, the trail makes a long and gradual descent into an attractive forest. Where the trail passes by a nearby boggy area (at approximately 1.7 miles from the trailhead), the footing can become somewhat wet. Emerging from this area, the trail climbs briskly through the forest up a rise and enters a broad grassy field (with power lines) that you cross to arrive at Mt. Pleasant Road. To avoid this rather anticlimactic turn-around at a road with a house in view, you can cross the road and reenter the woods to hike toward Mt. Pleasant, 1.8 miles further. That would, however, make your total round-trip mileage 8.2 miles, which would make it a Boomer Rating Three hike.

Punctuation Oddities

If the origin of the Georges River Land Trust is to be found in the name of St. George River, punctuation purists may wonder why the land trust spells its name *Georges* and not *George's* River. Anybody have an explanation?

Another way to avoid crossing the field to the road is simply to turn around after climbing the last rise in the forest, right before reaching the grassy area. You'll still have a nice walk in the woods—one, by the way, that is equally good on snowshoes.

Other Hikes in the Area

√ This hike is in the Ragged Mountain Section of the Georges River Land Trust, a 9.5-mile section of mountain path offering long views from Ragged, Bald, and Spruce mountains.

√ Of the three, we prefer the climb to Spruce and the walk beyond in the woods, because, after the Overlook, we've almost never met anyone else on the trail, even in high summer. The trail is also less steep than the climb to Ragged and Bald.

√ Besides Ragged, the GRLT includes two other sections, to the south: the Oyster River Bog Section and the Thomaston Town Forest Section.

√ Another section of the Path is the Frye-Hogback Section. In this book, we've included two hikes from that section: Hogback Mountain and Frye Mountain in Boomer Rating Three.

Overview
Boomer Rating Three
Upping the Ante

For us, hikes rated at this level are some of our favorites. They are for days when we don't have the time or inclination to knock ourselves out but want to be out in nature and still get some worthwhile exercise. They are ones that we often repeat, or that, as in the cases of Frye and the Sheepscot Headwaters Trail Network, represent relatively recent additions to our list. We think that you'll enjoy them, too.

In general, a Boomer Rating Three means that the hike's challenges are relatively contained, unlike most of the Fours and Fives. In comparison with a Boomer Rating Two, a Boomer Rating Three requires more effort, perhaps more time to complete, and more serious commitment. But do carefully read the description, because what we consider a challenge might not always coincide with your definition.

In this group of Featured Hikes rated in the mid-range, we've included a threesome in central Maine (Frye, Hogback, and Northern Headwaters), an old favorite in Acadia National Park (Cadillac by the South Ridge Trail), and two other wonderful Acadia hikes on the "quiet side" (Great Pond to Great Notch and Valley/South Ridge to Beech Mountain), plus a great hike to (but not through) Mahoosuc Notch—which would have to be a Boomer Rating Five, at least!

In addition, we describe a little-used trail that gives a superb view of the Acadia range (Schoodic Mountain), a pleasant walk in the Bigelows (Cranberry Pond), and two very photogenic hikes—Lower Lone Mountain near Phillips and, in the Mahoosuc mountains, Lower Wright Trail. There are also two well-known view hikes: Table Rock in Grafton Notch and Bald Rock in Lincolnville, plus two relatively unknown ones in the western mountains (Success Mountain and

Surplus Pond); finally, we've chosen an excellent ramble through an enchanted forest in the Rangeley area (Sabbath Day Pond).

What makes this selection of hikes so appealing to us is their variety. None requires a massive expenditure of physical effort, but all will bring roses to your cheeks, so to speak. The longest is a 9.1-mile hike (Frye Mountain), but many fall in the five to seven-mile round-trip category. Some are even shorter—Success Overlook, at 3 miles round-trip, or Table Rock in Grafton Notch for a 2.2 mile round-trip—with each also having an elevation gain that will likely leave you puffing at least a little. Both of these hikes, together with Bald Rock, exceed the relatively moderate elevation gain of 650 feet per mile, but as fairly short hikes, they'll give you your reward much faster, and you'll feel virtuous about working your heart and lungs.

Another hike, Surplus Pond Trail, also offers a surprising amount of variety in terms of trail scenery, and its one-way distance of 1.8 miles includes only one quite steep section down to the pond and back. On the other hand, the second part of Sabbath Day will challenge you to descend and ascend steep slabs of ledge or boulders, especially over Bates Ledge, even if otherwise the footpath is fairly level.

Note that while vertical altitude is calculated as the difference between beginning and highest point, when there is a lot of repeated ascent and descent throughout the hike, your body is going to feel much more exercised than the simple number of feet in vertical rise would suggest. Even the Northern Headwaters Trail, which appears to have an extremely modest rise of 280 feet, will seem more demanding because there is so much up and down, and the trail itself is not well-trodden.

Some of the Boomer Threes can be lengthened—for instance, Success, Table Rock, Lower Lone, Great Pond to Great Notch, and Lower Wright. But if you do that, you'll turn them into a Four or Five in terms of challenge, which is not a bad goal, of course, but not what this section is about.

Below are fifteen superb hikes. Note that they show *total round-trip* mileage and one-way elevation gain. Following the Featured Hikes in this section, we list "Other Hikes," also belonging to the category of Boomer Rating Three.

Hike	Round-trip miles	Vertical gain
Bald Rock (Lincolnville)	4.2 miles	750 ft.
Cadillac by South Ridge Trail	7.0 miles	1300 ft.
Cranberry Pond	5.2 or 7 miles, depending on starting point	1070 ft.
Frye Mountain	9.1 miles	570 ft.
Great Pond to Great Notch	6.6 miles	558 ft.
Hogback Mountain	5.0 miles	455 ft.
Lower Lone Mountain	5.8 miles	795 ft.
Lower Wright Trail to North-South Junction	5.0 miles	1000 ft.
Mahoosuc Notch Trail to Notch	5.0 miles	800 ft.
Northern Headwaters Trail	3.5 miles	280 ft.
Sabbath Day Pond Trail	7.4 miles	500 ft.
Schoodic Mountain	5.5 miles	1000 ft.
Surplus Pond Trail	3.8 miles	750 ft.
Table Rock	2.4 miles	900 ft.
Valley Trail and South Ridge to Beech Mountain	3.0 miles	769 ft.

Bald Rock Mountain (Lincolnville)

For a fine bird's-eye view to Penobscot Bay and a string of well-known Maine islands, do consider this hike for a crisp day in the fall or on snowshoes in winter.

Driving directions (DeLorme 14, C-4): Take ME-173 from Lincolnville Beach for 2.3 miles, turning left onto Youngtown Road. In 200 feet, turn left into a parking area with room for ten vehicles.
Total round-trip distance: 4.2 miles.
Vertical rise: 750 ft.
Highest point: 1100 ft. on Bald Rock Mountain.
Miscellaneous: No restroom or water at the trailhead or along it.
Map: AMC Maine, Map 4, Camden Hills, A-2.

The challenge and the payoff. Since two-thirds of this hike takes place on a multi-use road, you may have to share that part of the hike with the kind of "traffic" you don't usually expect to find on a woodsy path. Still, during fall when the leaves are changing colors, this is a nice outing, just as it is in winter when you do the hike on snowshoes. Those who love islands or who are acquainted with the islands in Penobscot Bay, will enjoy roaming the ledge summit and identifying them with a map.

Description of the hike. Directly behind where you parked your car, the trail begins on the Multi-Use Road, which has recently been improved from its formerly rutted state. This broad dirt road is closed to all but service vehicles, being reserved for hikers, bicycles, horseback riding, and snowmobiling—quite a bit of potential traffic in itself.

You will continue up this road, which climbs moderately, passing on the left a trail sign for the Frohock Mountain Trail and continuing for 1.3 miles, until you see the cut-off for Bald Mountain to the left.

In an open clearing immediately after you turn, you will see an old foundation about 10 x 15 feet for a cabin.

Note that the mileage to the summit given on the trail sign at the cut-off is inaccurate. The correct distance is 0.8 mile, during which you will be climbing about 550 feet, enough to make you sweat, especially on a humid or hot day. At one point, you are aided by a long series of rock steps; then the trail continues its climb on a wide path covered with pine needles and lots of roots and small rocks. As you approach the summit, the canopy of the forest gives way to sky. Skip the first path to the right and take the next one, where you will be able to choose your perch from amongst several different levels of ledge. There is a lean-to immediately before the summit, to the left and down a slight slope.

Once at the summit, take out your map and spot the islands of Penobscot Bay, including Islesboro and far-off Deer Isle.

What's in a Name?

As noted above, this hike gives you a view onto Penobscot Bay. Penobscot is an Indian word meaning "rocky part," "descending ledges," or "descending rocks," as Brian McCauley explains in *The Names of Maine*. Anybody who hikes in Maine inevitably gets a lot of experience of the "Penobscot" kind.

While you could return by the 2.1–mile Frohock Mountain Trail (near the lean-to) to the Multi-Use Road, this trail is very steep. We've found it best just to turn around and retrace our steps.

On the other hand, should you want to extend your hike, you can do so soon after the Bald Rock side-trail junctions with the Multi-Use Road, with a left onto the Cameron Mountain Trail for 1.9 miles and then going to Zeke's Lookout in about one-third of a mile. for views of Bald Rock Mountain. You can return to the Multi-Use Trail from Zeke's Trail in about 1.1 additional miles and then would have 2.5 miles to cover to get back to your car. Make sure, however, to have a map and compass. When we did this a number of years ago, we had a lot of trouble following the trail, which was beginning to disappear.

Mountain flower

Cadillac South Ridge Trail (Acadia, East Side)

A classic Acadia trail, this hike on the island's highest mountain has it all—forest, expansive ocean views, and Maine's specialties, roots, rocks, and ledge, plus super views. Ignore the tourists at the top by finding your own spot on the vast summit ledges.

Driving directions (DeLorme 16, 4-B & C): Going south on Route 3, past Otter Creek, and across from and just beyond the turnoff for the Blackwoods Campground, you will see the trailpost for the Cadillac South Ridge Trail. Park on the side of this busy road.
Total round-trip distance: 7 miles (signs on trail indicate 7.4 miles).
Vertical rise: 1300 ft.
Highest point: 1530 ft. on Cadillac Mountain
Miscellaneous: No restroom or water at the trailhead, but both are available at the summit, as well as a gift shop open during tourist season. **Note:** The Island Explorer buses do *not* operate to the summit of Cadillac Mountain.
Map: Acadia NP, East Side, I-14, H-13, F-13.

The challenge and the payoff. The hike's challenge resides in the roots and rocks on the trail, and the steady climb, plus, in the last half-mile, a couple of sections of rock boulders to negotiate sometimes with hands as well as feet, and once with an iron rung. But although the trail gains 1300 feet over its 3.5 mile length, there are interludes throughout of level walking—respite for the lungs and legs—with the result that frequent stops to rest are unnecessary. And the ambience, starting with the shady forest of mixed conifers and deciduous trees and rising to sparser vegetation as you proceed up the granite slopes, leads to a greater sense of exhilaration than of fatigue, as you access an ever more expansive panorama of islands, coast, and ocean.

Description of the hike. From the trail post on Route 3, you climb up several steep rock stairs to access the well-maintained footpath that begins by meandering gently up through the forest over roots, rocks, pine needles, and slabs of ledge. Shortly, the trail climbs more steeply over rock and by boulders. After one mile, you will see the first trail sign for Eagle's Crag, a loop of 0.3 mile off to the right. We normally skip it, continuing straight ahead. Within several minutes, the first views of the ocean began to appear over your left shoulder. A second signpost (also giving the chance to access Eagle's Crag) tells you that you have climbed 1.2 miles and that it is now 2.3 miles to Cadillac's summit.

Views continue to open up as you ascend and pass through stubby pines growing in patches of soil on ledge, or through low pine forests. A helpful hint: when you need to take a high step up a ledge rock, it sometimes helps to lean into the rock, using your back hiking pole to propel you forward. Only a few times toward the top of the trail will you have to use your arms to help power your step.

A little over two miles from where you started, you will come to a large rock rubble. Pass it by, keeping to the right side. Off to the left is a pond known as The Featherbed. One particularly dry summer, we were surprised to see that it was dry-as-dust, the result of global warming, we surmised. Above the pond area, just off the trail, is a well-placed bench, beckoning you to take a rest before carrying on for the last 1.2 miles up to Cadillac.

Continuing, you pass by the Pond Trail to the left (west) and the Canon Brook Trail (onto which we once wandered by mistake; see the textbox) to the right or east. You will have a couple of steep sections of ledge to negotiate, and then, as you continue to climb, you'll glimpse the first cars shimmering on the Park Loop Road about 0.5 mile away.

Do note that while the trail approaches the Park Loop Road, it will veer to the right, so that you do not have to cross any traffic. You are still 0.25 mile from the summit. There will be three patches of rock to climb, one with a rung, the others requiring arm power. You will continue through a shrub forest and arrive at a gravel road. Turn left and reenter the woods. There will be some more ledge and rock to climb, and then finally you emerge in the open. We usually go off-trail at this point to avoid the enormous parking area that disgorges hoards of tourists in the summer. Well short of the parking lot, there are miles of ledge on which to wander and catch the sea breezes.

A Word to the Wise
Cadillac South Ridge Trail, though well-marked by blue blazes on trees and rocks, as well as rock cairns, requires some attentiveness, especially when emerging from or entering the forest, particularly on the descent. It is entirely possible for the first-time—or even, we admit with a blush, the previously initiated—visitor, to wander off track and get on some plausible-seeming but wayward trail. This is exactly what we once did at the level of the Featherbed Pond, ending up on the steep, wet, and ledgy Canon Brook Trail that, to our chagrin, brought us out on Route 3 some two miles north of our car. On our last hike on Cadillac, we noticed the presence of more signs requesting that hikers not tamper with rock cairns or create new ones, which led us to believe that maybe others had been misled as we had been. Our best advice: follow the blue paint blazes rather than the cairns.

So, find a great spot and break out the sandwiches. You'll probably soon be joined by a seagull, alighting nearby in hopes of being offered some tasty morsel. Don't, of course. When he finally realizes nothing is forthcoming, he'll fly off to catch a downdraft and soar over the magnificent landscape in an entertaining and marvelous one-man show.

The last time we did this trail—one of our all-time favorites—we were out on a glorious sunny day in summer, at the same time as some thirty or so members from a hiking club in Iowa. They represented a variety of ages, shapes, and levels of hiking capability, yet had the kind of enthusiasm that was infectious. Perhaps the reason for the flatlander Iowans' lightheartedness was the unaccustomed elevation of Acadia's highest mountain, at all of 1530 feet. But as you descend the mountain by the same route taken to climb the mountain, you, too, may feel that exhilaration, if not their veritable giddiness, with the sea in front of you and your hair blowing in the breeze.

The Featherbed on South Ridge of Cadillac, Acadia

We've hiked this trail in all seasons and can definitely say that fall and late spring are the best times to be out there. The winds can blow pretty strongly up on the open ledge, but it is so invigorating!

Cranberry Pond (Bigelows)

Along the way to peaceful Cranberry Pond—a perfect place for lunch—you'll pass a picturesque brook with a bench at its bend and a beaver pond where you may catch a lucky glimpse of some affable fellow at work or play.

Driving directions (DeLorme 29, C-3): Access the trail from ME-27, five miles south of Stratton, where there is an AT parking lot on the south side of the road. Cross the highway for the trailhead in order to head north on the AT toward Horns Pond (4.2 m.) and Avery Peak (7.6 m.). You can also shorten the hike by nearly 2 miles by driving 0.75 mile further north on ME-27 to Stratton Brook Pond Road. Turn right on the dirt road and arrive at the trailhead on the left in one mile. Park off the road.

Total round-trip distance: 7 miles beginning from ME-27; 5.2 miles from Stratton Brook Pond Road.

Vertical rise: approximately 1070 ft.

Miscellaneous: No restroom or water at the trailhead, but there is a privy at the Cranberry Stream campsite. Note that most hiking guidebooks have you climb to Cranberry Peak at 3213 ft. from the Bigelow Range trailhead in Stratton, but our hike opts for a different destination and lops off 1100 feet of climbing, making its goal a quiet pond rather than a sometimes busy summit.

Map: AMC Maine, Map 2 Rangeley/Stratton Region, B-3.

The challenge and the payoff. After a couple miles of easy walking, you will climb about 1000 feet in the last mile and a half, which means that you'll probably break a sweat but that it won't be too grueling. You'll feel fully compensated when you reach the Pond and find a good perch above the water from which to relax and enjoy the tranquility.

Description of the hike. This description begins from ME-27. After crossing the highway, you walk for 0.9 mile through the forest on a well-worn path heading toward Stratton Brook Pond Road. Cross the road and continue easy walking on a clearly defined path of mostly gentle ups and downs. You cross one brook and a flight of log steps, followed by a drag road and another set of log steps, then Dick Brown's Bridge. Soon after, there is a trail box where you sign in. About a mile from Stratton Brook Pond Road, you come to the very pleasant Cranberry Stream campsite with privy and water, on the right. A few minutes further on, there is a bend in the stream (on the left) with a well-placed bench—a welcome sight especially for those who have descended the very steep 3.2 miles from the Horns Pond lean-tos.

Does Size Matter?

In the New England context, what's the difference between a *lake* and a *pond*? Moosehead Lake is definitely a lake, and so are Mooselookmeguntic and Flagstaff. No disagreement there. But what about lots of other bodies of water, like Cranberry Pond, which look like lakes to the rest of the country but are called *ponds* by New Englanders? To wit, Thoreau's Walden Pond in Massachusetts.

Within minutes after leaving the bend in the stream, you will begin climbing fairly steeply for approximately a mile. As you near one rise, you will hear water gurgling and can look down on a pleasant glen. The terrain now becomes level as you pass a beaver pond on the right and perhaps catch sight of one of those active fellows swimming in his private pool. For photographers, the still pond with trees reflected in the water is a very pretty shot, and with a good telephoto lens you might also catch the swimming beaver's cute little face. After the pond, there will be another quarter hour of climbing before, at 2495 feet, you reach an intersection in the trail. Cranberry Pond is a mere 0.2 mile further to the left.

Since this is an out-and-back hike, you'll retrace your steps. For another day, you might consider one of these variations:

All About Beavers

Beavers and giardia unfortunately often go together, so, like everywhere in Maine, don't think that a supposedly clear-looking pond is safe. It isn't, and giardia can make you very, very sick.

Speaking of beavers, did you know: they can chew through a six-inch tree in about fifteen minutes; they are especially fond of poplar but will also go for white birch and maple; they mate for life during their third year; an adult beaver typically weighs in between 35-40 pounds; their young (kits) are born in the spring, and the yearlings act as babysitters for the parents; most live to be about ten years old; beavers are considered second only to humans in their ability to change a landscape. Leave it to Beaver(s).

- At the trail intersection for Cranberry Pond, you can also turn right, as we did one day, to access Horns Pond, less than two miles away. But even on a cool day, this option makes for a real workout, since Horns Pond stands at 3250 feet and you started out at about 1430 feet on ME-27. That means a rise of more than 1800 feet in under two miles, and it will be over numerous rocks and boulder ledges that will challenge both your lungs and knees. For us, however, it was an interesting experience on an overcast day, when the forest seemed like a scene out of Tolkien, dark and brooding, with moss-covered rocks, their deep green coats offset by the black mud of the pathway. In addition, there were boulders the size of cabins, with gaping cavern mouths, beckoning like an evil witch. Well, it was a very dark fall day.
- An easier way to the Horns is by way of the Stratton Brook Pond, as described in Boomer Rating Four.
- A second option involving Cranberry Pond is to go just south of the town of Stratton to access the Bigelow Range Trail for Cranberry Peak (3213 ft.) and then come out by the Cranberry Pond Trail we have just described. There is the inconvenience, however, of being four miles from your car, which means that you either have to hoof it or to hitchhike,

as we did. In these times of high fuel costs, few will want to take the expedient of coming in two cars and spotting the second one. Total distance for this option would bring you to 8.3 miles.

History Tidbit

History buffs will be interested in knowing that the Bigelow Range was named for Major Timothy Bigelow, who climbed Bigelow Mountain to scout the territory ahead of Benedict Arnold's campaign through Maine to Quebec, in fall and winter 1775.

Frye Mountain (Georges Highland Path)

An excellent hike for when you have the inclination for a longer but still moderate walk through a woods that speaks of history with its old stone walls and other reminders of earlier times.

Driving directions (DeLorme 14, A-2): Frye Mountain is located off ME-220, heading north just past Polands Corner and near the Frye Mountain State Game Management Area. There are two approaches: the first, from Walker Ridge Road to the east, off ME-220; and the second, a bit further, an unmarked entrance, also on the east side of 220, which leads through the woods to Walker Ridge Road. If the gate is closed at the Walker Ridge Road, hikers can also park near the Frye Mountain State Game Management maintenance building and hike from there.

Total round-trip distance: 9.1 miles from Walker Ridge access; about 11 miles from ME-220 access.

Vertical rise: 570 ft.

Highest Point: 1139 ft., Frye Mountain.

Miscellaneous: There is neither restroom nor water at the trailhead.

Map: Georges Highland Path: Frye-Hogback Section, available from Georges River Land Trust, or usually at trailhead. Web site: www.grlt.org

---

The challenge and the payoff. You will likely find few other people on this hike that passes through a pleasant, varied woods with a meandering and picturesque stream. But because it is on multi-use land, you should most definitely wear blaze-orange during hunting seasons. Why not just keep both hat and vest in the trunk of your car so that you're always prepared?

Description of the hike. This hike is located in the 5240-acre state-owned Frye-Hogback Section of the Georges Highland Path. If you start from ME-220, you will follow the blue blazes through the woods for about a mile of mostly easy climbing or level walking. The trail is easy to follow because of the blazes, though it is not necessarily well trod. After passing a stretch of stone fences and other remains from a past era, you will glimpse through the woods, to the right, a gravel road used by ATVs and others. This is Walker Ridge Road, where you could have begun the hike. Cross to the other side of the road and reenter the woods.

Soon you will see a trail information sign with a map that you can either pick up or study on the spot. Continue walking and within minutes, Bartlett Stream will appear on the right. You will make two easy crossings of the stream, the first time very soon after seeing it and the second after first crossing a drag road and stepping over a stone wall. The stream itself offers many picturesque scenes. The hike proceeds through a variety of landscapes, including broad, expansive wooded areas set in beds of ferns as well as others of young firs. Because of the tall trees and lack of sunlight, you will see many mossy areas. As the hike begins to climb, the scenery changes, with more open areas and mounds of mountain lichen.

At 2.2 miles from the Walker Ridge Road access point, and closer to 3.2 miles from ME-220, you will see a sign posted on a tree, to the left of the trail, announcing the Frye Mountain Loop Trail. You are now at 1000 feet, having already covered most of the hike's modest ascent. The sign says the loop is 4.7 miles; we measured it as closer to 5.5 miles. In any event, you have your choice either to go north immediately toward the summit (1139 ft.), which you come to in less than a mile, or to take the southern route, losing and then regaining a couple hundred feet of altitude. Both are fine. We've always taken the northern route.

After completing the circuit, you head back for your car by the same trail, happy with your long, but relatively easy hike, ready to return again soon.

More on the Area

- The headwaters of the St. George River, near Frye Mountain, are fed by streams, ponds, and wetlands, as the waterway winds its way more than fifty miles to its mouth on the coast of Port Clyde (one of the take-off points for the ferry to Monhegan Island) where it enters Muscongus Bay. In this 225-square-mile watershed, there are lush forests, working farms, rolling hills, blueberry barrens, rock coast, and typical, small Maine communities.

- As noted for the Featured Hike, Northern Headwaters, also in this section, hiking trails on the Georges Highland Path and the Sheepscot Headwaters Trail Network can be linked, into a super-long hike that requires spotting a car or taking more than one day. You could, for instance, start with the Northern Headwaters Trail, followed by the Bog Brook Trail, and its link-up to the Hogback Connector, then continue on to Hogback and Frye mountains on the Georges Highland Path.

- Do make sure, however, to have a recent map and a GPS. We've occasionally had trouble following some of these trails, which do not tend to be heavily traveled. You can usually pick up a map at the trailhead. Or contact SWLA, P.O. Box 155, Freedom, Maine 04941, or phone 207-589-4311.

Great Pond Trail to Great Notch
(Western Mountains, Acadia)

A lovely, peaceful hike for all seasons, first on a tree-shaded path that runs alongside Great Pond and then in a stately forest on a pine-needle path bordered by stones, laid down decades ago by trail builders.

Driving directions (DeLorme 16, C-2): On the western side of Mount Desert Island, take ME-102 to Seal Cove Road, which you follow for 0.6 mile, turning right onto Long Pond Road for 1.1 miles, until the dead end at the pumping station.
Total round-trip distance: 6.6 miles.
Vertical rise: 558 ft.
Highest point: 640 ft. at Great Notch.
Miscellaneous: No restroom or drinking water at the trailhead. Park to the right of the birch tree by the Pond; we once got a ticket for parking to the left of the tree. If all the parking spots are taken, you can park your vehicle well up and off Long Pond Road, above the pumping station.
Map: Acadia NP, West Side, J-6. The full name is "Acadia National Park, Trails, Carriage Roads, Hiking, Biking," by Adventure LLC. It's very legible and gives mileage for all hikes on the Island. Don't hike Acadia without it!

Description of the hike. Begin behind the pumping station, which puts you immediately on the Great Pond Trail. Note that maps designate the body of water as Long Pond and the footpath as Long Pond (Great Pond) Trail, while the signposts on the trail all refer to it as Great Pond. You are going to walk along the lake for two miles, so ignore both the first trail sign to the left, which would put you onto Cold Brook Trail, as well as the next signpost, also to the left, for the Perpendicular Trail.

> **The challenge and the payoff**. Finding a parking spot at the height of tourist season may be the biggest challenge, since there is room for only about six or seven vehicles in the parking area by the pumping station. Except for once in August, however, we've never found this to be a problem because, after all, you are on "the quiet side" of Acadia. The only other rather small challenge may be that after rains or in spring, the trail bordering parts of the pond can be wet. No big deal, right? Anyway, the hike itself is most enjoyable, because for very little effort, despite the total round-trip mileage, you get the double reward of lake and forest, plus a great sense of tranquility. And you may even have, as we did once, the unusual opportunity to photograph a loon, placidly bobbing in the water about 25 feet away—the closest we'd ever been to this storied bird.

Your walk by the lakeside is for the most part on a wide, flat, and well-maintained gravel path. Considered to be an especially fine example of shoreline path building, requiring back fill and extensive stonework, the trail was completed in 1936 by the Civilian Conservation Corps. Especially in the summer, you'll appreciate the shade provided by the tree-bowered path and enjoy the sound of gently lapping water. You'll pass several rockslides on your left, and climb over rocks. Perhaps, you'll even have the opportunity to see a loon or to make the acquaintance of another small creature, like four-year old Rocky, the powerhouse chihuahua, whose master proudly told us how the little fellow had recently triumphantly finished a sixteen-mile hike. Just imagine how those tiny four legs must have been churning!

About an hour after starting the hike—depending, of course, on how often you stop to get a particularly picturesque photo or to chat—the trail pulls away from the lake to enter the woods, where it climbs moderately through a rock-scattered fir forest. Within a few minutes, you cross a well-constructed log and timber bridge over boulder-strewn Great Brook. The trail then begins to rise somewhat more up a rocky trail, sometimes with roots, other times softened by fir needle duff. But it remains a beautiful forest-shaded path, well trodden and flanked by rocks obviously laid by route builders decades ago.

Loon at Great Pond, Acadia

When you reach the intersection with the Western Trail, on your right, you will be 0.4 mile from the Great Notch. On this stretch of the trail, you'll be encountering roots all over the footpath, so keep your head down and watch your step.

The Great Notch is actually a crossroads, with a couple of log benches and a trail register, plus signposts giving the option to continue in several directions, including to both Mansell and Bernard Mountains, though from opposite directions, and the Western Mountain Road. We think that the Great Notch makes a perfect turn-around spot, but if you're seeking more challenge, check out our description in the section on Boomer Rating Four for the hike to Bernard Mountain by Great Pond Trail. Interestingly, although that hike is shorter than this one, it is definitely much more challenging. The one we've just described is for days when you want something more gentle.

Getting to Know Loons

~ Loons can weigh up to fourteen pounds, which is very heavy for a flight-capable bird. Their heft comes from the fact that they have solid rather than hollow bones. What this means is that while their solidness helps them in diving for fish, it makes getting airborne much more difficult. Sometimes to get aloft, they have to flap their wings while "running" across as much as a quarter-mile of open water. Once in the air, however, they can reach speeds of 90 mph. Pretty amazing!

~ No one who has heard the call of the loon forgets the haunting sound, although experts say that there are actually four different types of vocalizations: *wails* in order to stay in contact with each other; *yodels* for defending territory; *tremolos* when feeling threatened or defending chicks; and *hoots*, which are intimate calls between family members, spouses or chicks. The guy we saw in Great Pond was just chilling out, making no sound as he lazily bobbed in the water.

Hogback Mountain (Georges Highland Path)

For a quiet morning or afternoon excursion, take this pleasant and various hike to travel back into early Maine history in Waldo County, in a forest with remnants of old stone walls and even three nineteenth-century tombstones standing near a magnificent 200-year old oak tree.

Driving directions (DeLorme Map 14, A-1): From Route 3 and traveling north on ME-220, about 0.3 mile past the intersection with Walker Ridge Road, you will see on the right (east) a short road leading to a forest path (one of the access points to the Frye Mountain hike). Don't park here but rather well off the pavement on ME-220. Directly across the road is the unmarked trailhead for Hogback, almost obscured by vegetation, and marked only by planks crossing a boggy section.

Total round-trip distance: approximately 5 miles.

Vertical rise: 455 ft.

Miscellaneous: No water or restroom at trailhead. Part of the Georges River Land Trust, the Hogback Section is multi-use land, which means that logging operations may have made changes to the trail. To get the latest information and a map, contact Georges River Land Trust in Rockland at 207-594-5166.

Map: Georges Highland Path: Frye-Hogback Section, available from Georges River Land Trust or at the trailhead. Web site: www. grlt.org.

Description of the hike. After parking your car on the east side of ME-220, cross to the west side of the road, where you should look for beaten-down grasses and wooden planks laid end to end crossing a marshy area. This is the trailhead. Subsequently, the hike begins by climbing gently into a very pretty woods whose forest floor is graced by ferns and moss-covered rocks and crossed occasionally by tumbling stone fences.

The challenge and the payoff. The biggest challenge may be in following the trail, especially if recent logging operations have left the path encumbered with debris or even totally obscured. On one visit, we had some trouble with the trail, finding it ambiguously marked. Also the color of blue used for the blazes was sometimes difficult to see on a cloudy day or in the shadow, and some blazes were visible only from a specific angle. Therefore we counsel vigilance, especially when leaving the forest to cross a road or on reentering the forest from a logging road. In addition, when we were there one August day following plentiful rainfall, the trail was in places totally overgrown with grasses, brush, and ferns. Such route-finding challenges aside, you'll find a lot of appeal in the fact that this hike features a great combination of nature and history.

As you proceed, you will be going up a flank of the mountain and then around it before descending through a nice forest. Approximately 1.6 miles from the trailhead, just before crossing the unsigned Mountain Road, be on the lookout, on the left, for three gravestones in a small clearing, and about ten or fifteen feet off the trail. We missed them on the "out" trip, though easily spotted them on the return, probably because they were illuminated by a sunbeam; on the return, they'll be about 100-150 yards after leaving the road when you reenter the forest.

On one of the gravestones, slightly tipped by the passage of time, we read: "Samuel Howard, 1796-1870, and Lucy Ripley, his wife, 1798-1888." The second tombstone is more faintly inscribed, "Louisa J. Carr, 1836-1894," while a third carries the words, "Samuel J. Howard, died February 8, 1885, age 19." Towering in the background is a majestic oak tree that likely bore witness to these burials over a hundred years ago. We enjoyed constructing various scenarios based on these names and dates, pondering what the relationships had been and what dramas might have lain behind the terse facts carved on the tombstones.

But back to your out-trip. After traversing the road and reentering the forest, you will cross some seasonal creeks and a couple more stone walls. You will also cross skidder roads, now grassy walkways, but still suggesting earlier economic activity. About two miles into the hike, the trail passes across flat ledge and a grassy open area, then trends downward shortly before making a slight rise to arrive at the goal, the Hogback Overlook.

We took a GPS reading of 1156 feet at the Overlook, some 45 feet above the reading given on the Georges Highland Path map but within the margin of error for GPS readings. The Overlook is a fine place for lunch, but be careful of the ledge, which becomes slippery when moist and could lead to a dangerous tumble over a steep bluff into the brambles. From the Overlook, you have a nice view out onto forested hills, a couple of very private houses nestled in the trees, a field and pond, and then some far-off mountains.

A Word to the Wise

Multi-use land has its pros and cons. As a hiker, you may encounter hunters, trappers, and loggers, who have a legal right to exercise their activities, as much as you do. So, while it's great for hikers to have access to new trails, there is always the risk of competing interests. Which is why we recommend that you check the Web site of the Maine Department of Inland Fisheries and Wildlife (Maine.gov/ifw) to know when to expect hunting season. Alternatively, hike on Sundays, when hunting is forbidden. If you do go during hunting season, choose blaze-orange clothing and not anything that could confuse you with a deer, so that you are not mistaken for Bambi's mother.

When you've finished your lunch or photographing or rest stop, continue in the same direction along the ledge before reentering the woods. You are now completing the western side of the Hogback Loop (the entire loop is 1.4 miles), going north. At first, the trail descends gently from the Overlook, then arrives at a grassy section. As you emerge from the woods onto the grassy road, turn right. About twenty yards from there is a signpost marking the Hogback Loop (which you've just completed) and the Hogback Connector Trail, heading west and northwest before dropping south to link up with the Bog Brook Trailhead, which is part of the Sheepscot Headwater Trail Network. This gives you the opportunity to lengthen your hike if you wish, but make sure to have with you a recent map. This entire area is criss-crossed by former logging or farm roads and can be confusing if you accidentally get off the blue-blazed trail. We found that the blue blazes were easy to follow in the woods, but significantly less so on the road.

To continue with the hike we have been describing, when you arrive at the trail post, turn to the right, down the grassed-over road for roughly 0.3 mile. You are looking to rejoin the wooded trail where earlier you saw the tombstones. This part can be confusing; hopefully it will be better marked than when we were there. The entry into the woods will be on the left, but when we were there, the blue blaze was poorly placed and not really visible from our approach. It was just a few yards before another grassy road coming in from the right. As we suggested earlier, the number of formerly used roads can create uncertainty.

After you have entered the forest, with the family cemetery now on your right, continue to be very observant so that you do not miss blue blazes. If you realize that it's been too long since the last one, immediately retrace your steps to the last blue blaze and look again. We didn't and got lost, ending up bushwhacking and losing a lot of time. We encourage you to be more heedful than we were, because at this point the trail is simply the same one you originally took. Note that in high summer, after rainy periods, the trail can grow very grassy—we went through places where the ferns were up to the waist!

An Observation

Note that four of the hikes described in this section are contiguous: Northern Headwaters, Bog Brook, Hogback, and Frye. The first two are part of the Sheepscot Headwaters Trail Network, while the latter two belong to the Georges Highland Path. Members and volunteers from both groups work together to protect and preserve the natural resources of the area and subscribe to the philosophy that the land can be shared by many different parties.

"Where's the trail?" After a big rain on Hogback

Lower Lone Mountain (Phillips/Madrid)

A delightful and little-used section of the AT, passing through an especially fine forest, with creeks and streams and myriad tiny waterfalls in the spring, cool pools in the summer, and a spectacular show of color in the fall.

Driving directions (DeLorme 19, A & B-3): From Phillips, on Route 4, turn north onto Route 142. Continue for 2 miles until, on the left, you arrive at East Madrid Road, which is a paved and dirt road passing a few houses. At 6 miles from Route 142, turn left onto Potato Hill Road, which becomes narrower and is used by logging trucks. At a fork, stay to the right. You will follow this road for 4 miles. Occasional skidder roads take off from the side, and several open spots show active logging operations. You will leave your vehicle at approximately 12 miles from the beginning of Route 142, parking in an area on the left of the road where the grasses have been beaten down.

Total round-trip distance: 5.8 miles.

Vertical rise: 795 ft.

Highest point: 2297 ft.

Miscellaneous: No restroom or water at the trailhead. You can purify water from Sluice Brook at points along the hike, the first opportunity being approximately 1.3 miles from your car, then later when you reach the bubbling creeks near Barnjum Road, roughly 1.6 miles further on.

Map: AMC Maine, Map 2 Rangeley/Stratton Region, D & E-3.

Description of the hike. Leave your car and begin walking down the road, which grows increasingly narrow, rutted, and rocky. Follow it for nearly one-and-a-half miles, or about one-half hour of straightforward walking. When you reach Sluice Brook, with water streaming across the road and down a steep hillside, toward Orbeton Stream, the trailhead will be across the stream, immediately to the right. With a few steps up into the forest, you will be on the trail, now with Sluice Brook to your right and on the left an AT trail post indicating that Lone Mountain (3280 ft.) is 3.1 miles ahead. You won't be going that far on this hike, which will, instead, turn around at the Barnjum Road crossing.

The challenge and the payoff. The access road to the hike, Potato Hill Road, can be rough at times, and you must follow it for four miles. During or after heavy rains, it should be avoided, unless you've got four-wheel drive and like adventurous driving. Otherwise, if you take it slow, there should be no problem. In terms of the hike itself, you will not be gaining a lot of altitude and so will really be able to enjoy the beauty of a forest that you will very likely have to yourself. In the spring, you will be delighted by the sounds of water forming tiny eddies and sparkling fountains, while on a crisp day in the autumn, you'll not find a better place to enjoy the changing colors.

We have always found the walk through the woods very appealing, partly because there is not much vertical gain but especially because the woodscapes are so varied and pleasant. At times, the wide trail opens on either side to park-like, sparsely forested areas, while at other times, it wends its way through thicker trees and areas much favored by moose. Regardless of the season, we have almost never met anyone else on the trail, although one summer the stillness of the forest was occasionally broken by the sound of helicopters from a U.S. naval operations area on practice escape and rescue missions. More pleasing, of course, are the songbirds, especially in the morning.

We especially remember one spring day in mid-May after there had been heavy rains in the state. The road coming in to the trailhead had been tricky, but the trail was fine, especially because of the many bog bridges. The temperatures were in the 50s and 60s—perfect for hiking—and, since it was so early in the season, the wetness had not yet attracted bugs. As we walked through the moisture-laden woods, wrapped in great clouds of mist, and listened to the birds chirping and heard frogs croaking and saw many little brown toads jumping off the trail, we knew we were experiencing nature in its most renewing sense.

Wildlife Antics

During the entire hike you'll be in prime habitat for **moose**, a fact you will quickly note by the great piles of poop they choose to leave on the trails or even on the bog bridges, often near the beaten-down grasses of their sleeping yards.

These large, gangly creatures usually don't make their presence known by any other means, keeping clear of humans on the trail, though sometimes they can be heard crashing through the forest, or, more often, sighted along Maine highways.

But on one occasion, one of the authors did have a most unusual encounter with a cow moose, while doing his AT Monitor duties. He'd set up his tent along the trail corridor of Lone Mountain and had just exited the tent to begin heating up water for hot chocolate, when all of a sudden he looked up to see a moose about twenty feet away. His hair rose on end; he hadn't even heard her.

She just stood there, stock-still, staring at him. So he spoke to her, trying amiably to suggest that she "carry on." She continued to hold her ground until, after a few minutes, she circled behind him while continuing to stare. Then she went up the hillside, snorted a couple times, and returned, this time about forty feet away and looking pretty tense.

Was she planning to charge? Was she thinking she was protecting her young? Was she intensely curious about the interloper's strange yellow tent, his freeze-dried scrambled eggs . . . *him*?

Deciding the better part of prudence was to clear out and leave her be, he quickly donned his pack and high-tailed it to Barnjum Road. When he returned a couple of hours later, there was no sign of Miss Moose, nor had she disturbed the campsite or left any "calling cards." Apparently, she had just been trying to figure out who or what this stranger in her neighborhood was, and when he was no longer there, simply decided to go on her merry way.

A decision, he, too, made, by packing up his tent and ending his duties on the mountain for that day.

Throughout the forest, and especially as we approached the sylvan area right before Barnjum Road, there was the constant sound of water as the melting snows turned creeks into tinkling waterways with multiple miniature waterfalls cascading over doll-sized ledges. This marvelous area of bonny brooks, crossed by a bridge, is a place where you will want to spend some time before turning around to retrace your steps.

A nice add-on option, however, is to go another couple hundred yards to exit the woods on Barnjum Road and then to turn left, taking the logging road for about 200 yards to open areas where you have panoramic vistas of beautiful mountain scenery as the road continues to rise. Walk as long as you like before taking the same route back to your car that you used on the "out" trip.

Typical Maine creek

Lower Wright Trail to the North-South Junction
(Mahoosuc Range)

On this highly scenic hike in the Mahoosucs, you'll be in the near constant company of the waters of Goose Eye Brook, pouring over picturesque ledge, cutting channels, and creating beckoning pools and waterfalls for your visual and aural pleasure.

Driving directions (DeLorme 10, A-2 and 3): On US-2, at 2.8 miles north of Bethel, turn onto Sunday River Road and set your odometer. You will be going 9.5 miles before leaving your car. At 2.2 miles, Sunday River Road forks to the right (on the left is Skiway Road, which leads to the Sunday River ski complex). At 3.8 miles, you will see the picturesque Artist Covered Bridge on the left. At 5.6 miles, you pass the Outward Bound Newry Mountain Center. At 6.5 miles, the road turns to hard-packed dirt and gravel. At 7.8 miles, turn left across two closely spaced steel bridges, then immediately take the first right, passing by two old camps close to the road. At 9.3 miles, cross Goose Eye Brook on a wooden bridge. In another 0.2 mile, you will see the trailhead on the left. The parking area is ahead, on the right.

Total round-trip distance: 5 miles.
Highest point: 2200 ft.
Vertical rise: 1000 ft.
Miscellaneous: No restroom or water at the trailhead.
NB: Depending on the condition of the trail, and if no improvements have been made to it since we were there, this hike would rate as a Boomer Rating Four.
Map: AMC Maine, Map 7 Mahoosuc Range, C-2.

Description of the hike. Note that the beginning of the Lower Wright Trail was rerouted in 2008, so that if you took this hike at an earlier period, be aware that it now follows a different route.

> **The challenge and the payoff**. The trail is often wet, eroded, and studded with plenty of encumbrances—in addition to roots, there are nearly invisible stumps ready to trip the unwary. In parts, the trail is not well marked, the blue blazes being few and far between; some of the bog bridges are rotted through, and you'll be crossing and re-crossing the brook. But for excellent photography of water over broad ledge, picturesque bends in the stream bed, and a variety of dynamic water—from powerful, gushing jets to rivulets and tinkling fountains—you'll be pleased to have discovered the beauties of this corner of the great Mahoosuc Mountains.

After leaving your car and entering the woods at the trailhead, you will see a sign indicating that the trail on the left goes down to the water (over a root-impeded path). Do not take this trail if you want to go to the North-South Junction, because it will eventually peter out. Instead, take the trail on the right, which launches you on the Wright Trail. As you will soon discover, this trail follows a former road, which has been trenched to allow water to run downhill. It is above the Goose Eye Brook, which is to your left and down through the trees.

After about twenty minutes of steady and moderate climb on the road, look for a blue blaze on the left, which leads down through the woods. The trail descends over stone steps to a creek, then continues over ground that climbs moderately at times and at other times is flat. In a little more than a quarter-hour, you come to more stone steps, this time going up, and shortly thereafter, you make a second creek crossing. Within the next half-hour, there will be a third crossing of the brook, followed by some wooden steps going up the slope. Take advantage of the times when the trail approaches the waters of Goose Eye Brook and offers good vantage points with views onto pretty pools and waterfalls.

If the trail has not been improved since the last time we hiked it, it can become problematic, especially following heavy rains, since a number of the bog bridges have rotted through, boards laid over muddy areas are sometimes broken, and without careful plotting of your steps, you may slip and land in the muck. Further difficulties may be encountered in places of uneven footing or where the footpath is seriously eroded. A great deal depends on whether the trail maintainers have made a recent visit or not.

Just before you reach the Branch, you will see, on the right, leading back into the woods, a campsite. Very soon thereafter, you'll be at the Junction, which is a pretty and bowery spot with a small waterfall in the background. There are a couple of well-placed logs where we never fail to take a breather. This is the terminus of this hike, but if you want to go further, you make the choice of crossing the water and going left, up the South Branch, or going right up the North Branch, again by crossing the water. If you're interested in doing either, take a look at our description in Boomer Rating Five, which may or may not dissuade you!

You'll make the return trip to your car by retracing your steps. If the season is right, you may be tempted to take a refreshing dip in one of the scenic pools that you spotted on the way in.

Some Further Observations

This trail is *not* named for our good friend, Milt Wright, but it is one of his favorites. And ours, too, perhaps because there is a brewery and restaurant not too far away, at the intersection of Sunday River Road and US-2.

Both authors agree that the very best season to photograph the Lower Wright Trail is autumn, when the leaves turn red and golden and drift down, ever so artistically, in declivities in the ledge or in tiny pools of water ringed by green and rust-colored mosses. For the best photographing, take the trail to the water at the beginning of the hike (the one we told you not to take for the hike itself), and be sure to bring along a tripod for possible low-light conditions.

Mahoosuc Notch Trail (Mahoosuc Range)

Every AT thru-hiker knows about the notorious Mahoosuc Notch and either fears its approach or revels in its special challenges. For our part, possessed of a healthy disinclination for confronting the precarious, we haven't tackled the full Notch. Instead, we've done this fine hike right down to the Notch, where we've been properly awed by the train wreck of rocks and boulders and fallen timber, happy to leave its actual assault to braver folks.

Driving directions (DeLorme 18, E-1): Going north on ME-26 through Grafton Notch State Park, continue, until a bit under 3 miles past the parking area, you arrive at York/Success Pond Road on the west side of the highway. Drive on this road for over 8 miles, keeping an eye out for the Speck Pond Trail (on the left); about 1.5 or 2 miles *after* the trailhead for the Speck Pond Trail, you will come to a sign for the Mahoosuc Notch Trail. Turn left, and in about one-half mile you will come to a grassy parking area, on the right, with room for about four cars.

Total round-trip distance: 4.5 to 5 miles.

Vertical rise: about 800 ft.

Miscellaneous: No restrooms or water source at the trailhead.

Maps: AMC Maine, Map 7, Mahoosuc Range, C-2.

The challenge and the payoff. Remember we're talking only about the trail *to* the Notch, not the Notch itself. If you think that you might be tempted to have a "go" at the Notch, make sure to wear sturdy shoes and leave the pooch at home, since dogs—to say nothing of some of their masters—tend to get very nervous about having to scale the jumble of boulders that poke this way and that. For people like us, we suggest stopping at the Notch, which still makes for a very worthwhile short hike through a pleasant woods and over a few seasonal stream beds, all for fairly moderate elevation gain.

Description of the hike. Since the state lines are very close at this point, you will actually begin hiking in New Hampshire for about one-quarter mile before entering Maine. At the beginning, the footpath is wide and well trodden. As it narrows, you see Shelter Brook strewn with boulders and come upon a very pretty glen with mossy rocks.

About forty minutes into the hike, you cross the creek once and then again, and the trail becomes more rugged and eroded. There will be a third crossing, until about an hour after you left your car, the trail will pull away from the creek, and head into the woods, leveling out.

We found the woods very pleasant and didn't meet a soul on the trail, even though it was a Sunday in late September. Most AT thru-hikers will be staying at the Full Goose Shelter if they are going northward toward Katahdin or, if headed south, the Speck Pond Shelter. Which is why this hike makes for a lightly used trail, great for the day hiker.

In about an hour-and-a-half from your car, you will come to an opening and an AT sign, signaling that the Full Goose campsite is 1.5 miles to the right while the Notch is to the left. This is a good place to stop for lunch or a snack, because the rest of the trail to the Notch, which is just five minutes further, provides no opportunity for sitting. Shortly beyond the sign, you will descend over some rocks to the bottom, then up the very root-encumbered trail to the unbelievable sight of the Notch—a jumble of rock slabs and fallen timber that truly looks like nothing so much as a massive train wreck. The white AT slash painted on one rock tells you where the "trail" is.

After spending a quarter-hour taking in with amazement the first yards of the famed Notch, we headed back the way we had just come. When we arrived at the opening with the AT sign, two women from North Carolina were just descending from the Full Goose Shelter, explaining that they had gotten something of a late start because they had been celebrating their six-month anniversary on the trail. We laughed with them about how the Notch would make this one anniversary they would never forget—especially because now it was threatening rain, which caused us to fear for their safe passage over slippery rocks, though it didn't seem to faze them at all. "No sweat," they told us, undaunted, as they set forth with bright smiles, leaving us to feel more than a little wimpy.

"How do I even start hiking?" First challenge of the Mahoosuc Notch

What Our Hike Avoids, But What Braver Souls Take On

The Mahoosuc Notch is considered by many to be the toughest mile of the AT. It's been known to frighten grown men or at least make them swear off (or *at*) the AT.

Composed of enormous boulders that have fallen from the cliffs on either side, the Notch has been described as a "ferocious tangle of rocks . . . as big as houses and railroad cars," according to thru-hiker and author Jan D. Curran (*Onward to Katahdin*, Rainbow Books, 1999).

Not only do Notch hikers face the constant challenge of getting over, under, and between these truck-size rocks, but they also must occasionally pick their way along narrow ledges with overhanging boulders, making it easy to bump a backpack and lose balance, resulting in a potentially serious fall.

It's hard for us to believe, but some people do actually find crossing the Notch "fun"!

Northern Headwaters Trail (Waldo County)

As you walk through this quiet, undulating landscape with its stands of tall trees and ruins of old stone fences, turn your thoughts toward a time long past when the area was abuzz with the farming activity of numerous families working the land.

Driving directions (DeLorme 14, A-1 and 22, E-1): From ME-3, turn north on ME-220. Continue for 3.4 miles and turn left on Burnham Hill Road. At a Y-corner, continue right on Halldale Road for 1.6 miles until, on the left, you come to Whitten Hill Road and see the yellow-gold trailpost of the Sheepscot Headwaters Trail Network. The Vose Cemetery is further ahead, on the opposite side of the road. Leave your vehicle, parked well off Halldale Road, or, if the road looks okay for your vehicle, drive up the gravel-and-dirt Whitten Road 0.25 mile and park in a (sometimes) cleared area of the field.
Total round-trip mileage: 3.5-mile loop, with the opportunity to take side trails or to link up with other trails of the Sheepscot Headwaters Trail Network and the Georges Highland Path.
Vertical rise: approx. 280 ft.
Highest point: 600 feet.
Miscellaneous: No restroom or water at trailhead. Make sure to obtain a map from the Sheepscot Wellspring Land Alliance, or at the trailhead, since new trails are still being cut. **NB:** If you decide to hike during hunting season, wear blaze-orange clothing, since hunters have the right to use this property. Better yet, hike only when it is *not* hunting season, or on Sundays, when it is illegal to hunt.
Map: Sheepscot Wellspring Land Alliance Trail Guide, usually available at trailhead.

Description of the hike. At the top of Whitten Hill Road, you will see a trail box that usually contains maps provided by the Sheepscot Wellspring Land Alliance. Cross the grassy field and enter the forest where there is a large wooden sign dedicating the trail to the memory of Helen Antignani. The Antignani family were out-of-state landowners, and, upon the death of his wife in March 1999, Mr. Antignani chose to deed this property to the Sheepscot Wellspring Land Alliance with the proviso that the trail be dedicated to his spouse.

The challenge and the payoff. The modest challenge of this hike concerns footing in some parts, primarily because the footpath is not yet fully pounded in, particularly on the spur trails. Therefore, not only do you often have to navigate the network of roots above ground but also, sometimes, determine the exact route between the trees which are marked with blue blazes for the main trail and red for the spur trails. The flip side of an unbeaten path is solitude and an undisturbed ecosystem that provides the habitat for many species of birds and mammals. Even if you don't make any sightings (morning is the best time, of course), the fact that you'll probably have the trail to yourself is a reward in itself, giving you ample time with your thoughts or to contemplate how a former bustling farmland in rural Maine became a quiet forest.

Watch your feet as you enter the forest, because there is a great tangle of roots above ground, radiating out from the trees like a giant's splayed digits, just waiting to trip you. Shortly, you pass into a more open section of grass, and soon the trail will offer the option of turning left or right, since it is a loop hike. Our choice is to turn right, because we find the first half of the hike the most interesting.

You are now heading downhill and will soon come to a stand of exceptionally grand fir trees not cut for at least sixty years. A few minutes later, a trail sign gives the option of taking the Goose Ridge Trail to the right on a red spur trail. Eventually this trail will continue on to Freedom. We took it to the trail sign for the Mink Run Cutoff, which leads back up to the main trail and its blue blazes.

On the main trail, continue through an attractive stand of tall trees, set in a relatively clear forest floor, and in a few minutes, you are at the headwaters area on your right. This is a particularly picturesque spot when the water is running over mossy boulders and rocks. It's enjoyed by many different creatures, as we can testify, since once while we were there taking a break, suddenly two Saint

Bernard dogs accompanied by a Mastiff came bounding out of the woods, their owners just behind. First one dog, then the second tested the waters, and finally the third, who had been holding back, joined them in a side pool. When they'd had enough, they merrily clambered out of the water to greet us on the bank, with great showers of water, as they vigorously shook off. Thus involuntarily "refreshed," we re-hoisted our backpacks and carried on, while they barreled off to find their mistresses.

Frolicking dogs at Northern Headwaters

Caution Required

Based on personal experience, we want to emphasize that it's important to heed the warning about wearing orange in hunting season. Once in October, we were surprised to see a bow-and-arrow deer hunter stealthily step out of the woods, because he'd "heard a noise"—probably us—and thought he would be bagging a deer. He had a legal right to be there, but so did we. It made us think twice about being in the woods during hunting season, orange caps or not.

After leaving the brook side, cross the creek bed. On this part of the trail, the blue blazes are sometimes replaced by blue plastic tape or tags. The trail now climbs a bit into a higher area, then changes direction and pulls back into the forest. Soon, you pass an old stone wall on your left. At another turn, marked by two vertical blue blazes (the double usage means that the trail turns), you cross the walls. Throughout this area there are many fine old trees, just asking you to pick one and make up a story about what it has seen.

You continue on old farm or logging roads and pass more stone fences. When you come to a field, turn left and skirt the forest for some three hundred yards before reentering the woods on the left, when you will see a pole with blue tape and a tree likewise bearing blue. You will now be moving downward through the forest, and a lot of deadfall and tangled roots may impede rapid progress. Keep a constant eye out for the blue plastic or blue blazes so that you do not stray from the trail.

At about one-and-three-quarter miles from the start, the trail intersects the Whitten Hill Trail, marked with orange blazes and tape. The short Whitten Hill Trail crosses Halldale Road to connect with the Bog Brook Trail (described as a Feature Hike in Boomer Rating Two). So, on a day when you have the time, this would make a fine combined hike of two loops and about six-and-a-half miles, bringing you back across Halldale Road to finish the last section of the Northern Headwaters Loop.

Just before closing the loop of the Northern Headwaters Trail, you will see a cellar foundation on the left and shortly thereafter will turn right to conclude the hike, perhaps in a contemplative turn of mind about how quickly nature reclaims the land when the footsteps of men disappear.

On Stone Fences

New England stone fences have a rich and romantic history. For an illustrated history of the region's stone walls, take a look at William Hubbell's *Good Fences: A Pictorial History of New England's Stone Walls* (2006), published by Down East Books. Hubbell dates stone walls to the Ice Age and charts their history to the present, disussing building techniques and how the ravages of men and nature destroy the walls. If you want to concentrate on the stone walls of Maine, turn to W.H. Bunting's *A Day's Work: A Sampler of Historic Maine Photographs, Parts I and II*, published by Tillbury House in 1997, which shows antique photographs and contains much anecdotal information.

Sabbath Day Pond (Rangeley)

With its trailhead located opposite one of the most spectacular views in Maine, Height of Land, six hundred feet above Mooselookmeguntic Lake, this hike is all about beauty as it winds its way over varied terrain and through great stretches of fairyland forest and beautiful birch glades to three different ponds.

Driving directions (DeLorme 18, A-4): Take ME-17 to Mooselookmeguntic Lake, which is 11 miles south from Oquossoc Village and 26 miles north of Rumford. Park on the west (lake) side of the road but *not* at the overlook, which is intended for sightseers. Instead, leave your car a few hundred yards south of the overlook, near the Bemis Stream Trailhead. Walk back to the overlook area where, on the opposite side of the road, you'll find the trailhead, which climbs to the forest abruptly from the highway. Watch for fast-moving traffic, especially on the return, since the end of the trail drops you directly onto the road.
Total round-trip distance: 7.4 miles.
Vertical rise: 500 ft.
Highest point: 2700 ft. at Bates Ledge.
Miscellaneous: No privy or water at trailhead.
Map: AT in Maine, Map 6: Maine Highway 27 to Maine Highway 17.

> **The challenge and the payoff.** While a great deal of the hike covers meandering, gentle terrain, the footing over roots and through a great deal of wetness, plus steep rises and descents on ledge or broken slabs of ledge particularly at Bates Ledge, will give your leg muscles and knees a real workout. Hiking poles will help make the descents easier on your lower extremities, while the stretches of beautiful woods with tall trees and a ground-cover of brilliant moss and sometimes "nursery" trees will make you feel that you are in an enchanted forest.

Description of the hike. The trail departs on the east side of ME-17 and is marked by the AT symbol, splashed in white on the rocks. Climb sharply up several rock steps to enter the forest. Within a few yards, you will see an official AT trail sign indicating that the Sabbath Day lean-to is 3.8 miles away. You will have no trouble following the trail route, which is clearly marked with the AT's white blazes.

For the first ten or fifteen minutes, you climb steeply up over roots and rocks and root-covered ledge, trying to find your purchase and being careful not to rely too much on roots or limbs or even small trees, which may have been loosened by all those hikers who preceded you. You are climbing toward the unmarked wooded summit of Spruce Mountain, which stands at 2530 feet and is 0.8 mile from the trailhead.

After the first quarter-hour, the trail levels off, even going downhill, followed by several short steep sections over rocks. In somewhat over a mile, you will cross an ATV trail, after which you reenter the woods. This is a particularly pleasant stretch, with a series of bog bridges protecting the undergrowth and keeping your feet out of the mud. On either side of the trail are young trees, and behind them, arising from the mossy forest carpet, are stands of tall trees through which there is an occasional glimpse of the contours of nearby mountains. In the dappled sunlight, the quiet of the woods seems to suggest a fairyland forest, straight from the pages of a child's book.

At 1.6 miles, you will glimpse little Moxie Pond (in Abenaki, "dark water") to the right as you skirt its north shore. Soon after, the trail makes a moderate climb, passing through a beautiful white birch forest set in a blanket of ferns. On our last hike in the fall, we marveled at how beautifully the white or silver trunks of the trees set off the colors of the autumn leaves.

At 2.7 miles you reach Bates Ledge, which is both steep and made up of slabs of rock ledge that can be tricky to negotiate. This is the most demanding part of the hike. There is a steep climb of nearly 200 feet over these huge slabs. Far down, to the right, you will see Long Pond, where you are headed. Once you have made it to the top, you will plunge even more steeply down the other side—about 300 feet in less than 0.5 mile—toward the Pond. Let out your hiking poles to save your knees, and know that at the bottom, after crossing a brook, you will come out to a perfect spot on Long Pond where there is a little, bitty sand beach, about a yard in width, and a couple of AT wooden benches. We ate our lunch at this idyllic spot, made even more so when we heard the call of loons. As we looked out over the rippling water sparkling in the sunlight, surrounded by low-lying mountains with trees carrying tinges of soft fall colors, we thought that this hike had been pretty close to perfect.

A Fall Museum

We have done this hike in every season, and each has its special beauties, but recently when we hiked the trail on a Saturday at the height of fall colors, we had the entire trail to ourselves. Other areas in Maine, such as Grafton Notch, are justly famous for their autumnal finery and changing colors, but precisely because so many leaf-peepers will clog those well-known trails and jostle you every time you want to photograph, we recommend the Sabbath Day Pond Trail. The quality of the color palette—from golden peach-pink to every hue of red, deep burgundy to brilliant garnet, burnt-orange and luminous yellow—all set against the white bark of the birches and beeches and the green of the firs and pines is like being in an artist's studio, or in what could be called, the museum of nature.

To arrive at Sabbath Day Pond, continue on the trail, which pulls away from Long Pond, and then skirts Sabbath Day Pond, the smaller of the two ponds, which are joined by a creek. (According to Brian McCauley's *The Names of Maine*, the origin of the hike's namesake is attributable to a group of early fur trappers who met in this area to keep the Sabbath.)

At 3.8 miles from the start, you'll see the sign for the AT Sabbath Day lean-to, which is 200 feet back in the woods. This lean-to was rebuilt by the MATC in 1993 and can accommodate eight overnighters. We've never been there when either the lean-to or the tent platform below it had any occupants, but we do know that it is one of the most popular in Maine. One Christmas Day, when we came out in the snow, the rough-hewn log table, piled high with snow, appeared to be quietly waiting for spring and the hikers who would arrive in a few months.

Sabbath Day Pond lean-to on a snowy Christmas Day

A Winter Hike

Another way of approaching Sabbath Day Pond in the winter is over the snow from ME-17, about a mile south of where the AT trail described above, begins. Because this route is mostly flat, the walk out to the Pond is quite easy either on foot or by snowshoe. We don't recommend it for other seasons, however, because it is extremely wet and boggy. But over snow in the winter, you'll have a great outing.

When you've enjoyed the scene, turn around and retrace your steps. The ascent of Bates Ledge may seem even steeper, but it will be followed by the beauty of the birch glade and the quiet majesty of the magic forest. Then you will descend Spruce Mountain and end your hike abruptly at those last rock steps that drop almost right into the passing traffic on ME-17. Be careful!

Schoodic Mountain (East Franklin)

From the summit of Schoodic Mountain, you will have a magnificent view of Frenchman's Bay and the Acadia range, offering an impressive overview of one of the nation's most popular national parks.

Driving directions (DeLorme 24, E-4): Despite its name, this hike is **not** on the Schoodic Peninsula, but rather out of East Franklin. From Route 1, driving north on ME-200 (also known as Bert Gray Road), turn east on Gen Cobb Road (General Cobb), which you will follow straight up a hill past some houses for 0.5 mile. At this point, there is a large enough area on the left to leave your car, below extensive blueberry barrens. You will begin hiking up the road. See exact directions below.

Total round-trip distance: roughly 5.5 miles.

Vertical rise: 1000 ft. to the summit.

Highest point: 1069 ft., summit of Schoodic Mountain.

Miscellaneous: No restroom or water at trailhead. **NB:** It's worth repeating that you should not confuse this hike on Schoodic Mountain with Schoodic Head, which is on Schoodic Peninsula.

Map: None. We found the trailhead by asking at a nearby school and then on the access road encountered a local who gave us further directions, incorporated below.

The challenge and the payoff. There are two challenges to this hike: route-finding at the lower level and steepness, which is concentrated in the last one-and-a-half miles in which you will be climbing on both shale, which can cause sliding, and ledge. To counter the first challenge, follow our directions exactly. Exercise care and use your hiking poles to help with the second. The payoff is great—extensive 360-degree views from an expansive summit and an unusual and excellent view of the Acadia range.

Description of the hike. Begin walking up the rough road, past a seasonal cabin on the right and over a culvert. After about one-half mile you will come to railroad tracks. Cross them and turn right, continuing on the road. In five minutes, when the road appears to go straight, go left instead. In another one-half mile, be on the lookout to the left for an orange ribbon tied to a tree limb, which marks the beginning of the trail. Leave the road and walk up this forested trail. In a few minutes, you will come to an open area with evidence of use by ATVs. Turn left up a gravel-and-rock rise that shortly becomes ledge. At the left turn, you will have climbed more than three hundred feet and will still have another several hundred feet to ascend in the last 0.75 mile to the summit.

Until you get fairly high on the mountain, there are practically no trail indicators. Then there are cairns, rather than blazes, to follow. The climb is steep, so, every so often, turn around, because the views backward keep getting better and better. As you approach the summit, you will see the microwave tower and continue to climb toward it. Pay attention to the way you approach the tower and to the relationship of the views down to the broad bog and over to Cadillac and other mountains in Acadia, so that on the descent you are sure to reenter the woods at the right spot.

Once on the summit, circle around to take in the 360-degree views, especially, of course, out to Mt. Desert Island, but also down onto Tunk Lake to the east and Donnell Pond to the west, plus far-off mountains. Since the main view is onto Acadia National Park, find a great spot near the shelter of a rock—it can be very windy on the bare summit—and soak in the beauty. You would be hard pressed to find a more impressive panorama.

Once, as we scouted the summit on a really excellent day in August, we saw a fellow with a long gray beard down to his chest, carrying something like a butterfly bag and a spearing pole. Of course, we wondered what he was doing. Was it some kind of real or quasi-scientific research, or was it trash collection? Curious, we approached him several times, but he always skedaddled away. So that mystery remains, while the memory of this hike with its manifold visual rewards at the summit continues.

If you took your bearings coming up, as we advised, when it's time to leave, re-locate your set of cairns to descend the mountain and reenter the forest by the same route in order to get back to your car.

Further Intelligence

There is at least one other route up the mountain from the village of Tunk Lake, but we believe that the route we've described is the most scenic.

According to Brian McCauley in *The Names of Maine*, "Schoodic" may be either Abenaki or Malecite, meaning "trout place" or "point of land," or even "opened by fire," in the sense of a "clearing of land." Certainly the "point of land" definition seems to fit Schoodic Peninsula, whereas the "clearing of land" (though not by fire) might well work for Schoodic Mountain, which is largely open ledge.

While you're probably going to use your camera mostly for views from the summit, don't forget the blueberry barrens, where you left your car, which, especially in the fall, are also highly photogenic.

Surplus Pond (Andover)

A pleasant hike with just a few steep pitches along a segment of the AT, featuring a great variety of landscape, including a fine woods, rolling terrain, and a secluded pond.

Driving directions (DeLorme 18, D-2): The approach to the hike can be made either from ME-120 out of Rumford or by taking ME-5 northward from US-2. The former is perhaps the more pleasant. In either case, when you arrive at the village of Andover and its one and only significant intersection, continue (or turn) westward on East Hill Road, also known as East B Hill Road. After 8 miles, you come to the AT crossing, marked by a sign on the right. A short distance past this sign is a downward-sloping parking area. Park either here or on the broad shoulders of the road.

Total round-trip distance: 3.8 miles.

Vertical rise: 750 ft.

Highest point: 2250 ft.

Miscellaneous: No restroom or water.

Map: AT in Maine, Map 7 Maine Highway 17 to Maine-New Hampshire State Line.

The challenge and the payoff. After the initial climb up an embankment from your car, you will encounter largely moderate grades, one brook crossing and some bogginess during the wet season, plus a brief encounter with rock slabs and a steep downward path to the level of the pond at the end. The payoff is in the variety of restful forest scenery and in the goal: the pond itself. An added "plus" is that since the hike is short, you can easily lengthen your outing on either end. Across the road from where you parked for the trailhead, you can take the AT in the opposite direction toward Dunn Notch and the popular Dunn Falls area (see Boomer Rating Two). Alternatively, at Surplus Pond, you can continue on another couple miles toward Wyman Mountain, to the east.

Description of the hike. The trail climbs steeply up an embankment, then, after about a hundred feet from the beginning, makes a sharp turn to the right. After that, it settles into a steady, moderate ascent through a mixed forest of hardwoods and conifers, heading eastward (or "northward," from the AT thru-hiker's perspective), along the flank of Grady Mountain.

In less than a mile from the start, you cross a stream. During spring and early winter, you'll find areas of boggy trail and some mud and roots to deal with. From there, the trail meanders upward, becoming somewhat steeper after crossing a large, open glade, about half a mile further on. This park-like area, with open uphill and downhill views of sparser forest, is a particularly pleasant stretch.

Approaching the hike's end, there is a sharp descent of nearly 250 feet in about a quarter of a mile to arrive at the pond. Here, the trail makes tight switchbacks over a rocky, eroded footpath down to Surplus Pond. Your hiking poles will be a great benefit here. At the pond, the trail skirts the south end of the water, where in mid-November we once found ice in the lake and snow along the shoreline. Even in early May, you may still find snow hanging on in the shadier parts of the pond. Of course, this can be a plus, because it also means that there won't be any bugs out to annoy you. The inviting-looking cottage on the southeast bank of the pond, and to which a forest road leads, was "grandfathered" into the AT corridor and was slated for removal by 2010.

Since this is an out-and-back hike and probably won't take much more time than two and one-half hours to complete, you might consider continuing on the trail beyond the road or extending your outing, after you arrive back at your car, by taking the trail on the other side of East B Hill Road for about a mile to Dunn Notch for a view of a spectacular sixty-foot double waterfall. This would bring your hike to just under six miles, in all, and would also add some views to your pleasure.

Alternatively, you could begin your hike at Surplus Pond and hike toward East B Hill Road (and perhaps on to Dunn Notch). If you take this option, turn right off East B Hill Road onto the signed Burroughs Brook Road, just past a bridge, about five miles from the Andover intersection. Then proceed three miles northward to Surplus Pond, holding left at intersections with other dirt roads.

The road's condition, when we drove it, posed no problems for an ordinary passenger car.

Whichever way you approach the hike, you will be covering the same terrain twice unless you "spot" a second vehicle. However, in these days of fossil fuel conservation awareness, such a choice should not be considered "environmentally correct."

Wildlife Antics

We recently read an entertaining account on the Web by Milt Gross, an AT corridor monitor, about two "close encounters" he had along the boundaries of the Surplus Pond trail with Maine's iconic mammal, the moose.

Gross writes that as he was tramping the corridor (well off the trail) to verify the integrity of the property survey line, he was suddenly confronted by a huge bull moose. Stopped in his tracks, Gross wasn't sure what to do. As he remained uncertain, the big guy decided to turn around and go the other way, leading Gross to conclude that *this* moose had "read the book" concerning encounters with humans. An added benefit was that this forest fellow actually provided a service, because the route he took was the very survey line that previously had been eluding the AT corridor monitor!

Soon after, a second bull moose appeared. However, this one clearly hadn't "read the book," because he remained intent upon coming straight at Gross. Quickly the man ducked behind a tree, his knees knocking, imagining the peeved beast starchly saying to himself: "What is this diminutive creature with those terrible-looking legs doing in my forest?" Yet, once again Gross was spared an unwelcome confrontation as the moose continued on by. This led Gross to remember having heard that a moose's range of vision doesn't extend to much beyond twenty-five feet. Thank heavens!

Table Rock (Grafton Notch State Park)

For one of Maine's iconic views on a famous state Scenic Byway and the great spread of mountains in Grafton Notch State Park, take this hike, popular throughout the year but especially during leaf-peeping season, when the forests are aflame with color.

Driving directions (DeLorme 10, A-3 and 18, D-1 & 2): From the intersection in Newry at which Route 26 departs from US-2, take ME-26 northwest for 12.1 miles to the Grafton Notch parking area on the left side of the highway.
Total round-trip distance: 2.4 miles.
Vertical rise: 900 ft.
Highest point: 2448 ft.
Miscellaneous: At the parking lot, there is a privy but no available water. Note that this is a day-use fee area. If you have a Grafton Notch State Park sticker, display it on your car dashboard so that you're legally parked.
Map: AMC Maine, Map 7: Mahoosuc Range, C-3.

The challenge and the payoff. After an easy start, the trail climbs fairly steeply to a side trail with rocks and boulders and a ledge face, where your ascent will be assisted by seven iron rungs that you will climb like a ladder to gain access to the Overlook. There, some nine hundred feet above the valley, you will have superb views onto the great forests of Grafton Notch, cut by ME-26, an impressively scenic roadway going up the Bear River Valley. If you come in winter, the scene will resemble a giant Christmas card. But at any time, really, it is one of the top sights of Maine.

Description of the hike. Walk out of the parking area and turn left. On the opposite side of the road is the trailhead, indicated by a sign with the AT logo. This is the trail to the Baldpate Peaks, but for this hike you'll be cutting off on the second spur trail leading to Table Rock, two miles short of West Baldpate (see Boomer Rating Five).

First, you pass over a boggy area on pressure-treated boards. Immediately thereafter, at 0.1 mile, you will see, on the right, the first opportunity to access the Table Rock Loop trail. There is also a second turn-off ahead at 0.9 mile, which we suggest you take. Since this hike is a loop, you can, of course, make either choice, but the second turn-off makes for a less steep approach. For our loop, you will return by the southern spur trail.

On the main trail going up to the second cut-off, you climb about seven hundred feet and will encounter roots and rocks and possibly patches of wetness, plus a little brook or two. You turn off to the right when you see the sign indicating that it is half a mile to Table Rock. This trail is fairly level for some yards, then crosses a brook and climbs more steeply, becoming flat again, and then climbing steeply over boulders. You come to an open spot and see a ledge face to ascend. It may be slightly awkward, but seven iron rungs serving as a ladder will help you up.

A famous Maine State Scenic Byway: Grafton Notch

Once up, you will walk a few yards with forest on either side and then come to the Overlook, which juts out like a giant ledge table, giving you an unusual perch and excellent views up Grafton Notch and the Bear River Valley, as well as over to Maine's third highest mountain, Old Speck (4180 ft.). If you've come with small children or during the wintertime, be very cautious about the edges, because you are more than nine hundred feet above the valley floor and there are no railings!

Even though the hike to Table Rock is a relatively short one and can be made shorter if you use the first steep side trail to the Outlook, it may whet your appetite for more hiking and/or sightseeing in this area. If so, take a look at Boomer Rating Four for the Eyebrow Trail and Boomer Rating Five for Baldpate Peaks, as well as Old Speck in "Other Hikes" in the same category. Or visit Grafton Notch State Park headquarters in Newry, Maine, for maps and suggestions.

Trail Savvy

For experienced hikers and lovers of the outdoors, it's hard to remember that some people seem unaware of elementary trail and nature etiquette. Especially at heavily visited areas like Table Rock, the rules are all the more important:

- Stay on marked trails.
- Don't make your own switchbacks.
- Carry out what you carry in, including gum and candy wrappers.
- Smoke only when stopped and carry out cigarette butts (But why on earth are you smoking in the woods, anyway?!).
- Do not pick flowers or carry out rocks or stones.
- Go prepared with proper clothing and with water and food so that if you decide to lengthen your hike, or there is a sudden cloudburst, you are adequately prepared.

Valley Trail to Beech Mountain (Acadia West Side)

A real gem of a trail through a beautiful, majestic woods on the quiet side of Acadia—one not to miss, perhaps less for the views on top, though they are nice, than for the beauty of the forest and of the trail itself.

Driving directions (DeLorme 16, C-2): Traveling south on ME-102 before you get to the village of Southwest Harbor, turn right onto Seal Cove Road and follow it for 0.6 mile, then take a right onto Long Pond Road. After 1.1 miles, the road dead-ends at the pumping station, where you park.

Total round-trip mileage: 3.0 miles.

Vertical rise: 769 ft.

Highest point: 839 ft.

Miscellaneous: No water or restroom at the trailhead. Park at the pumping station where there is room for six or seven cars; overflow can park above the pumping station, well off the road.

Map: We recommend for all hikes on Mount Desert Island that you purchase the excellent topographic map by Adventure LLC entitled "Acadia National Park, Trails, Carriage Roads, Hiking, Biking," available at stores in the Park. On this map, the Beech Mountain hike is on the West Side fold, at I & J-6.

The challenge and the payoff. On your way up, you will be climbing some 769 feet, most of which comes after the first 0.4 mile. There are a couple of series of steep uphill climbs, plus switchbacks along sets of rock stairs moving sharply uphill. You will work your heart and lungs, but in fact, the stair-like aspect of many parts of the trail makes the footing easier. Moreover, this is a beautiful trail, much of it through a cathedral-like setting. On the way down, when you're not huffing and puffing, you'll be especially able to appreciate the care taken in building the trail, one of the best in Acadia for beauty and lack of crowds, even in high summer. Just be sure to have your hiking sticks.

Description of the hike. If you have parked in front of the lake, turn around and you will see the trailhead for the Valley Trail to Beech Mountain directly behind you. (The trail that goes along the right (east) side of the lake is the West Ridge Trail, another way up Beech, but we do not recommend it. On the left side of the lake is the Great Pond Trail, used for the Bernard Mountain and Great Pond to Great Notch hikes, described elsewhere in this book.)

The first 0.4 mile on the Valley Trail is a largely level, very moderate climb through a tall-tree woods, which emerges on a gravel road and, just ahead, a crossroads. Walk to the intersection of the crossroads, and turn left. Reenter the woods at the trail sign on the right.

You will now begin climbing more sharply, but it's only one mile, and you can pause often to enjoy the sight of such a striking forest of tall, straight conifers. The trail is often moss-bordered because these tall trees let only a little sunlight filter through. After 0.7 mile, there will be a sign indicating that a left (along South Ridge Trail) will take you to the top of Beech Mountain. Sets of rock stairs now switchback the way up. You'll be grateful that the trail builders made your climb that much easier by their efforts.

As you near the top, views to the ocean and the coast begin to open up. Now the trail is moving by and over ancient boulders, along ledge and a smooth rock surface. Shortly, you arrive at the top of ledge-covered Beech Mountain with an unmanned fire lookout tower. It is no longer possible to climb the tower, but you can roam the broad summit to get views of the Canada Cliffs and Beech Cliffs, as well as, further to the east, Somes Sound.

Since you probably saw few people on the trail coming up (another benefit of the hike), you may be surprised to see other folks on the top. They probably came up the roughly half-mile trail from the parking area at the end of Beech Hill Road or possibly from the Canada Cliffs side to climb the north end of the South Ridge Trail.

Trail Builders
All of us who enjoy Acadia trails owe a debt of thanks to men like the visionary George Dorr, trail architect Ben Breeze, and the Civilian Conservation Corps (CCC) teams who worked in the 1930s on Mount Desert Island. Two CCC camps were established on Acadia, with Camp 158 (located just south of Great Pond) responsible for the masterpiece trails on the western side, including Valley Trail. For more on trail builders, see *Trails of History: The Story of Mount Desert Island's Paths from Norumbega to Acadia*, by Tom St. Germain and Jay Saunders (Parkman Publications,1993).

While deer and other small forest creatures can be found in Acadia, we saw only one four-legged creature. At the summit was a large group of vacation hikers who had brought along the family dog and lavished attention on him, serving him both food and water from a collapsible dish. We assumed that as responsible owners, they were also following Park rules and kept him leashed so that if he caught wind of deer or some other interesting critter, he wouldn't go tearing off.

Variations
While it is possible to make this a loop hike by going up the way we have described above and coming down the West Ridge Trail from the Beech summit, or vice versa, we counsel against it. The West Ridge Trail is slightly shorter but often has bad footing, such as eroding dirt on steep pitches, and it has none of the rock stair steps you find on the Valley Trail. Moreover, aside from a high-up view of Long Pond and Mansell Mountain, the West Ridge Trail offers little of the beauty and none of the majesty of the Valley Trail.

Other Hikes
Boomer Rating Three

Borestone, Elliotsville (DeLorme 41, E 4 & 5)

If it's fall and you're looking for a great hike with views and autumn leaves to photograph, Borestone is the mountain for you. You park 1.3 miles below the Audubon's Visitor's Center, walk up the Bodfish Road, and, if you are not a member of the Audubon Society, which owns the mountain, pay a several-dollar entrance fee. From the Center, which is on the shore of Sunrise Pond, the trail climbs for about one mile through a beautiful, old-growth forest, uncut since the late nineteenth century, to attain the rock ledges of Borestone's West Peak. One-half mile further is East Peak (2000 ft.), and in order to push yourself up the ledges, you'll need a little leg power. But for the splendid 360-degree views, including those of Saddleback, Baker, Elephant, and Big and Little Moose mountains, you'll be glad you did.
Round-trip mileage: under 5 miles.
Vertical rise: 1200 ft.
Map: USGS Sebec Lake quadrangle, 15 min. series, or USGS Barren Mountain West quadrangle, 7.5 min. series.

Little Harbor Brook, with option to Sargent Mountain by Amphitheater Trail, Acadia (DeLorme 16, C-3)
This is a very nice hike on an underused trail, beginning alongside an unusually pretty brook, and climbing, but not too steeply, to 360-degree views of lakes and ocean. It is one of the multiple ways of going to Sargent Mountain (see also "Other Hikes" in Boomer Rating Four), but if you don't have the time or energy to make the round-trip hike of 9.4 miles, you can stop at the Little Harbor Bridge and still have a delightful outing of less than three miles. As always with Acadia, do arm yourself with a good map, since the trail is

somewhat difficult to follow in spots, and if you inadvertently get off it, you need to have an idea where you are.

The trailhead is 3.3 miles southwest of Seal Harbor on Route 3, immediately after a small bridge, where you'll see a grassy spot to park your car on the right side of the road and a little sign naming the trail. You will begin on the Harbor Brook Trail, taking it for 0.7 mile. This is a very scenic area, perhaps even more so, oddly enough, on the return, and you're apt to want to just mosey along. Continue until intersecting with the Asticou Trail, where you turn right (east), taking this trail for just 0.2 mile until it meets, on the left, the first carriage road. Walk on the carriage road, going north for about 0.4 mile, until you come to the Little Harbor Bridge, a possible turnaround point, or where you will pick up the Amphitheater Trail if you're aiming for Sargent Mountain. Take the Amphitheater Trail to the intersection with the Birch Springs Trail, which you ignore, turning right (east), instead, on the Sargent Mountain Trail. You climb this trail, sometimes fairly steeply, for 1.2 miles to the 1373-foot summit where you will enjoy glorious views. From beginning to end, from brook to lakes to ocean, this is a hike in which water views take center stage.

Round-trip mileage: under 3 miles to Little Harbor Bridge; 9.4 miles to summit of Sargent.

Vertical rise: about 200 ft. to Little Harbor Bridge; 1350 ft. to Sargent Mountain.

Map: Acadia NP, East Side, J-11.

Little and Big Niagara Falls, Baxter State Park (DeLorme 50, D-4)
If you're visiting Baxter State Park and want to do an easy piece of the AT, we'd suggest that you get on the trail for Abol Bridge, stopping just beyond Big Niagara Falls for about a three mile out-and-back walk, or longer if you want. What makes this trail so attractive is, first, its relatively level and easy footing and, secondly, the opportunity, as you walk alongside the Nesowadnehunk Stream, to make early Maine history come alive from docent signs describing old log-driving days, how toll dams worked, and telling tales of the colorful log drivers who risked life and limb on the roiling logs. This is a particularly good and easy ramble that can be combined with the Sentinel Mountain hike, described below, for an all-day outing in Baxter State Park.

Round-trip mileage: 3 miles, or more depending on how far you continue.
Vertical rise: 120 ft.
Map: AMC Maine, Map 1 Baxter State Park/Katahdin, lower right inset: Kidney and Daicey Ponds area.

Nesowadnehunk Stream, Little and Big Niagara Falls, Baxter State Park

Little Wilson Falls, Monson (DeLorme 31, A-3 and 41, E-3 & 4)
There are a couple ways of getting to Little Wilson Falls: the long way on the AT from ME-15 or the short way, north of Monson using the Elliotsville Road for 7.7 miles and accessing a woods road maintained by the Maine Forest Service, which leads to the Little Wilson Campsite, a favorite of Boy Scout troops. For the first, you'll be undertaking about a twelve-mile round-trip hike, while the second is a short three miles, involving mostly a road walk to the falls.

For our money, only the longer hike on the AT makes hiking sense. We look upon it as a pleasant choice for when you don't want to deal with vertical rise (although there are plenty of roots and other impediments on the trail to slow progress). The walk through the woods is enjoyable, especially in spring with new green, and in fall when the leaves are changing color, and you pass by lakes and ponds. Naturally you can turn back at any time, making your goal a walk in a pretty forest rather than the falls themselves.

Round-trip mileage: from 3 to 12 miles.

Vertical rise: 550 ft.

Map: USGS 15' Sebec Lake.

Schoodic Peninsula, Acadia (DeLorme 17, B-1)

Not very many people know about hiking possibilities on the Peninsula, and that is what makes such hiking opportunities all the more attractive. As you drive along the one-way Park loop road, on which there are not many places to park, you will come upon four fairly short hiking trails: **Alder Trail** (0.6 mile of level and easy walking), **Anvil Trail** (1.1 miles), **East Trail** (0.5 mile, steep), and **Schoodic Head Trail** (0.6 mile). If you park at Blueberry Hill on the southeast side of the peninsula, more or less opposite Schoodic Island, you can access the Alder and Anvil trails, which link to the other two. It is also possible, roughly opposite Pond Island, to park on the right of the loop road, then cross over to the other side and enter by foot through a gated road, which leads uphill and accesses the trails. Once, on snowshoes, we had a bracing hike by this approach up to higher land and great wintry views.

Note that while Schoodic Peninsula is just four watery miles east of Bar Harbor, it will take you nearly an hour to travel by car the forty-five miles. If you're coming from Ellsworth, go "Down East" about nineteen miles on US Route 1. In West Gouldsboro, take a right and head south to Route 186. Continue about six miles before turning right for the Peninsula. After Frazer Point, where there are restrooms and picnic facilities, the road becomes a one-way loop of six miles in length. Do note that in summer, as elsewhere in Acadia, you're likely to be sharing the road with lots of bicyclists.

Round-trip mileage: from 1 mile to 2.2 or more if several trails are combined.

Vertical rise: from 180 ft. (The Anvil) to 440 ft. (Schoodic Head).

Map: Check online.

Winter at Schoodic Peninsula

Sentinel Mountain, Baxter State Park (DeLorme 50, D-4)

Once when we wanted to hike Russell Pond Trail, but the Roaring Brook parking lot had already closed—and we'd gotten to the Togue Gate by 5:40 AM!—we went, instead, to Daicey Pond to do the Sentinel Trail hike. An unexpected but very fine side benefit of our 4:00 AM arising in a motel in Millinocket was that we were on the trail for a 7:15 AM start. Which meant that when we took a side trail to the Lily Pad Pond, we got to see a beaver out for an early morning swim and to note the interesting herbal/medicinal smells arising from the bog. Returning to the trail, we walked along Kidney Pond before pulling southeast into the forest to climb Sentinel Mountain, whose summit stands at 1837 feet. From the summit loop, we took in the views of many ponds, plus Doubletop, West, OJ-1, and Katahdin. It was, we decided, a fine backup hike.

Round-trip mileage: about 7.4 miles.

Vertical rise: 800 ft.

Map: AMC, Maine, Map 1 Baxter State Park/Katahdin, D-1, and lower-right insert: Kidney and Daicey Ponds area

Thuya Gardens to Jordan Pond House, Acadia (DeLorme 16, 3-C)

This is a very pleasant hike with a special twist, since it can be broken by a stop at the Jordan Pond House, famous for its popovers served with strawberry jam. In good weather, it is delightful to join the throngs on the lawn for afternoon tea and for views onto the two mountains known as the "Bubbles," which lie at the north end of the pond. Of course, if you want those incredibly light popovers, you need to make sure that the seasonal restaurant is open, so mark these dates: mid-May through late October.

You begin the hike from the back of beautiful Thuya Gardens (see the Featured Hike in Boomer Rating One), exiting through a gate onto a connector path going northeast. This path leads you to the Asticou Ridge Trail, which crosses low-lying Eliot Mountain in pleasant fashion. You will note that the trail is very well built, often with stairs of both natural stone and cut granite. Follow this trail northward for 0.6 mile, turning right (east) when you intersect the Asticou Trail. In the next 0.5-mile section, there is some moderate steepness. However, the remaining 1.2 miles to the Around Mountain Carriage Road, where you come out near the Pond House, are generally easy going. After the traditional popover interlude, return by way of the same trail to "walk off" the calories and get another chance to enjoy a very nice woods.

Round-trip distance: 5.4 miles.
Vertical rise: 340 ft.
Map: Acadia NP, East Side, I-10 and H-11.

Overview

Boomer Rating Four:
Earning Your Spurs!

Assuming that by now you're in pretty good shape, what's to keep you from biting off an even tougher challenge—a Boomer Rating Four?

For this category, we've chosen favorite hikes throughout the state, from Acadia National Park—the Acadia and St. Sauveur loop, The Bowl and Champlain, and Bernard Mountain by Great Pond—to northern Maine with Big Moose Mountain; plus several hikes in western Maine—in Grafton Notch (The Eyebrow, and Success Mountain), and Caribou Mountain in Evans Notch.

We tell you about a couple of splendid hikes in Oxford County—first, Rumford White Cap, and then Bald and Speckled Mountains; two in the Mount Blue area, Blueberry and Tumbledown; a lovely and little traveled section of the AT on the Lone Mountain Trail outside of Phillips; Burnt Mountain in the Sugarloaf area; and, finally, a hike to beautiful Horns Pond in the Bigelows.

All of them are great, each for a different reason, whether it's the beauty of the woodlands or the pleasure of the waters of creeks, lakes, or a mountain tarn, to say nothing, of course, of impressive summit views. Those we've included in the category "Other Hikes" are no less splendid, but most of them are well enough known to have made it into other hiking books. So, for them, we content ourselves with just a short description.

What are the criteria for assigning a hike a Boomer Rating Four? Primarily, the ranking has to do with vertical gain or loss in relatively few miles. For instance, you have to negotiate more than 1800 feet over a couple miles for the Tumbledown hike. Or sometimes there is a steep climb only over a short section, as with the rock faces of Bernard (which is otherwise a moderate round-trip of 6.2 miles), or the cabled section of The Eyebrow, which is not for the faint of heart and whose name alone should suggest something of the unusual nature of this hike! Or the challenge may come in the quality of the footpath, as for instance with the large boulders to climb up and down on the Champlain Trail, or an eroding trail of dirt and shale (Acadia and St. Sauveur, in parts), or multiple water crossings (Caribou).

The fourteen Featured Hikes in this section range in round-trip length from super short (2.1 miles for The Eyebrow), to fairly long—up to ten or twelve miles for Lone Mountain, though for this one you can cut short your outing at any point, since it is not a view-destination hike. Most of the hikes, however, fall in the five, six, or seven-mile round-trip range.

In sum, a Boomer Rating Four depends on the effort expended (without reaching quite the "exquisite" level of physical output required by a Boomer Rating Five), whether the challenge is in unrelenting steepness or steepness over a single section, negotiating boulders or rock faces, or multiple water crossings. These hikes may or may not be an all-day affair but will definitely let you know that you've worked your body. We can't imagine doing any of them without hiking poles, although you will have to stash the sticks, or hand them off to a partner, when climbing up or down some stretches of boulder. And while we frankly confess to using a dose or two of ibuprofen to counteract stiffness before and after these hikes, we also feel inordinately proud when we've accomplished these bruisers.

Listed below are the hikes with total round-trip distance and vertical rise. To get a real sense of the vertical challenge, divide the round-trip mileage in half, and then look at the vertical gain. Anything over 750 feet per mile can be considered a workout; more than that, and you're in for some real sweating, even on a cool day. At the end of this section, we include five "Other Hikes" that also meet the criteria for a Boomer Rating Four, because we suspect that once you get the hang of it, you'll be eager to keep right on bagging peaks.

Hike	Round-trip miles	Vertical gain
Acadia and St. Sauveur Loop	4.7 miles	1161 ft., including for two summits
Bald and Speckled Mountains	5.4 miles	1800 ft.
Bernard Mountain, by Great Pond	6.2 miles	980 ft.
Big Moose Mountain	7.0 miles	1810 ft.
Blueberry Mountain	3.4 miles	1300 ft.
The Bowl and Champlain	4.8 miles	1058 ft.
Burnt Mountain	6.0 miles, approximately	1840 ft.
Caribou Mountain	6.9 miles	1888 ft.
The Eyebrow	2.1 miles	900 ft.
Horns Pond	9.2 miles	1876 ft.
Lone Mountain	9.2 miles	1806 ft.
Rumford Whitecap	4.5 miles	1540 ft.
Success Mountain	4.8 miles	1800 ft.
Tumbledown Mountain	3.0 miles	1863 ft.

Acadia and St. Sauveur Loop
(Acadia, West Side)

For great views onto Somes Sound, this is a fine loop hike, first through a very pretty woods up to Acadia Mountain and then down and over to Saint Sauveur, so that you can "bag" a second summit.

Driving directions (DeLorme 16, C-3): As you leave the Thompson Island causeway heading for Acadia, bear right at the fork after the light for ME-102. Continue seven miles. There is a parking lot on the right side, also serving Echo Lake. Note that there is considerable traffic on ME-102 during high season.
Total round-trip distance: 4.7 miles.
Vertical rise: 1161 ft. (combined total).
Highest points: 681 ft., Acadia Mtn.; 679 ft., St. Sauveur.
Miscellaneous: There are restroom facilities at the parking area; none elsewhere on the hike.
Map: Acadia NP, West Side, H & I-7.

The challenge and the payoff. This is a hike for people "up" for climbing a couple non-technical boulder faces and making a steep descent on rock ledge. It is also for those in pursuit of the beauties of forest and Sound waters—coupled, in the summer, with aromatic pine needles and wafts of sea air. The descent over to St. Sauveur is steep, and the trail in places is crumbly. **NB:** Coming off St. Sauveur, do *not* be misled into descending by the Ledge Trail, which is both very steep and goes to the wrong parking area. Keep on the St. Sauveur Trail, which is an easier descent and drops you where you want to be—across from your car.

Description of the hike. You find the trailhead across from the parking area on ME-102 and climb some rock stairs to access the trail. From there, it is 0.1 mile to the turnoffs for Acadia Mountain and St. Sauveur. If you take the left to Acadia Mountain, it will be

0.9 of a mile to the summit. The St. Sauveur trail, which is less steep, arrives at the summit in 1.3 miles.

For Acadia Mountain, the trail starts out over rocks and roots but in the beginning is like a pleasant walk in the woods. Soon after crossing a stream, you come upon an eighteen-foot boulder to climb up (or go around, as some hikers have done). It is the first of several challenges. The next boulder front to ascend has steps. Do note that steel-tipped hiking poles can slip on rock. Either have your hiking poles rubber-tipped or try to lay down as much boot sole as possible to minimize slipping. And, of course, on a wet day or after a rain, exercise extra caution.

The trail climbs steadily until you reach the summit at 681 feet. There you can spread out to left and right to find your own spot from which to enjoy the views and/or lunch. To continue the loop, you will go right, through steeply descending rock. For short folks, wary of falling or jolting their knees, some of these descents may require easing yourself down on your bottom or using your arm power. But since hiking isn't like the sport of bouldering, in which both form and style count, just do what you have to. Age has its benefits; you'll be applauded for just being out there, not ridiculed for lack of grace!

Acadia and St. Sauveur Loop, Acadia

As you descend, there will be excellent views of sailboats in the Sound, and with the use of a telephoto lens, you'll be able to make some great shots of graceful sails against the blue waters. The trail descends steeply and often roughly, sometimes through large boulders, while at other times it winds through pine groves and low-lying bushes.

At the junction with the Man 'O' War Brook Fire Road, descend by the Valley Peak Trail (rather than Flying Mountain Trail, which is closer to the water). From the junction with the fire road, you'll be going downwards a further 0.8 mile where there is a short link over to St. Sauveur Mountain (679 ft.). If you miss it, you'll add another 0.7 mile to the hike, but at least the Valley Peak Trail gives you an opportunity to circle back on the St. Sauveur Trail after 0.3 mile.

History Tidbits

There is a long and uncertain history about how Acadia got its name. What is sure is that seventeenth-century French kings and explorers played an important role in its early history.

Later, in the early twentieth century, the U.S. Federal Government established Sieur de Monts National Monument and in 1919 re-christened the area Lafayette National Park in honor of the famous Marquis.

Ten years later, however, the name was changed back to Acadia National Park, as stipulated by a landowner on Schoodic Peninsula who was willing to make a considerable gift of land on condition that the name be re-changed.—Not exactly a case of renaming French fries "freedom fries," but along the same lines?

St. Sauveur Mountain, itself, was named for a sixteenth-century French colony located nearby.

As you come off St. Sauveur, remember to avoid the Ledge Trail, because it goes to the wrong parking area and is 0.6 mile from where you left your car. The last 0.1 mile of the correct way down will be familiar, because this is the way you came.

Variations

For a longer hike, the St. Sauveur Trail can be linked to Flying Mountain Trail. But in our view, Flying Mountain is not really worth it, and if you attempt to return by the Valley Cove Road between April and August, you may find parts of the road closed because of nesting falcons.

Probably because the Acadia Mountain Trail leads to great views, it is one of the most popular hikes in the Park, at once relatively short but giving a good workout, and leading to a signature Maine seascape. However, if you want the views, but don't want to deal with steep descents on rock ledge and boulder faces, just do the St. Sauveur portion, simply making sure to go beyond the marked summit to the ledges overlooking Somes Sound for fine views. That would give you a total hike of 2.2 miles and a vertical gain of 531 feet.

Bald and Speckled Mountains
(Oxford County)

A "two-for-one" hike—meaning two summits with views onto two pond, and acres and acres of forest, giving the sense of remoteness despite the relative proximity of Maine's largest city within an hour's drive.

Driving directions (DeLorme 11, A-1): Traveling west on ME-219 from its intersection with ME-4 in North Turner for just over 12 miles, turn right (north) onto Valley Road. Follow this road for about 2 miles, turning left on Labrador Pond Road. You will skirt the southern edge of the pond for one mile. Then fork right onto Greenwood Road, for about 0.3 mile and then left at a junction onto Black Mountain Road. After slightly over 0.5 mile, take a left fork again, this time onto Redding Road. Follow it for about 5 miles, passing Shagg Pond on your right. One-half mile after the pond, you will see a parking area on the left side of the road, which can accommodate four or five cars. The trail begins directly across the road.
Total round-trip distance: 5.4 miles.
Vertical rise: 1800 ft.
Highest points: Bald Mountain, 1692 ft.; Speckled Mountain, 2185 ft.
Miscellaneous: No water or privy at the trailhead. **NB:** This hike should not be confused with the Caribou-Speckled Mountain Wilderness in Evans Notch.
Map: USGS Mt Zircon quadrangle, 7.5-min. series.

The challenge and the payoff. For a steep climb of a total of 1800 feet, which is actually increased because you climb *two* mountain tops in 2.7 miles, you get ledge, bluffs, and pond views, plus a good workout on this hike in Oxford County, home according to MountainZone.com to 475 mountain summits and peaks.

Description of the hike. After parking, cross the road and begin your hike by proceeding up the forest lane. Follow this route for about 0.5 mile, and you will come into sight of Little Concord Pond, glimmering through the trees ahead. Short of the pond, however, you will turn off on a blue-blaze trail at a sign on your right welcoming you in the name of the trail's maintainers, who cheerily tell you that the summit of Bald is one steep mile away and that it will probably take an hour or more to get there. Note that from Bald to Speckled summit, you'll be going another 1.3 steeper miles.

After the trail maintainers' sign, start the stiff climb, going over rocks and ledge that can be slippery following rains. After a mile, the trail levels out and you'll have fine views of the valley below and of beautiful 65-acre Shagg Pond. Since you will have been climbing steeply—and there's more ahead—pause at vantage points to look down on Shagg and Abbott ponds. Though Shagg is not large enough for water-skiing, you are likely, on a summer's day, to have a bird's-eye view of bathers and boaters enjoying their sylvan idyll. The pond also supports canoeing and fishing, while rock climbers use Shagg Crag.

Fall trail on the way to Bald and Speckled Mountains

Your next objective is Speckled Mountain, which, seen from a distance, presents impressive bluffs. Speckled is nearly 500 vertical feet higher than Bald, and you'll be covering 1.3 miles to get to this second summit.

From Bald, bear left at the cliff's end and descend the steep col between the two mountains. As you climb the other side, you'll be passing over areas of ledge and through a scrub-like forest. The final assault to the summit requires yet another steep climb, which means that on a warm or humid day, you'll definitely need to be mopping your brow. Once on top, however, you'll be able to catch a breeze and revel in the fine views spreading out in all directions as far as the White Mountains.

Since this is an out-and-back hike, return by the same trip in reverse. You'll be praising yourself all the way down for accomplishing a demanding half-day outing that offers good exercise for heart, lungs, and legs.

All those Names and Numbers

Duplicates, triplicates, quadruplicates, and so on. If you study a map of Maine, you'll soon discover that our forefathers seemed to suffer from a deficit of creativity in naming mountains.

There are, for instance, nine or more Bald Mountains, at least two Speckled Mountains, several Pleasant and Peaked Mountains, a number of Spruce Mountains (plus a Spotted Spruce), and even two Elephant Mountains. There are at least three Saddlebacks, plus a Saddleback, Jr. There is a Moose Mountain and a Big Moose Mountain. More than one Caribou Mountain, as well as duplicates for Burnt, Pisgah, Ragged, Round, Russell, Schoodic, Snow, and Sugarloaf Mountains.—Which is why we give the DeLorme coordinates for all *our* hikes!

And we haven't even started on lakes and ponds bearing the same names: Clear, Pleasant, Long, Mud. At least there appears to be only one *Spider* Lake.

Colors come into play, too: Grey Mountain, Grey Brook Mountain, several Black Mountains (also a Black Nubble), Green Mountain, Mt. Blue, and Blue Hill.

Not all mountains are so prosaically name, however. For instance, there are Burnt Jacket Mountain, Quaggy Joe Mountain, Nighthawk Mountain, and Big Brawn, to say nothing of those with Indian names.

Bernard Mountain by Great Pond Trail
(Acadia, West Side)

A great loop hike on the "quiet" side of Acadia with a little of everything—pleasant shoreline walking, a beautiful forest, steep rock faces to shimmy up, a rapid descent through the forest, a bit of forest road-walking—and outside of tourist season, you're almost guaranteed to have the trail to yourself.

Driving directions (DeLorme 16, C-2): Traveling south on ME-102, before you get to the village of Southwest Harbor, turn right onto Seal Cove Road and follow it for 0.6 mile, then take a right onto Long Pond Road. After 1.1 miles, the road dead-ends at the pumping station where you park.
Round-trip distance: 6.2 miles.
Vertical rise: 989 ft.
Highest point: 1071 ft. at summit of Bernard Mountain.
Miscellaneous: No restroom or drinking water at the trailhead. Parking is limited at the pumping station, accommodating a maximum of seven cars. In high tourist season, you may need to park your vehicle above the pumping station and well off the road. Don't risk a ticket by parking parallel with the lake or to the left of the birch trees.
Map: Acadia NP, West Side, I & J, 4-5. Really the only map for hiking in Acadia. It will set you back a few bucks but is worth it.

Description of the hike. You access the trail from behind the pumping station and proceed for two easy miles by the shore of the pond known as Long Pond, though the trail markers all refer to it as Great Pond. Passing both side trails (Cold Brook and Perpendicular), you continue walking alongside the lake until the trail leaves the lake to pull into the woods.

Within ten minutes, you cross an attractive log and timber bridge over Great Brook and climb moderately through an unusually fine forest on a trail often bordered by boulders and mounds of mountain lichen.

The challenge and the payoff. The area named Knight Nubble, between Great Notch and Little Notch, presents three rock faces that must be negotiated in part with both hands and feet touching the "ground." It's steep, no doubt about it, but not dangerous, provided you proceed with prudence and don't try to undertake the scramble in inclement weather. If you look at it in the right way, it's actually kind of a kick, and only reinforces the rewards of this hike, which come in the quietness of the west side of Mount Desert Island, the calm beauty of the lake, and the sense of history in walking on a beautiful, forest-shaded path flanked in part by stones laid down by the trail builders of yesteryear. It's not the views but the beauty and peaceful nature of the hike that make it, for us, a favored destination.

Even on a gorgeous August day at noon, we had this part of the trail to ourselves and often paused to inhale the aroma of fir needles in the sun and to admire the care with which this path, like others in Acadia, had been constructed by trail builders endowed with an aesthetic sensibility.

After you have traveled 2.9 miles from your car, you come to a signpost and choose the Great Notch option. The Notch itself is 0.4 mile further on. The trail is now covered with tangles of roots, which will impede your speed. At the Great Notch crossroads, where you can sign the trail register or take a quick rest on a couple of log benches, go right toward Knight Nubble, which is 0.2 mile further ahead. Bernard Mountain is 0.1 mile beyond that, but first you must climb the steep and narrow path to the Nubble and then negotiate three rock faces.

Your first reaction on seeing the rock faces may be, "Oh, no!" But it's not as difficult as it looks. The first face is the shortest and easiest, and the second is not too hard either. However, the third "nubble" is the longest and most demanding, and it took us ten minutes to negotiate it, which meant stashing hiking poles and drinking bottles and placing a camera in a backpack so as not to endanger its lens.

Kayaker along the shoreline at Great Pond, Acadia

We call this a "four-point" climb, since all four appendages were nearly always in contact with the climbing surface. It may not have been too graceful, but we got there, and so can you!

Once on top of Knight Nubble (930 ft.), you go only a few yards before you see to the left an Overlook. This is a nice, somewhat secluded spot off the trail, with natural ledge and a view to the southeast. We lunched here but left sooner than we would have wanted, since there was a pesky squirrel who kept attempting to conduct stealth raids. Please, please don't feed these guys, since it only turns them into forest delinquents!

From the top of the Nubble, you descend forty feet for Little Notch at 890 feet. Within a few minutes, you'll see a sign to the right, for another Overlook with views toward Indian Point and the west shore of Mount Desert. None of the viewpoints on this trail is anything to write home about, but ocean views are really not your reason for doing and enjoying this hike, anyway. Shortly after this Overlook, you come to the viewless summit of Bernard, marked by a cairn and sign indicating that it lies at 1071 feet.

Tidbits from History

Bernard Mountain was named for an eighteenth-century governor of Massachusetts, Sir Francis Bernard, at the time when Maine and Massachusetts were a single entity. Mansell Mountain derives its name from Sir Robert Mansell, who was a Naval commander for King James I (1566-1625). The King gave Mansell the coastal area of Mount Desert, and then Mansell bought the entire island of Mt. Desert for 150 English pounds. Though he immediately renamed it for himself, he subsequently seemed to lose interest in his purchase. In the 1920s, long after the island had reverted to its original designation, the legendary George Dorr thought that Mansell deserved to have a namesake—but a modest one. And so the *second* highest mountain on the western side became Mansell Mountain. Mansell stands at 949 feet, while Bernard beats it at 1071 feet. In fact, the real peaks are on the east side of the Park: Cadillac (1530 ft.), Sargent (1273 ft.), Dorr (1270 ft.), Pemetic (1248 ft.), Penobscot (1194 ft.), and Champlain (1058 ft.).

The descent on the Bernard Mountain South Face Trail is rather stiff, which means, of course, that your big toe may be pressing too hard against the end of your boots (the remedy is to tighten the laces), and arthritic knees may be expressing their objection, so you might want to pop an ibuprofen about now. Ignore the West Ledge Trail to the right (leading to the Western Mountain Road), and continue left for Mill Field.

Don't be fooled into expecting a real field. In essence, Mill Field is just a woodsy parking area. When you exit the woods at this parking area, continue walking on the road, passing the Gilley Field sign. After ten minutes or less, you will reenter the woods at the Cold Brook Trail, a wide fire road, which is pretty much flat.

The trail sign mistakenly says that Long Pond is one mile beyond, but actually it is only 0.4 mile, so you'll arrive back at your car in a quarter-hour or so.

Note that there are other options on this trail for extending or varying the hike. You could, for instance, at the Great Notch crossroads, also bag Mansell Mountain, which is about a half-mile to the east, and return to ascend Bernard; or from Mansell you could descend by the Mansell Mountain Trail (0.8 mile) down to Cold Brook and 0.4 mile back to your car. Study the map for other alternatives, but know that the one described above is our favorite.

Big Moose Mountain
(formerly Big Squaw Mountain)

A pleasant hike through the woods, climbing to an abandoned warden's cabin, then a steep mile-long ascent by rock steps to an overlook with expansive views onto Moosehead Lake and to far-off mountains, including Katahdin, Maine's highest at 5267 feet.

Driving directions (DeLorme 41, D-1): To reach the trailhead, take ME-6/15 northwest from the Greenville town center for exactly 5 miles. (If you see a sign for the Big Squaw Ski resort, you have gone a bit too far.) Turn left onto a gravel road. A trail information sign about Big and Little Moose mountains is on the left. To reach the trailhead, continue driving about another mile. The trailhead is on the right along with a parking area.

Total round-trip distance: 7.0 miles; or, with the scenic overlooks, about 7.5 miles.

Vertical rise: 1810 ft.

Highest point: Big Moose Mountain, 3199 ft.

Miscellaneous: 1) There are no restroom facilities at the trailhead. 2) Some maps and books still identify this mountain by the politically incorrect Squaw Mountain nomenclature.

Map: USGS 15' Greenville. You probably don't need it, since the trail is very clear and there are no ambiguous points.

> **The challenge and the payoff.** On the last mile from the abandoned warden's cabin, you will huff and puff to reach the summit, climbing 942 feet, often over a series of rock steps. But both the start and finish of this hike are on relatively flat land, the forest is very nice, and at the top there are great views onto forty-mile long Moosehead Lake. In the background, the view of well-known and well-loved Maine mountains, including Katahdin, is your reward for all that toil and effort.

Description of the hike. The trail enters the woods and rises briefly over roots and frequent wetness (hence, several bog bridges) before leveling out, then climbing steadily, but reasonably, over 868 feet to the still-standing former warden's cabin, 2.5 miles from the trailhead. Note that the blue blazes can be infrequent.

On the day we were on the trail, we met one of the cabin's former occupants, who, some 75 years before, as a year-old baby, had spent the first of what would be many summers at the cabin. His dad, a forest warden, was charged with making the daily run to the lookout tower at the summit, one mile beyond the cabin. To help the family make ends meet, his mother brewed root beer with water from nearby Big Squaw Brook and made her own bread for sandwiches to sell to hikers and campers. Today, their two-room cabin, with privy uphill, is a natural midway resting point, and scores of hikers have left their autograph on its walls—an odd sight, undoubtedly, for the man who spent his boyhood there.

The trail continues opposite the cabin, with the brook on the left. You cross a narrow wooden bridge, then soon a log ladder before the series of rock and/or log steps that provide footing up the mountain. It's steep, no doubt about it, but the steps are very well placed. And every so often, there is a more or less flat stretch where you can breathe more easily and marvel at all the work that went into constructing these steps.

Since it's only a mile from the cabin up to the summit, we kept thinking—hoping—that we were approaching the top and kept being fooled until, suddenly, we saw solar panels followed immediately by the abandoned lookout tower, both of which are cabled down to the rock ledge. From this vantage point, the views are great, but getting a photograph might be hard, since if you want a wide-angle shot, the cables will get in your way. Still, the views extending from Mount Kineo to Katahdin, with Gulf Hagas and White Cap Mountains and even the Bigelows, plus the entire expanse of famous Moosehead Lake, are very fine indeed. On our hike, we had the added drama of storm clouds moving above the lake, while patches of sun lit up the far-off mountains. If you want more views, you can take a short extension beyond the tower to another ledge high above a picturesque mountain tarn, Mirror Pond.

On your ascent, you will have noticed two side paths leading to scenic overlooks. As always, our advice is to skip such additions on the out-trip and decide on the return whether to do them. Doing both will add another 0.3 or 0.5 mile to the total of your hike, but since the views at the summit are so much better, we don't really think the sidetrips are necessary, especially on the way down.

In terms of total time, most people can do this hike in about four hours. But with conversation, rest stops and lunch, plus time at the summit, and the slight extension from the summit for a view onto Mirror Lake, you may spend, as we did, about four hours and forty-five minutes. You'll return to your car by the same trail, happy to have gotten to know this Big Moose.

Moose antlers for sale by the side of the road

Moose Musings

- There are an estimated 30,000 moose in Maine, including one by the name of Lenny, who is said to reside in Scarborough and is composed of 1700 pounds of milk chocolate.
- Lenny's weight more than doubles what an actual adult male moose weighs—on average, 800 pounds, while his lady friend tips the scales at 600.
- The life expectancy of a bull moose is seven years; the cow moose outlives him, typically reaching eight years of age before going on to the great, green forest in the sky.
- Moose shed their horns every year in February and start regrowing them in April. In winter, collectors tramp through the woods to collect the horns, shine them up a bit, and then offer them for sale. One summer, we saw roadside sellers near Rumford, offering beautiful sets of moose horns for from $70 to $250 per pair.
- Did Moosehead Lake get its name because, from nearby Mt. Kineo, the lake looks like a moose's head? Or does Mt. Kineo look like a moose lying down when viewed from Moosehead Lake? Those are all theories that have been proposed. More likely, the name is explained by the actual presence of so many moose guys and gals in the area.

Blueberry Mountain (Weld)

The splendid 360-degree views of Mount Blue State Park, Tumbledown and Little Jackson and Webb Lake make your exertions on this tough trail, relentlessly straight up, definitely worthwhile.

Driving directions (DeLorme 19, C-1 & 2): From Weld Corner, drive north on ME-142 (Phillips Road) for 1.5 miles until you see, on the left, a sign for Blueberry Mountain Bible Camp. Take this rock-and-dirt road for 1.8 miles. Given the condition of the road, you will need to go very slowly. At its terminus is the main building, a lodge, for Bible Camp attendees. Park opposite the lodge, where there is room for several cars. Unless camp personnel indicate otherwise, the trail is accessed beyond the lodge and barn from an athletic field, which you cross in order to enter the woods. The entrance point from the field was not clearly visible when we were there, but look for beaten-down grass, diagonally or northeast from where you crossed the field, and then for blue blazes on rocks or trees.

Total round-trip distance: About 3.4 miles.

Vertical rise: 1300 ft.

Highest point: 2962 ft. at Blueberry summit.

Miscellaneous: The Bible Camp has been generous about allowing hikers use of their access road and parking area, so keep them happy *before* arriving at the Bible Camp by filling your canteen and using a restroom. There is no water on the trail.

Map: AMC Maine, Map 6 Weld Region, D-3.

Description of the hike. After entering the forest from the athletic field, you will be on an old logging trail that soon narrows and begins to climb steeply uphill. It takes a good twenty minutes of relentless climbing before the trail gives a hint of flattening out briefly. In another twenty minutes, after a further steep rise, you reach an area where you can at last see the sky rather than just the trail and trees. There are a couple of good boulders here to sit on and to rest up for the next section, which starts out flattish and even downhill before turning back into a sharp uphill climb, at times requiring you to pull yourself up by arm strength.

159

> **The challenge and the payoff.** This is not a trail for the occasional hiker because it is constantly uphill and constantly steep. In addition, the footpath is eroded in some places, while in others you may need to use your arms to haul yourself up. But the ascent is short—only 1.7 miles—and while you may need, as we did, two hours to get to the summit, it offers superb views. In fact, we were so elated by the sights—and by the breeze, since it was, after all, another of those steamy August days—that we ended up spending nearly an hour at the summit, exulting in the expansive views and the fact that we had the whole top all to ourselves—a frequent plus of Maine hiking.

The first view of mountains comes into sight as the trail opens up a bit. Scattered throughout the nice mixed-wood forest (pines, hemlock, firs, cedars and beech, maple, white and yellow and gray birch, and ironwood), alongside the trail, are large boulders. There are also, of course, given the name of the hike, blueberries—or rather, *fool's* blueberries, being the right color, but on a stem rather than on a bush. We didn't see many of the real ones. Perhaps they had all been picked clean by early August.

Within another one-half hour, you reach a flat top with lots of ledge to traverse, and then, following blue blazes on rocks and the rock cairns, you come to one really large cairn, the obvious terminus. You made it! Good for you! From the top, you can look over to two other hikes described in this book, Little Jackson and Tumbledown, the first rated as a Boomer Rating Five, and the second a Boomer Rating Four.

As we headed downward, we were surprised to encounter several groups of hikers from nearby Mount Blue State Park. By their look of exhaustion, they obviously hadn't realized what they were getting into, and were barely able to muster the energy to ask how far away the top was. We encouraged them, but were happy not to have begun *our* hike at the hottest part of the afternoon, as they were.

On the descent, we shaved one-half hour from our ascent time, picking our way down very carefully, since when your legs are jelly-like, it's easier to take a spill.

At the bottom, we figuratively high-fived, re-dosed with ibuprofen, and hit our water-cooler for a refreshing iced tea. We hear that on the three hundred acres of this pristine wilderness, all manner of animals and fowl roam, including deer, bear, moose, rabbits, coyotes, martens, turkey, partridge, hawks, owls, and hummingbirds. We didn't see any, but maybe you will. Our happiest sight, at the end of a great hike on this steamy August day, was of our air-conditioned car.

Blueberry Lore

- The blueberry, sometimes also known as the bilberry, whortleberry, and hurtleberry, is Maine's state berry.
- Maine leads the world in the production of wild blueberries, the best ones for pie-making. Wild blueberries, unlike the larger, grocery-store variety, are smaller and vastly more flavorful.
- A clever Mainer, Abijah Tabbut, invented the blueberry rake in 1822, while early American colonists made gray paint by boiling blueberries in milk.
- It's been said that if all the blueberries grown in North America in one year were spread in a single layer, they would cover a four-lane highway stretching from New York to Chicago. Who ever figures out these things?!
- Lowbush wild blueberry, which grow about 6 to 18 inches high and produce up to 4000 pounds per acre, are periodically renewed by nature through lightning strikes or brushfires that serve not only to prune bushes and control weeds but also to fertilize the soil.
- Blueberries are both good and good for you. High in fiber and antioxidants, with vitamins A and C, zinc, potassium, iron, calcium and magnesium, they are also low in calories. Which is our rationale for that second piece of pie!

The Bowl and Champlain Mountain
(Acadia, East Side)

Spectacular views of Frenchman Bay—second to none on the island—made all the sweeter because you used your own legs and worked your lungs to get to this superb viewpoint.

Driving directions (DeLorme 16, B-4): From Bar Harbor, take ME-3 south past the Jackson Laboratory, turning left onto the Park Loop Road. Pass through the Entrance Station and continue for the turnoff to Sand Beach, which is a major parking and transportation hub where you will leave your car. To access the trailhead, leave the parking lot on foot, turning right onto the road, and in a few yards, you'll see a sign for the trailhead across the road.

Total round-trip mileage: 4.8 miles.

Vertical rise: 1058 ft.

Highest point: 1058 at the summit of Champlain Mountain.

Miscellaneous: Restroom and water are both available at the trailhead parking lot for Sand Beach.

Map: Acadia NP, East Side, H-15.

The challenge and the payoff. On a trail with lots of rocks and ledge, you'll be getting to know the pink stone of Acadia close up, as you have to stash your hiking poles and come nose to nose with it while you haul yourself up the rock at several points on the trail. But your efforts are repaid many times over by the views down onto the Bowl and out to the ocean as well as those from on top of Champlain, which are unbeatable—stunning, really.

Description of the hike. After leaving the parking lot at Sand Beach and turning right onto the Park Loop Road, you walk for only a few yards before seeing the trailhead on the opposite side of the road. The blue-blazed Bear Brook Trail starts off on rocks and continues on them, in one form or another, most of the way. Your first destination

162

is the Bowl, which is 0.8 mile ahead. Within ten minutes, you will see a trail sign indicating that the Bowl is accessed in two directions. If you take the right, you'll be faced by the challenge of The Beehive with its heart-stopping and strenuously steep climb on iron rungs and ladders as well as an iron bridge. Being acrophobic, we've never been tempted, instead choosing the left turn over ledge. Likely, you will, too.

At 0.5 mile from the Sand Beach parking lot, a trail sign indicates that the Bowl is 0.4 miles further. In 0.2 mile, you will see another trail post, offering the chance to go to Gorham Mountain along a ridge to the left. Ignore it and take a right here for the Bowl, which is only 0.2 mile further, and you'll pass through a lovely birch forest.

Shortly, you begin a descent to the pond, which you will follow along its southern shoreline, sometimes on raised planks. On our last time out, in mid-August, we spied what we called "the last lily of summer" floating amongst lily pads and absolutely had to photograph it, which required moving off the trail through brambles and bushes—probably an infraction of the rules, but one that we excused in the name of art. Further on, there is a small "beach" area where you can "legally" approach the water's edge.

Views onto pond and ocean, Bowl and Champlain Trail, Acadia

When you move away from the pond, the trail is at first flattish before crossing a brook and climbing to a crest. In less than a quarter-hour of climbing, you arrive at an open place with the first expansive views behind you. Note that the view onto the Bowl gets better and better as you climb. You will haul yourself up on boulders, then pause for great views back to the Bowl and off to the ocean. Make sure your camera batteries are fresh and you have lots of space on your memory card!

You do not see the summit of Champlain at this point but rather a series of intermediate summits as you move steadily toward your goal on the well-marked trail, climbing up and over Acadia's pink rock and passing through picturesque groves of pine trees. Unless you have long legs or springy thigh muscles, you'll be using your arms to haul yourself up the rocks on several occasions. About a quarter-hour before arriving at the summit, the trail descends into a short pine forest with blueberry bushes and increasing amounts of ledge. The final stretch up a long expanse of easily walkable ledge is quite pleasant, and your goal is plainly in sight.

> **History Lessons**
> Why "Frenchman" Bay? According to Brian McCauley in *The Names of Maine* (Acadia Press, 2004), it is because of all the French ships during the American Revolution that would gather here to fight the British.
>
> Another small history lesson: Champlain Mountain is named, of course, for Samuel Champlain (1567-1635), the French explorer who called the island he discovered, "Isle des Monts déserts," for the simple reason that the summits of most of the mountains seen from the sea were "destitute of trees," with "only rocks on them," as he wrote in 1604.
>
> Champlain, who was once the Governor of Quebec, is also credited with discovering Lake Champlain, which lies mostly in what later became northern New York state.

In all, it took us about an hour and forty minutes to get to the top, moving along at a steady, but certainly not fast, clip. The point, however, as you know, is not how fast you go, but how much you are enjoying it, even those pesky rock climbs, when you have to figure out the best way to plant your arms and feet.

At the summit, the eye is magnetically attracted to the eastern views embracing the impressive entirety of Frenchman Bay dotted with islands and sailboats, while to the west are Dorr Mountain (1270 ft.) and just a bit of the top of Cadillac (1530 ft.) whose long South Ridge you saw to your left during much of your way up to Champlain. (See Boomer Rating Three for the hike to Cadillac.)

You will note that hikers arrive at the summit of Champlain from several other trails, including the 1.2-mile Beachcroft Trail accessed from Route 3; the one-mile long north stretch of Bear Brook Trail; and the heart-pounding, sheer-sided Precipice Trail, considered the most difficult on the Island and closed the last time we were there because of dangerous conditions. It is therefore possible to climb Champlain by the route we have just described and descend either by Beachcroft, which is very steep, or by north Bear Brook, provided you have transportation on the other end.

On the other hand, retracing your steps is fine, because you have excellent views nearly all the way down. This time, in the area of the Bowl you will probably note small colored dots—people—on The Beehive Trail, another sheer-sided cliff with grades similar to the Precipice Trail. (Both trails were built by the same individual who obviously liked his trails to be dramatic.) Return to your car in the Sand Beach parking area, which in the busy summer months fills up by midday with those who want to loll about on a pretty sandy beach instead of earn, as you just did, a Maine seacoast favorite: lobster, corn on the cob, and coleslaw, topped off with a slice of blueberry pie.

Burnt Mountain (Sugarloaf area)

In the shadow of Maine's second tallest peak, Sugarloaf (4237 ft.), Burnt Mountain offers a relatively unknown hike and a terrific 360-degree view of the Carrabassett Valley and surrounding mountains.

Driving directions (DeLorme 29, E-5 and D-5): Heading north on ME-27/16, out of Kingfield, you will go 15 miles before coming to the huge sign for the Sugarloaf resort. Turn left into the entrance and proceed up the road for 1.4 miles, taking a left on Mountainside Road (with condo complexes on either side of the road), and continue 0.7 mile to Bigelow Mountain Road, where you will take a left. (Ignore the earlier turn for Burnt Mountain Road.) Drive to the end of the road and park on the left side, making sure not to impinge upon reserved parking places for tenants. (If there is no room to park here, you will need to backtrack to the parking area at the Grand Summit Resort Hotel, which is a 10-minute walk to the trailhead.) After leaving your car, you will see, on the left, a wide ski trail (No. 21), which leads in a few yards to the trailhead for Burnt Mountain Hiking Trail.
Total round-trip distance: about 6 miles.
Vertical rise: 1840 ft.
Highest point: 3600 ft. at the summit of Burnt.
Miscellaneous: No restroom or water at trailhead. Note that on the AMC map, the mountain is identified as Burnt *Hill*.
Map: AMC Maine, Map 2 Rangeley/Stratton, C-3. You may also be able to download a map from www.PurpleLizard.com, cartography by Michael Hermann, 2003.

Description of the hike. When you leave your car, you'll see a small blue-and-white sign, pointing left, for the Burnt Mountain Trail. Cross a concrete-and-steel snowmobile bridge under which spill the waters of the West Branch of Brackett Brook. A few yards ahead, to the right, the Burnt Mountain Trail begins, with the brook down to the right. You'll be following a blue-blaze trail.

The challenge and the payoff. The primary challenge of this hike comes especially in its second half, when you're climbing steeply over a lot of rock—ledge, boulders, small rocks, and gravel—and the real summit seems to elude you because of two false summits. On the positive side, in the first half you're traveling through a beautiful forest of birches and golden leaves in the fall, and in all seasons, you have excellent views from on top.

After about a quarter-mile, you'll cross the stream on a hollowed-out log leading to boulders and rocks between which you must carefully move to reach the other side. The trail takes off, up and to the left, even though there is no blue blaze. Some 100 yards later, there will be another crossing of the brook before the trail leaves the brook. For the next hour, you'll be going through beautiful mixed forests. A right turn takes you along the crest of a mountain on a level trail. Shortly thereafter, the climb increases in steepness on a gravel-and-rocky trail.

As the trees get shorter and you climb a couple more steep pitches, you come to a rock with the first great view to the Bigelows, back behind you. It took us about two hours to arrive at this point, which seemed a good place to have a view with our lunch.

For the next thirty to forty-five minutes, you will be climbing through talus and jagged rocks. There is one false summit, then a second resembling a small rock mountain. The real summit, a bald, gently rounded dome, is somewhat further to the left, marked with a huge pile of rocks. When you get there, you'll definitely feel entitled to relax and take in the superb view.

Your immediate attention goes to the impressive slopes of Sugarloaf, Maine's signature ski-resort mountain, towering directly to the west and a little over a mile away. You'll have a great view of the whole ski set-up—the ski trails, chairlifts, and gleaming snowmaking pipes set into the mountainside. As your eyes track southward, Spaulding Mountain (4010 ft.) and the long summit ridge of Abraham (4050 ft.) come prominently into view. Do note that a potential side benefit of your location, in case you want to brag to someone about making the summit, is that, given the proximity of the microwave tower on Sugarloaf, you'll have peerless cell-phone connections.

A Word to the Wise

A couple of points: confusion might arise if you consult a map that identifies this mountain as Burnt Hill. It's a case of a different name but the same thing. The second possible confusion is that there is another hike in Maine with "Burnt" in its title: Burnt Meadow Mountains (in the plural), which is in the southwestern part of the state, in the vicinity of Brownfield (DeLorme 4, B-2). It, too, may be a worthy destination, but our featured hike take place in the Sugarloaf area. (Note yet another Burnt Mountain in Baxter State Park.)

We did this hike as an out-and-back, but if you are making the loop, make sure your route-finding skills are sharp. To do it, you traverse a broad plateau before descending into the trees, as the trail drops steadily. Lower down, you will cross ski trail No. 51 a couple of times before ending at No. 50, which eventually leads to No. 22, then to No. 21, which was the hike's starting point. Come equipped with a good map if you decide to do the loop. A shorter loop may be possible by taking Ski Route 51 west back to 21 and Bigelow Mountain Road.

Other Options

Sugarloaf/USA offers not only downhill skiing but also some 100 kilometers of cross-country skiing, an Olympic-size ice-skating rink, snowshoeing, golf, biking, and hiking, each in its appropriate season. In the non-ski season, hikers can use any of the ski trails to climb Sugarloaf. Alternatively, we recommend going up Sugarloaf by the AT route, accessed one mile north of the Sugarloaf complex on ME-16/27 from Caribou Valley Road, on the left, which you follow for 4.5 miles. (See Boomer Rating Five, Other Hikes.)

Caribou Mountain (Evans Notch)

A veritable "water delight" hike that allows you to enjoy the sights and sounds of two brooks—Morrison, on the way up, with its several waterfalls and picturesque flumes, and, on the descent, charming Mud Brook—a total misnomer for a lovely stream with no mud in it at all.

Driving directions (DeLorme 10, B-1): Located in the Maine part of the White Mountains National Forest, south of Gilead on US-2, the trailhead is accessed by taking ME-113 south for 4.8 miles to arrive at a large parking area with restrooms on the left and the trailheads on the right. Two sets of trail signs give you a choice for the loop. On the left is the Caribou Trail, which arrives at Caribou Mountain in 3.4 miles. On the right is the Mud Brook Trail, which is 0.1 mile longer to the summit. Our hike describes beginning with the route to the left.

Total round-trip distance: 6.9 miles.

Vertical rise: 1888 ft.

Highest point: Caribou Mountain, 2850 ft.

Miscellaneous: Note that this is a fee area and that you are expected to pay on the honor system, leaving a stub on your windshield. Alternatively, if you have a Golden Age Passport, display it on your dashboard and hike for free.

Map: AMC White Mtns., NH & Maine, Map 5 Evans Notch, E-13.

> **The challenge and the payoff**. You'll encounter steepness, roots and rocks, plus multiple stream crossings both on the out-trip and the return. However, the grade tends to be nicely paced rather than presenting bursts of steepness or constant pull-ups by arm power. Moreover, the rigors are repaid by really splendid views of many mountains and thousands of acres of forest from the summit, by waterfalls along the trail, and two attractive, boulder-strewn brooks that offer many scenic spots to eat lunch or dabble your feet in the cool water.

Description of the hike. The trail is marked by yellow blazes. Taking off on the Caribou trail, in short order you will cross Morrison Brook four times as you proceed up the wide, well-beaten forest path and past some popular scenic spots along the creek. After the fourth stream crossing and about thirty minutes, the trail becomes steeper and narrower, the footpath sometimes eroded. At 1.5 miles (for us, about fifty minutes into the hike), a sign announces that you are entering the Caribou Speckled Mountain Wilderness of the White Mountain National Forest.

Shortly thereafter, you arrive at one of the beauty spots of the hike, 25-foot Kees Waterfall, where you cross the stream once again and then again very soon. Do note, in crossing brooks, that before plotting your course through water, you should try to judge the stability, slant, and slipperiness of the stones as well as the depth and current of the water. It certainly helps to have hiking sticks extended appropriately to steady yourself and/or to test the footing. Make sure, before taking your first step, to plan the next one or two steps so that you know where your momentum should carry you. If your hiking boots are properly waterproof, your feet won't get wet until the water rises up to the upper laces—which is one of the real advantages to wearing hiking boots rather than sneakers.

As you continue, you will see two more falls, which, at high-water times, can be quite dramatic, particularly one that drops over and down through huge blackened boulders from two directions. There will be at least two more stream crossings, for roughly eight in all, before you hit the Mud Brook junction. Take a right here. You have now completed 2.9 miles of the hike and are 0.5 mile from the summit.

Now you will climb quite steeply over rocks for most of the remaining distance. But the effort will be worth it when the first open views appear on the right, becoming much more impressive as you proceed up the ledge. The summit is not marked by a trail sign, but you are now at 2850 feet, and very likely will need to hold your hat in the whipping wind as you revel in 360-degree views including, to the south, the north end of Lake Kezar, beyond to Speckled Mountain (2906 ft.), East Royce Mountain (3114 ft.) to the southwest, and in the distance, far beyond, Mount Washington (6288 ft).

A typical Maine trail

If the wind is too strong here and you haven't yet eaten lunch, save it for the nearby descent over the south ledge of Caribou (watch to see where the ledge seems to offer a sharp drop to the trail through a thicket of bushes). The south side is sheltered from the wind and offers an endless display of forested mountainsides, virtually uninterrupted. It's just you and the great White Mountains. On a clear, windy day, with fluffy clouds sometimes dimming the sun, we had a sweeping panorama of Maine and New Hampshire mountains—an amazingly "all-nature" view, without any visible works of man. No highways in sight, no towns—just the green, undulating folds of mountains. From this natural view-balcony, just after leaving the summit, you will plunge back into the forest for your return.

Facts and Legends of the Whites

- Most people associate the White Mountains with New Hampshire, but Maine also claims a corner of the Whites, accessed by scenic ME-113. The White Mountain National Forest ranges between the two states and covers almost 800,000 acres, including the largest alpine area east of the Rocky Mountains.
- Since the Whites look green to most of us, why call them the White Mountains? According to one legend, it is because in the old days, sailors out to sea in the Gulf of Maine saw these great mountains, which for eight months of the year were covered with snow, and so decided the name. A skeptic might ask how could sailors sight these mountains from hundreds of miles away? Well, it may be because the valley floor out of Evans Notch is no more than 600 ft. above sea level, while the Whites stand thousands of feet above. Then again, maybe in pre-global warming days, there was a lot more snow and the air was crystal-clear. Or is that why the sailor story is considered a legend?
- Since no one has ever thought that caribou roam this area, what explains the name of the mountain? The most likely story is that it's a corruption of the name Calabo, which shows on the 1853 Walling map of Oxford County.

The descent down the Mud Brook Trail involves more than half a dozen brook crossings, many just a hop and a skip to the other side. In fact, the cheerful brook will remain your companion until, one-quarter mile from the trailhead, it swings away westward. About ten minutes before the end of the hike, there are a number of gorgeous photo opportunities of the brook as it bends and burbles through a boulder field. Alas, without a tripod, it may be difficult to get a properly exposed shot. As we parted ways from the brook, we silently bade farewell to this fine friend who had accompanied us on our return.

Eyebrow Trail
(Grafton Notch State Park)

An unusual short climb up a very steep ledge face, assisted at times by fixed cables, for a bird's eye view over Grafton Notch. Not for everyone but interesting for those looking for an unusual challenge.

Driving directions (DeLorme 10, A-3 and 18, D-1): From the intersection in Newry at which Route 26 departs from US-2, take ME-26 northwest for 12.1 miles to the Grafton Notch parking area. From here you access the trailheads for Old Speck Mountain (3.8 miles, one-way), the Mahoosuc Trail (3.5 miles), and The Eyebrow (0.1 mile). Across the road are the trailheads for Baldpate and Table Rock (check out Boomer Ratings Five and Three, respectively).
Total round-trip distance: 2.1-mile loop.
Vertical rise: 900 ft.
Miscellaneous: 1) Across from the Grafton Notch State Park information and sign-in board at the parking lot, there is a pit toilet, up a short flight of stairs. 2) This is a day-use fee area, so pay to park, or display your season pass to the Park on the dashboard.
Map: AMC Maine, Map 7 Mahoosuc Range, C-3.

The challenge and the payoff. This may be as close to technical climbing as some people want to get. Without the fixed steel cables, rungs, and short ladder, it would be pretty hair-raising to negotiate the downward slanting ledge. But if you are careful and go on a dry day, the climb is not unduly dangerous. The payoff comes primarily in the bragging rights you'll claim after having scaled the mountain—even more than the view of Grafton Notch, which can be achieved for less effort from Table Rock across the road.

Description of the hike. After signing in, take the trail to the left of the trail board. (Since this hike is a loop, you will be returning from the trail to the right, but if you don't fancy pulling yourself up by the fixed cables, you could, of course, go up using the trail on the right (Old Speck Trail) and make your hike an out-and-back affair.) For the Eyebrow Trail, you enter the woods and walk for 0.1 mile to the start of the orange-blazed Eyebrow Trail.

Very soon the trail begins to climb up rock steps quite steeply, and then you reach the precipice section with its steel cables, intended to help you to pull yourself up the ledge by using arm power. The first and longest set of cables stops at a slanting ledge face that you must traverse, either using the steel foot rungs or carefully picking your way across, to a several-step aluminum ladder up over the ledge. If the rocks are at all wet, be very cautious so as not to slip since the downward slanting ledge could result in a bad accident. Once you are away from the ledge, you will continue climbing steeply but at least with more sense of security.

There is no defined summit, but rather a couple of cleared lookouts down to the parking lot and out over the Notch and surrounding mountains. As your eye follows ME-26 cutting its way through the great forest, you will certainly understand why this stretch of Route 26 through Grafton Notch State Park has been designated a "Maine Scenic Byway."

Soon after the lookouts, you'll begin the downward part of the loop. If you were nervous during the ledge challenge on the ascent, you will be relieved to know that the descent, while hard on the knees, is considerably less nerve-wracking. Note that when the trail junctions with the AT (the Old Speck Trail), do not turn right (which would put you on the *climb* to Old Speck), but just go downhill. You will cross and follow brooks and go by waterfalls, including pretty Cascade Brook. Remember that this AT trail, like all others, is marked by white blazes, and that a double blaze means that you need to make a sharp turn. In one spot by the big waterfalls, we thought that there should be a double blaze, but even without it, common sense and a clearly beaten trail indicated that we needed to turn right.

Taking it relatively easy, you'll complete the loop in three hours or less, and feel pretty proud about it. After all, you've just proved again that Boomers are game for adventure!

Further Observations

The first half of this hike is less a typical mountain hike than a not-quite technical climb, so be forewarned. One of us wasn't inclined to include it in the book, but the other one felt that we should offer a variety of different experiences and the Eyebrow Trail is certainly one such! We've put this hike in Boomer Rating Four, which is an indecisive average between a Five for the scary (for us) precipice crossing, and a Three for the rest. We suppose there are some folks who would consider it only a Three.

Why call it the *Eyebrow* Trail? Well, consider this: think of a craggy old-timer with bushy eyebrows that stand out from his face, all wild and untamed . . . . Get the idea?

Horns Pond Trail (Bigelows)

This is the best of three ways to get to beautiful Horns Pond, a mountain tarn created by glacier activity, by means of a trail that climbs through a pretty forest and makes you work, but not overwork, to reach your destination.

Driving directions (DeLorme 29, C 3 & 4): Going north on ME-27, pass the big Sugarloaf ski/outdoor entrance on the left, and continue 0.7 mile past the Wyman Town Line to Stratton Brook Pond Road, marked by a blue sign to the right. This is a generally good gravel road that you follow until the end, about 1.5 miles, where there is a trail information board and parking space for about eight vehicles. Before reaching the end of the road, you will see where the Appalachian Trail to Horns Pond crosses Stratton Brook Pond Road, but this is *not* the trail to take, since it is vastly more difficult—described as "rock-climbing" by a couple of Tennessee AT thru-hikers we met on one occasion.

Total round-trip distance: 9.2 miles.

Vertical rise: 1876 ft.

Highest point: 3215 ft. at the CCC lean-to.

Miscellaneous: No water or restroom at trailhead. Both are available further on in the hike. There is a new outhouse soon after crossing the Stratton Brook Pond outlet, on the left, and also one at the campground at Horns Pond. Water can be purified from the outlet and the Pond.

Map: AMC Maine, Map 2 Rangeley/Stratton Region, A-3.

> **The challenge and the payoff.** With an altitude gain of 1876 feet in over 4.1 miles, this hike is not overtaxing, and even when it climbs more steeply in the forest, you also have flat stretches, so that only occasionally do you need to stop to catch your breath. Plus, your reward doesn't wait until the end of the hike, but is present at both beginning and end with the level walk along pretty marshland and very nice woods. Naturally, Horns Pond, itself, whose size and setting are striking, is the frosting on the cake.

Description of the hike. You begin the hike to the left of the trail information sign at the parking area by walking 0.4 mile down the road to the Stratton Pond outlet, where you have views backward to Sugarloaf and ahead to the Horns and West and Avery Peaks. Old-timers remember that in the past it was possible to drive all the way to the outlet and across it by bridge. Now there is no bridge spanning this twenty-foot expanse of water and you must leave your vehicle at the above-mentioned parking area. You will cross the water where there is a log with stones piled against it, exercising care on the slippery rocks. Only once, in late spring, did we find the water too high to cross, since we did not want to be wet up to the knees.

Stratton Pond outlet crossing in the Bigelows

On the other side of the outlet, you are on the Fire Warden's Trail, which starts out wide and flat. Take it for 1.7 miles to the Junction for the Horns Pond lean-tos. In summertime, the walk is especially pleasant through a lush forest, though you do gain altitude in a couple of steep ascents, including one over ledge and roots that can be slippery in wet conditions. In general, however, the trail is in good condition, with a number of bog bridges, even if, inevitably, some are disintegrating from the wetness of the forest. The "up" side of all that moisture results in picturesque mossy rocks scattered here and there throughout the woodland. To the point where the trail junctions for the Horns Pond lean-tos, this is a Boomer Rating Three hike. Were you to continue on the Fire Warden's Trail, which becomes increasingly tough and has a reputation somewhat similar to the Old Speck Trail in Grafton Notch, it would quickly become an unremitting Boomer Rating Five rock-and-boulder climb.

But you've been wise and taken the trail we are describing. After signing in at the trail register at the Junction, where there are also a couple of well-placed logs for a rest, you turn left onto the trail for the Horns Pond leans-tos. You are now 2.4 miles from the next Junction with the AT trail and a further 0.2 mile from the lean-tos. During this stretch, you will be gaining most of your altitude, but as we said, the great thing is that there are also level places, which makes it all quite bearable.

Within a half-hour—at our speed, which, as you know, is not alarmingly fast—you will cross stones at a steep waterfall that tumbles down over the side, then, immediately, a log bridge across a gully. You continue climbing and cross a seasonal brook. A short time later, on the left, is a brown trail sign at eye level indicating a spur route to a viewpoint. Generally, our approach is to skip the spur trails unless we have knowledge that the view is too great to miss, because we like to focus on the main goal and fear depleting our energy on the "appetizers." So, skipping the spur trail, within minutes, you come to a broad creek, conveniently offering rocks on which to sit while you bathe your toes in the brook or enjoy the natural "air-conditioning" of a cool breeze traveling down the waterway.

As you carry on for another fifteen or twenty minutes, you'll have a view of Sugarloaf off to the left, with its characteristic striations marking the ski trails down the mountain. About one-half hour later, you hit the Junction with the AT, at which point you turn right. After a quick 0.2 mile, you arrive at the historic CCC lean-to, no longer in active use, but retained for day-hikers. One summer afternoon, we shared the shelter with a group of challenge-hike high-school kids, to sit out a rainstorm that had been heralded by a couple strikes of lightning touching down not too far from the trail and which had spooked us all.

Safety Tips

- How many drops of iodine does it take to purify a quart of liquid? With liquid 2% tincture of iodine, add *five drops per quart when the water is clear and ten drops when the water is cloudy.* Let the water stand for at least thirty minutes before drinking. (Rick Curtis, *The Backpacker's Field Manual*).
- Where are you safest in a storm with lightning? Not under the tallest tree in the forest, for sure! But lightning may not always choose just the tallest tree, as we witnessed when it struck ground in a forest of same-sized trees, only yards from the trail.
- Experts tell us that during a lightning storm to seek low ground and sturdy shelter but to realize that no place may be really safe.
- If caught in the open, never lie flat on the ground, but rather crouch with your feet together and your weight on the balls of your feet. Keep your head lowered and cover your ears.

From the lean-to, Horns Pond is a few hundred yards down the trail on the left marked by a sign. Above the lean-to and to the right are the Caretaker's quarters, encased in plastic on a raised tent platform. There, one happy soul spends his or her time from May to October, teaching the leave-no-trace ethic and overseeing the area with its popular tent sites for AT thru-hikers and others as well as "managing" two state-of-the-art outhouses.

Hikers going on to the Horns, North and South, or to Avery and West Peaks—it is possible to bag them all in one extended hike—will not tarry too long at Horns Pond, despite its beauty. But *you* can, since all you need to do now is turn around and retrace your steps. Hopefully your experience will be more leisurely than our last one: we had to race down the mountain in pelting rain and then a constant drizzle, which finally convinced us after years of hiking to buy rain covers for our day packs!

Trail History

Many have been the times we have applauded the legacy of works performed by the Civilian Conservation Corps during the 1930s. The day lean-to shelter at Horns Pond is one such excellent structure, solidly built and carrying the history of decades and decades of hikers, whose names are sometimes carved into the logs and whose tales of battling the nightly excursions of mice running over sleeping bags are legion. In places like Maine, the CCC has left a real legacy on American trails.

Lone Mountain (Phillips/Madrid)

Here's a stretch of the AT that hardly sees any day hikers and whose rewards come in the first half while the challenges are bunched in the second. In spring and summer, the first half is sheer delight because of the presence of water in creeks and streams and miniature waterfalls, while the second half will test you mettle and prove that the summit isn't always where you get your reward.

Driving directions (DeLorme 19, A & B-3): From Phillips, on Route 4, turn north onto Rte. 142. Continue for 2 miles until you arrive at East Madrid Road, on the left, which is a paved and dirt road passing a few houses. At 6 miles from Rte. 142, turn left onto Potato Hill Road, which becomes narrower and is used by logging trucks. At a fork, stay to the right. You will follow this road for 4 miles. Occasional skidder roads take off from the side, and several open areas show active logging operations. You will leave your vehicle at approximately 12 miles from the beginning of Rte. 142, parking in an area on the left of the road where the grasses have been beaten down.
Total round-trip distance: about 9.2 miles.
Vertical rise: 1806 ft.
Highest point: 3280 ft. at Lone Mountain.
Miscellaneous: No restroom or water at the trailhead. Water will be near your route, from where you cross Sluice Brook, approximately 1.3 miles from your car, to the bubbling waters of Perham Stream near Barnjum Road, about 1.6 miles further on. Be sure to purify it.
Map: AMC Maine, Map 2 Rangeley/Stratton Region, D-3.

Description of the hike. When you leave your car, begin walking down the increasingly overgrown, rutted, and rocky road for about 1.3 miles until you reach Sluice Brook and falls, gushing on the right. As the water passes over the "road," it flattens out so that you will likely wetten only the tops of your shoes. Immediately to the right, up a few steps in the forest, is an AT trail sign signaling that Lone Mountain is 3.1 miles away, while the Junction with the Mt.

Abraham side trail is 4.2 miles, and Spaulding Mountain, at 3988 feet, is 5.9 miles. Our hike takes you just to Lone Mountain.

The challenge and the payoff. The challenge of the hike may come 1) in access to the trailhead, since Potato Hill Road, used by logging truck traffic, may be rough in spots or even just marginally passable by passenger cars after rains and 2) in making a demanding ascent to the viewless summit of Lone Mountain, merely marked by a simple sign and offering none of the usual repayment for your outlay of energy. But hey, you got your reward to begin with, first through an attractive woodland with a lot of variation and then at the charming pools and eddies and bubbling waters of Perham Stream near Barnjum Road, *and* you get to go back there, on the return. Plus, if you've chosen a cool spring day or a crisp autumn one, that 1000-foot pull up to Lone Mountain will seem, if not like a piece of cake, at least nothing compared to how we felt one steamy August day with temperatures in the high eighties.

You enter the forest, and the trail begins immediately to make a moderate ascent, roughly following the route of Sluice Brook for about the first twenty minutes, during which you enjoy the view and sound of the gurgling water as it tumbles over rocks. Following the AT white blazes on trees, you will shortly pull away from the stream, arriving at a grass-covered road about an hour and a quarter after leaving your car. Cross it and reenter the woods, which are pleasant, offering a lot of variety, with large open stretches and other places where the trail is embraced by a corridor of trees. At 1.6 miles, you arrive at a particularly picturesque spot with a couple of bridges over the burbling waters. This is a great place to take a breather, eat your lunch, or, on a hot day, dabble your feet in the icy water.

Very shortly thereafter, you will emerge from the woods to cross Barnjum Road, also used by logging trucks. If you've got lots of energy, you might consider turning left and walking up the road for a mile or so, because especially in the early morning, the experience is quite wonderful as you seem to climb into the sky and discover vista points along the way to surrounding mountains. Return to where you exited the woods and reenter on the other side, now on your left.

This part of the hike will be the most demanding by far, because you will be climbing more than 1000 feet in about 1.5 miles. We've done it in all kinds of weather, but only once in the humidity-laced heat of August found it to be something of a slog. However, you will feel so virtuous! And one thing is for sure: it's good heart and lung exercise.

Finally, after much output of energy, the physical trial comes to an end, and the "summit" will come upon you as something of a surprise—just a kind of flattish place with a sign to the left indicating that you are now at 3280 feet. Congratulate yourself, take a swig of water, then start on down the trail, taking a break whenever your legs become too "jelly-like." Remember that once you cross Barnjum Road again, it's all downhill and you will soon be near the happy waters of the brooks and in the tranquility of the Bambi-like forest.

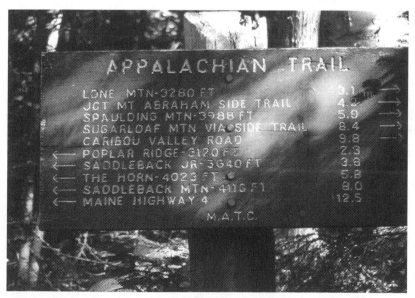

Lone Mountain trail sign

Angels of the AT

One of the reasons that AT trails are easy to follow, well blazed, and cleared of brush and downfall, is because of the volunteer Maintainers, who hit the trail every hiking season and keep it that way just for you.

The less heralded of AT volunteers are the Corridor Monitors, whose work may be less apparent to the hiker, but is just as essential. These are the folks who monitor an area typically 500 feet away from the trail on each side, checking for infractions, such as harvesting of wood, dumping of trash, or trespass by unauthorized ATVs or snowmobiles.

Each Monitor, like each Maintainer, is typically assigned a three or four-mile stretch of the trail, which actually means six or eight miles, since both sides of the trail must be monitored. As the Monitor checks for infractions, he must bushwhack through fallen timber and boggy areas to locate boundary markers set out by the National Park Service.

On the stretch of Lone Mountain monitored by one of the authors, it was necessary to locate nearly three-dozen boundary markers. Hence, the task could be a multi-day affair, requiring a campsite out in the wilds that on occasion might even be broken by an adventure with a forest creature. For a detailed account of the same, see the Featured Hike for Lower Lone Mountain in Boomer Rating Three.

Rumford Whitecap Mountain
(Rumford Center)

From a uniquely beautiful summit—an extensive white granite dome, broken at intervals by "gardens" of small evergreens, blueberry bushes, and other appealing vegetation—there are magnificent 360-degree views, taking in some of the Northeast's most impressive western mountains, including Old Speck.

Driving directions (DeLorme 18, E-4 & 5): Heading westerly on U.S. Rt. 2, in Rumford Center, turn right at Andover Road; then, at 4.6 miles, right onto East Andover Road. In less than 0.25 mile, you will see a cleared parking area on the left. Directly opposite and across the road, there is a small brown sign indicating the entrance to the trail behind a red cattle gate.
Total round-trip distance: approximately 4.5 miles.
Vertical rise: 1540 ft.
Highest point: 2200 ft. on Rumford Whitecap Mountain.
Miscellaneous: There are no privies at the trailhead or anywhere on the hike. As always, bring your own water.
Map: At the parking area, study the posted map that shows three color-coded trails. Our hike takes you up the orange Trail 1 and, on the return, down the yellow Trail 2. You will take the green connector trail over the bridge, and return to your car in 0.25 mile by the orange trail.

The challenge and the payoff. The first mile or so of this hike is relentlessly uphill, and the descent by the yellow trail over a couple stretches of slanting ledge is very steep, so you'll really be using your knee "brakes." The reward, however, is quite wonderful. As you arrive toward the top, you'll be struck by the unusual aspect of this mountain, which is a one-of-a-kind for Maine, with garden-like patches of wind-bent pine trees set amidst blueberry bushes and other low-lying shrubs. The actual "white cap" refers to the ledge of the expansive rounded summit, from which you will have truly super views.

Description of the hike. If you have not taken this hike since fall 2007, note that the Mahoosuc Land Trust, which has ownership of portions of the mountain, has done some trail re-routing and re-marking. Now there are three color-coded trails, orange and yellow (accessible from the parking area on East Andover Road) and the blue trail (off Coburn Brook Road, several miles further north). The loop hike we describe goes up the orange trail (Trail 1) and returns by the yellow trail (Trail 2, Starr Trail).

Cross the road and go around the red cattle gate to begin walking up an old, grassy road. Soon, on the right, there will be a trail register where you sign in. When you come into an open area, ignore the road on the right and look, instead, on the left, for the orange trail marked by orange paint or ribbons. At first the trail follows a wide, needled path before becoming gravel and rock and climbing briskly. In 0.25 mile you see the connector trail on the left, pointing to yellow Trail 2. You'll be on it for the return, but for the present continue on the orange trail, along a grassy road—sometimes level, sometimes downhill, at times crossing a seasonal creek or water runoff, and climbing over rocks.

Since you must climb more than 1500 feet in just under two miles, in warm weather you may be working up a bit of a sweat as you ascend the rock-and-boulder-strewn path and a long section of rock ledge without views. After about twenty minutes, you turn left into the woods, following which there is more ledge but also a more open feeling. You've climbed about 1200 feet at this point and still have another 350 feet to go. Five minutes later you come to the intersection on the left with the yellow trail. You are now about a third of a mile from the summit.

From this area on, it is necessary to keep an eye out for the orange blazes on the ground, which lead you toward the summit. Some confusion is possible, since there are remnants of former blazes and sometimes a plethora of cairns, plus the official marks for the blue and yellow trails. Just remember to watch for the color orange and to keep ascending toward the east. In blueberry season, expect to see folks with pails working the patches of fruit-bearing low bushes that dot the pre-summit.

With a little more effort, you'll arrive at the top and have your reward of 360-degree views. The true summit is a broad, sloping, bare area, distinguished at its highest point by a small brass U.S. Government marker in the granite. Eastward and less than a mile away, Black Mountain with its prominent radio tower is the primary feature. Southeastward, the eye embraces the town of Rumford, nestled between mountains, often marked by white plumes of steam rising from the paper mills. The best views, of course, are out to the west, to the mountains of Maine and New Hampshire.

Some Nineteenth-century Maine History
The town of Rumford (pop. 6472 in 2000) was originally called New Penacook Plantation. Its first paper-mill operation started up in 1873 and brought great prosperity to the area as witnessed by fine examples of Victorian and Edwardian architecture. You can get a sense of that earlier period by visiting Strathglass Park with its historic residences figuring in the National Register of Historic Places. The Park was conceived by an early owner of the Oxford Paper Company who hired an architect with grand ideas to build what at the time was considered to be the finest company housing in the nation. Enter the area of still active multi-story homes in brick, stone, and slate through an imposing arch bespeaking the grandeur of yesteryear.

Even on bright and sunny days, you may need to have a windbreaker on the summit. And certainly if you see storm clouds gathering and the sky darkening, you're going to want to get off the bald, exposed summit quickly so as not to become a target for potential lightning.

On the descent, watch carefully to follow the orange blazes or ribbons until after a third of a mile, you come to the intersection with the yellow trail on the right. The view in your "windshield" will now be of Old Speck as you descend to the southwest. Watch carefully for where you enter the woods. Within a half-hour, you come to some steep, downward ledge, which you negotiate for about 0.25 mile. Shortly thereafter, you come to the place where the yellow and blue trails intersect. After a few yards, turn sharply left to continue on the yellow trail. There will be another short, steep downward pitch, followed by the crossing of a couple of old skidder roads. You come to an overgrown road, very rough in places, and will see signs directing you to turn south.

Climbing to the top of Rumford Whitecap

In about twenty minutes, you'll see, on the left, a red sign indicating access to Trail 1 by way of the connector (green) trail. You will descend some recently constructed log steps and cross a bridge over a picturesque creek, which, in spring or after rains, tumbles down in a rush. From the other side, access the orange trail with a right turn in order to regain your car. If you miss the connector trail, you'll exit onto East Andover Road just a little north of the parking area. No harm done, because your car is still in sight, and in the fall, you may even be able, as we were, to nab a healthy snack off a nearby wild apple tree.

For some folks, Rumford Whitecap is considered to be a three or four-season hike. But in view of the vertical rise of this hike, we find it hard to imagine skiing the trail. In fall and summer, however, it's a wonderful and rewarding workout.

Covered Bridges

- If you want to extend your outing or are looking for a nice place to have a picnic lunch, drive north from the parking area for a couple miles on East Andover Road, passing Coburn Brook Road, and continuing another couple of miles (for a total of four miles) to the covered wooden Lovejoy Bridge, built in 1867.
- There were once 120 covered bridges in Maine, but only eight original ones remain today. Lovejoy, which spans the Ellis River, is the shortest at seventy feet.
- Speaking of covered bridges, one of the most famous is the Sunday River Bridge, known as Artist's Bridge, dating from 1872, located on the way to hikes described in Boomer Rating Three (Lower Wright to the North-South Junction) and Boomer Rating Five (Wright-Goose Eye Loop).

Success Mountain
(Grafton Notch/Mahoosuc Range)

From the summit of Success Mountain, you will have excellent 360-degree views of the mountains of western Maine, plus many great peaks of New Hampshire. In fact, this hike is actually in New Hampshire—though very close to the border with Maine—and is accessed from Maine by a scenic drive through Grafton Notch State Park.

Driving directions (DeLorme 18, D-1): Driving north on ME-26 at 2.8 miles beyond the parking area for the trailheads for Eyebrow, Old Speck, and the Baldpates, turn left on York Pond Road, which soon changes name and becomes the 21-mile long Success Pond Road, a wide dirt road owned by a logging company. To reach the trailhead, drive about 15.5 miles, giving logging trucks a wide berth and full right-of-way. You are looking for an unnamed turn to the left, between two boulders. Take this turn and drive back about 200 yards, keeping right at a fork, to a clearing where there is plenty of room to park your car. Just inside the woods, there is a small plaque nailed to a tree, which serves as a wordless identification of the trail.

Total round-trip distance: 3 miles for Success Overlook; 4.8 miles for the summit of Success Mountain.

Vertical rise: 1300 ft. to the Overlook; 1800 ft. to the summit.

Highest point: 3052 ft. at the Overlook; 3565 ft. at the summit of Mount Success.

Miscellaneous: No water or restrooms at the trailhead.

Map: AMC Maine, Map 7 Mahoosuc Range, C-2.

Description of the hike. From the clearing, enter the woods, where there is a small wooden plaque (with no trail name) nailed to a tree. The pathway appears to be a snowmobile route and begins to climb almost immediately. Maintained by a local club, the trail is wet and eroded in places but always easy to follow with its blue blazes. For one long stretch, you will climb straight up over moss-covered rocks and ledge.

The challenge and the payoff. This trail is pretty relentlessly uphill, often wet, and climbs up moss-covered ledge. But it's not an unreasonable output of energy if you just go to the Overlook. Moreover, we find that the real pleasure of the trail—beyond the great views both at the Outlook and at the summit—inheres in the mossy, vibrant forest glades alongside the route. Indeed, mosses and lichens—the sources of these colors—seem to cover everything that stays in contact with the forest floor, especially logs and stones. The sight of all these shades of green, especially when struck by clear sunlight, makes for an indelible visual memory along with the impressive rock face of North Cap.

A little under 1.5 miles into the hike (an hour and fifteen minutes at our pace), and after having climbed 1300 feet, you will see a trail to the right for the Outlook Loop. It is marked by yellow blazes and is a short path that continues climbing only very gently—a nice change, you'll agree—out to a broad ledge area. We definitely think that the outlook is very worthwhile and in itself makes a perfectly justifiable destination. There are several fine vantage points with views toward the far-off Presidentials. On clear days, you'll even see the plume of smoke from the cog railway climbing the flank of Mt. Washington on the right, and with your binoculars you can spot some of the buildings of the weather-station laboratory located there.

When we took this hike in late summer moving into early fall, we were struck by the beauty of the under-forest in many areas, with its great beds of ferns and beautiful green moss, as well as by the abundance of mushrooms, ranging in color from red-orange to dark tan, light-brown, and white. On the underside of some fallen timber, we saw fist-sized crystalline fungi while, along the trail, clusters of bright red ash berries provided a shock of color. There are, thus, lots of opportunities for the macro-photographer, though the low light in much of the forest area may require high ISO or, better yet, a tripod.

Success Mountain overlook with a view to New Hampshire

At the Overlook, the view of the sheer rock face of North Bald Cap is mightily impressive, and you may even imagine that it resembles Half Dome in Yosemite. Beyond North Bald Cap, you'll have an excellent view on a clear day of New Hampshire's most famous peak, Mt. Washington, at 6288 feet. Since you'll probably be alone at the Overlook, take your time before descending, if you just want a Boomer Rating Three-Plus hike, or going on to the summit for a Boomer Rating Four.

If you continue on to the summit of Success (only 0.75 mile further, after you regain the main trail), you will be rewarded with comprehensive 360-degree view of the entire White Mountain area of Maine and New Hampshire. To be sure, reaching the summit at 3565 ft. entails climbing another 500 feet, but it's nothing excessively challenging now that you have the "hang" of it. As you drink in the views, you can speculate as to the reasons behind the name of this mountain and what it may promise for those who attain it.

Return to your car by the same route, taking special care on the particularly steep and often wet and slippery downhill sections of rock ledge.

Regional Facts

√   Success, New Hampshire, is an unincorporated township of 59.2 square miles, located in Coos County, New Hampshire, directly east of Berlin and bordering on the state of Maine. As of the 2000 census, the township had a total population of two, a special distinction shared by only five other places in the United States. (Another is Twombly, Maine.) During the summer the population of Success increases, since there are numerous summer "camps" (houses or cabins) on Success Pond.

√   Upon leaving the trail, you will be much closer to Berlin, New Hampshire—only 5.4 miles from paved Hutchins Street—as opposed to the 15+ miles on Success Pond Road, which takes you back to ME-26. Of course, which direction you exit from Success Pond Road depends on where you are going next: Maine or New Hampshire.

Tumbledown Mountain (Weld)

This hike is all about rock for a steep ascent to a lovely alpine lake and with a bit more climbing, to great views that embrace several distant mountain ranges and Webb Lake.

Driving directions (DeLorme 19, C-1 & 2): From Weld Corner, take the Byron Notch Road. This gravel road leads to several trailheads, all of which will take you to Tumbledown. You will access the first trailhead by turning right, after the cemetery, on Morgan Road for the Parker Ridge trail leading to Tumbledown (as well as for the Little Jackson Trail; see Boomer Rating Five). The second access, the one we describe below, is the shortest way up to Tumbledown Pond. For it, continue on Byron Notch Road to the sign for the Brook Trail. Park on the side of the road. The third way up Tumbledown is at the trailhead a mile further up Byron Notch Road for the Old Chimney and Loop trails.
Total round-trip distance: 4+ miles.
Vertical rise: Roughly 1863 ft.
Highest point: 3086 ft. on Tumbledown Mountain.
Miscellaneous: There are no restroom facilities at the Brook trailhead; remember to be a leave-no-trace hiker and use those plastic baggies for toilet paper. This is a very popular trail on weekends, especially.
Map: AMC Maine, Map 6 Weld Region, D-2.

Description of the hike. The Brook Trail begins with a gravel-and-dirt road that climbs steadily. In about forty minutes you leave behind this overgrown road and enter the forest, following blue blazes. The trail continues more and more steeply over rocks and boulders. Indeed, this is a trail that is made of fallen rock in a great tumble—hence, its name. But remember that you don't have to race up the steep, rocky ascent like the twenty-year-olds who will pass you. Just set a reasonable pace, and after an hour and a half or two, depending on the number of breaks you take, you'll arrive at the last rock hurdles, over which you will need to scramble or be assisted up by a taller companion.

The challenge and the payoff. Rock, rock, and rock everywhere, from gravel road to a rocky path, from boulders to ledge. And there is the kind of relentless steepness that takes the occasional Sunday hiker by surprise and calls for pre- and post-dosing of ibuprofen for those with problem knees. But Tumbledown Pond is a worthy destination, a beautiful mountain lake at 2872 feet. Plus, if you climb just another 140 feet or so on the rock ledges of Tumbledown Mountain, you'll have a super view onto the pond, with Little Jackson (3434 ft.) in the background, and a great panorama of mountains all around, while in the distance Webb Lake stretches out.

And there, before you, will be beautiful Tumbledown Pond, complete with its own little island. On one August day, we spied a couple of young lads cooling off by swimming from the lake shore to the island. Other hikers found resting spots beside the lake, perfect for taking a breather or having their picnic lunch.

After a rest, cross over the rocks and boulders at water's edge, on the left, to continue your ascent as far as you wish up Tumbledown Mountain. First, you enter a forested enclosure with rocks. When the wind is too strong to picnic by the lake, people often take shelter in this grove of trees below the ledge.

From the grove, you exit out to ledge, on which you will be climbing the rest of the way through patches of tightly packed woods and shrubs. At this point, the trail is neither consistently nor clearly marked with the blue slashes. Lack of a clear trail might not be too great a problem in climbing the mountain, but we found it more problematic coming down, since rock cairns that can be spotted a few hundred yards ahead are not always a reliable sign that you should just follow them by going straight. A couple of times on the descent we had to correct ourselves, somewhat dangerously. Also, note that up on the bare summit the wind can be very strong. We heard reports that it was gusting at sixty miles an hour on the day we were climbing—enough to lose a bill cap, for sure!

Tumbledown Mountain stands at 3068 feet, or just about 200 feet above the level of the lake. We found that it wasn't necessary to climb the entire distance up for great views, so with the wind gusting so strongly and the temperatures quite cold, got our pictures and started the sharp descent off the mountain, agreeing that it had been a great outing.

On Knees

Unlike animals who walk on all fours, we two-legged humans often have trouble with our biggest weight-bearing joints, the knees. Do note that experts tell us that losing just five pounds will eliminate at least fifteen pounds of stress on the knees. The following hints from *Backpacker* magazine may also help.

- On the trail, lean your upper body slightly forward, especially when going uphill, because this slightly crouched posture keeps your hips and knees flexed, putting less stress on your ACL (anterior cruciate ligament) and more evenly disperses weight between your quads and hamstrings.
- Avoid maneuvers on the trail that put extra stress on your knees, such as full squats and long drops from ledges.
- Interrupt long downhill stretches with frequent rest breaks. Take shorter steps going downhill.
- And, of course, use trekking poles to reduce impact on your knees.
- At-home, strengthen leg muscles by focusing on the inner thighs and hamstrings with these exercises:

1. With ankle weights on, lie on your back, then lift the right leg while keeping the left leg bent and the left foot on the floor. Flex the right knee slightly and rotate your foot out, tightening your inner thigh and flexing the muscle.

2. For the hamstrings, stand and lift one weighted foot behind you until the lifted leg is bent at 90 degrees and hold for 5 seconds before slowly lowering the leg. Repeat each exercise 10-15 times.

Other Hikes
Boomer Rating Four

Bemis Mountain and Bemis Stream Trails (DeLorme 18, A-4)
This is a mountain with several summits and views from the long
Bemis Ridge as well as the open knobs. We propose a hike of under
10 miles (turning back at the Bemis lean-to) that still provides lots
of cardiovascular work in return for good views.

You can access this trail in a couple of ways. We've done it
from gorgeous Height of Land on ME-17 as well as from the Bemis
Track, a good-quality dirt road that intersects ME-17 on its west side,
seven miles south of the AT crossing at the map point, "Houghton"
(DeLorme 18, B-5). The latter approach not only gets you closer to
the trail but saves you from having to ford Bemis Stream. **NB:** If you
come from ME-17, do not park at the Height of Land Overlook, but
half-a-mile south on the west side by the Bemis Stream trailhead.

From here, the trail begins by making a sharp descent of about
700 feet down a grassy cliff side. At 0.8 mile, you arrive at Bemis
Stream, which must be forded. Two-tenths of a mile further, you cross
Bemis Track before making an extremely steep ascent, first to open
knobs with a view across the valley back to your car, and then, at 2.2
miles, to First Peak. This means that from Bemis Stream, at 1500 feet,
you climb up 1000 feet in just over a mile. The worst is now over,
although you will make a shorter climb to Second Peak, which is 0.9
mile further and provides views from the open ledges. At this point,
the trail levels off and you arrive at the Bemis Mountain lean-to after
two miles of relatively easy walking in comparison to what preceded
it. When we last hiked this trail, the upper part was exceedingly
muddy, but in recent years, trail maintainers have done a lot of work
to improve the footpath, constructing bog bridges and ladder-steps.
Round-trip distance: From ME-17 to lean-to and back, 9.2 miles.
Vertical rise: 1615 ft. from Bemis Stream to Third Peak.
Map: AT in Maine, Map 6 Maine Highway 27 to Maine Highway
17, and Map 7 Maine Highway 17 to Maine-New Hampshire State
Line.

Chairback (DeLorme 42, D-2)

For a very nice trail and good scenery in the backcountry, we recommend the Chairback hike. Take the Katahdin Ironworks road, following signs for Gulf Hagas. Leave your car in the same parking area as for that hike. Access the Chairback trail either by walking up the road for half a mile, where on the left, you'll see a former logging road, now grassed over, that climbs up and quickly narrows to a forest trail. Or from the parking area, enter the woods as for the Gulf Hagas hike, but do not cross the West Branch of the Pleasant River. Instead follow the trail until it exits onto the haul road. On the opposite side is the grassed-over road referred to above.

The trail climbs just under 1000 feet in about 1.5 miles, then becomes fairly level. At 1.7 miles, you can take a short spur trail to East Chairback Pond and from a vantage point high above the water, have a nice spot to take your lunch. At 2.8 miles, you'll be at the base of the main ascent of Chairback Mountain (2219 ft.), and will reach the semi-open ledges in 0.7 mile. Although the trail is often covered with roots, it is also fir-needled and much of the hike is along a pleasant ridge until, for the last 150 feet or so, you make a scramble up boulders. At 3.9 miles, you arrive at the summit of Chairback. For those with energy to spare, continue on for another 0.5 mile to the Chairback lean-to, and 0.4 mile beyond it, to Columbus Mountain, which stands at 2326 feet. We've always been satisfied, however, to stop at Chairback, since the ride out of KIW and back home is long.

Round-trip mileage: 7.8 miles.

Vertical rise: 1500+ ft.

Map: AT in Maine, Map 3 West Branch of the Pleasant River to Monson (Barren-Chairback Range, Wilson Valley Area).

Doubletop, Baxter State Park (DeLorme 50, D-4)

This is a steep climb on a sometimes eroded trail, but for your work, you are going to have superb views from its double summits. On a wonderfully windy, late-August day, we were thrilled by the view onto Katahdin, to which we had hiked just the preceding week.

Our hike started at the Nesowadnehunk campground from where we took the gravel road south behind the lean-tos, on the roofs of which fishermen had laid their waders to dry. We entered the woods, crossed the stream, and then climbed away from the brook valley on a crumbly dirt trail. At 1.7 miles, there is a steep climb along the shoulder, and at 3.1 miles, you'll reach the North Peak of Doubletop (3488 ft.), on which lie the remains of an old fire tower. Two-tenths of a mile further carries you along the level ridge to South Peak. As we picked our way around one of the knobs, we felt a bit exposed, since there was a sharp drop-off to one side. But views from North and South peaks were exhilarating in all directions, and we were especially delighted with the great view of Katahdin.

Round-trip distance: 6.6 miles.
Vertical rise: 2450 ft.
Map: AMC Maine, Map 1 Baxter State Park/Katahdin, C-1.

North Crocker (DeLorme 29, C & D-3)
On an early spring day, before the black flies and mosquitoes are active, this is a pleasant climb through a beautiful birch forest. It's 2700 feet up to North Peak (4228 ft.), and the trail rises steadily, but on a cool day, it never seems overwhelmingly hard. Still, our advice is not to bother with South Peak (4010 ft.), which will add on two miles, because all you'll really see at the top are the ski slopes of Sugarloaf, hardly worth the extra miles. In fact, overall, the rewards of this hike are not the views to other mountaintops—very limited, indeed, and almost nonexistent from North Peak—but the forest itself, brightly green against the white bark of the birch trees, on a fine May day.

Round-trip mileage: 9.8 miles.
Vertical rise: 2700 ft.
Map: AMC Maine, Map 2 Rangeley/Stratton Region, B & C-3.

Sargent and Penobscot, Acadia (DeLorme 16, C-3)
This is a good hike (except for one particularly difficult section) with beautiful views of water—lakes, sounds, and ocean—from the summits of these two mountains. Try to do it out of high season, because you will start off from the Jordan Pond House, and parking can be hard to find in the summer. The toughest part of the hike comes after a mere 0.3 mile,

From Doubletop a view of Katahdin

as you begin to climb the Penobscot Mountain Trail. For 0.2 mile, you ascend, almost vertically, rock ledges and boulders, at one point assisted by a handrail and footbridge. Exercise extreme caution, especially on the return, as you maneuver through boulders and boulder-drops.

That part aside, it's only a mile to Penobscot Mountain (1194 ft.), and then less than a mile to Sargent at 1373 feet, and the views are great, even if, from on high, Jordan Pond looks like an oddly rectangular body of water. As always in Acadia, watch carefully for blazes in order to keep on the right trail, especially as you look for the descent from Penobscot for the 0.2-mile section described above, which leads steeply down to the road. Too many people have built illegal cairns, and there are many misleading side-paths because of all the foot traffic the Park receives.

While both the length and relatively modest altitude gain of this hike could put it in Boomer Rating Three, the necessity to negotiate the steep rock ledges, with some straight vertical climbing, keeps it located in Boomer Rating Four for us.

Round-trip mileage: 4.6 miles.

Vertical rise: 1150 ft.

Map: Acadia NP, East Side, G & H 10-11.

Descending Sargent and Penobscot

Once you've reaped the glories and benefits of these Fours, we expect that you'll be eager to take on the Fives. After all, Boomers are an intrepid lot!

Overview
Boomer Rating Five
Super Strenuous, Super Rewards

Now that you've achieved your Boomer Four spurs, you're ready for the final challenge, right? And with a drum-roll, here you go . . . .

In this category, we group some pretty arduous hikes, but if you did the Boomer Rating Fours without too much subsequent recuperation time, you can probably do these. And you'll definitely be able to claim substantial bragging rights, since any of the Boomer Rating Fives could vanquish folks several decades younger. More importantly, you'll reap scenic rewards in great profusion, returning home with glorious views of Maine's beauties emblazoned in memory and on your photographs.

Just try to make sure that conditions for your hike are fairly ideal: long daylight hours to allow you ample time, moderate temperatures, low humidity, and no insect activity, because you are going to sweat and sweat plenty, even on a dry day. Pack a nutritious lunch, have plenty of water and snacks, take your ibuprofen or wear that knee brace, grab those hiking sticks, and hit the trail!

Why do we rate these hikes Boomer Rating Five? Primarily because most require climbs of more than 2000 feet in fairly short order (meaning, not that many miles), and sometimes, as with the Baldpates or White Cap, make an exceedingly steep haul over jumbled ledge and rock, or go straight up a wet and rocky creek bed. The Gulf Hagas hike scores a Five because while the ostensible vertical gain is not all that much, you go up and down so many times that the actual total of feet gained is vastly increased. Plus, not only is the footpath often eroded, slippery, and tangled with roots, but it also includes numerous rock escarpments, *and* you will even have to ford an icy stream, over slithery rocks and in a current, for half the length of a football field. Need we say more?!

Still, you earn your Boomer Five spurs by taking on some of the toughest trails in the state. We're not proposing the infamous Mahoosuc Notch, which requires crawling through jumbles of gigantic boulders or jumping from boulder to boulder, nor the acrophobe's nightmare, the Knife Edge in Baxter State Park, which involves a 1.1-mile traverse of a narrow ridge spine with sheer drop-offs on either side.

But we *are* talking about other trails in the Mahoosuc Range and in the Hundred-Mile Wilderness, whose very name is enough to make your hair stand on end. As you enter the woods north of Monson to access this 100-mile part of the AT, a trail sign alerts any unwary hiker to the fact that, "There are no places to obtain supplies or help until you reach Abol Bridge, 90 miles north," and "You should not attempt this section unless you carry a minimum of 10 days' supplies." Then, starkly, you are warned, "Do not underestimate the difficulties of this section." All that is missing are a few exclamation points. But this *is*, after all, a real 100-mile wilderness, the same one Bill Bryson so colorfully wrote up in Chapter 20 of *A Walk in the Woods*. And you won't hit Katahdin until you've pounded on for another 112 miles. Fortunately, we're not asking for that kind of commitment—though we are expecting you to be "up" for adventure.

Two of our Fives will take you into or near this Hundred-Mile Wilderness: the trails of White Cap and Gulf Hagas. They are definitely in the remote backcountry, and, for that very reason, are also wonderful. For five other hikes, you will be in the Grafton Notch/ Mahoosuc Range region: the Baldpates via the AT, Carlo-Goose Eye Loop, Speck Pond Trail from the New Hampshire side, Wright-Goose Eye Loop, and Puzzle Mountain on the Grafton Loop Trail. The last of our Fives' *Featured Hikes* is Little Jackson in the Weld area. That's a total of eight hikes guaranteed to put you through your paces, but wow, do they offer great rewards! We tack on six more possibilities in the section, "Other Hikes."

Hike	Round-trip mileage	Vertical gain
Baldpate, West Peak	7.2 miles	2298 ft. (**NB:** 1000 ft. in 0.8 mile
Carlo-Goose Eye Loop	7.7 miles	2170 ft.
Gulf Hagas	8.0+ miles	500 ft. (but don't be fooled!)
Little Jackson	7.0 miles	2300 ft.
Puzzle Mountain	6.4 miles	2360 ft.
Speck Pond	7.0 miles	2300 ft.
White Cap	7.5 miles	2078 ft. (two-thirds in less than a mile)
Wright-Goose Eye Loop	9.3 miles	2604 ft.

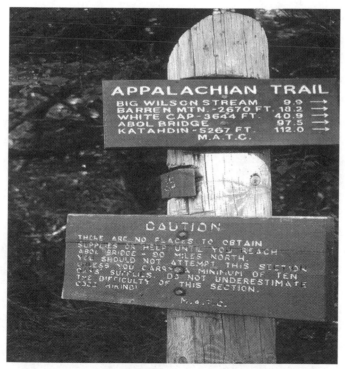

AT trail sign and cautionary language,
entry to Hundred-Mile Wilderness

Baldpate Peaks (Grafton Notch State Park)

A strenuous hike on the AT in the Mahoosuc Range, with the potential for glorious views from the two summits: one in a fragile alpine area, the other a bare mountaintop, both especially great in the fall when the forests below offer an artist's palette of colors.

Driving directions (DeLorme 10, A-3 and 18, D-1 & 2): From the intersection in Newry at which Route 26 departs from US-2, take ME-26 northwest for 12.1 miles to the Grafton Notch parking area, on the left side of the highway.
Round-trip distance: 5.4 or 7.2 miles (West Baldpate is 2.7 miles from the trailhead; East Baldpate, 3.6 miles; the AT lean-to is 2 miles from the trailhead; for the Table Rock Loop, see, Boomer Rating Three).
Vertical rise: to West Peak, 2180 ft.; to East Peak, 2298 ft.
Highest point: West Peak, 3662 ft; East Peak, 3780 ft.
Miscellaneous: At the parking lot, there is a privy but no available water. Note that this is a day-use fee area, or, if you have a Grafton Notch State Park sticker, display it for your right to hike.
Map: AMC Maine, Map 7 Mahoosuc Range, C-3.

The challenge and the payoff. This is a *hard* hike, much harder than the total number of miles would lead you to believe, primarily because after climbing 1180 feet to the level of the AT lean-to, you must make a further grueling ascent of 1000 feet in 0.8 mile to West Peak. It's a little like walking straight up a ladder, except that this "ladder" is often wet, eroded, made of ledge and piles of boulders that have to be negotiated. Even on a cool, dry day, you will still feel like the wet end of a mop! The primary payoff (aside from hopefully beneficial cardiovascular work) comes, as usual, in the excellent views from the summit(s). In addition, other pluses are the forest itself, the pleasant route that wends around a lower mountain flank on the approach to the lean-to, and the option of bagging two summits instead of one.

Description of the hike. The trailhead is on the other side of ME-26 from where you parked and is marked by a large wooden AT logo. Immediately after you leave the last pressure-treated board of the bog bridge, at 0.1 mile, you will see, on the right, the first opportunity to access the Table Rock Loop trail. If you have the intention of making either one or both summits, our advice is to skip both that trail *and* the second side trail 0.7 mile further on, so that you save your energy and time for the "main course—that is, the two summits.

Did You Know?

There are some nine mountains in Maine that carry the name Bald Mountain. So by adding "pate" to "bald," this mountain's name offers a welcome variation. It also accurately denotes East Peak, which is definitely a bald pate, while West Peak is merely in the "alpine stage" of baldness, that is, with krummholz—stunted trees—on its "cranium."

Like a lot of other trails in Maine, this one is super-encumbered with roots and frequent patches of wetness, smack in the middle of your route. Which means that you should forget the white socks and sharp-looking hiking trousers and just plow right through the wet areas, since good-citizen-hiker etiquette mandates that you stay in the center of the trail even when it's mucky. Fortunately, AT Maintainers often provide rocks or planks or sometimes even bog bridges over these problem patches in their effort to keep you from going off the trail and beating down more foliage on the sides. Look at it this way: puddles and mud in the woods let you return to childhood.

After about 1.5 miles of climbing, the trail levels off, even offering a beguiling downhill stretch, though it will soon exact revenge for this pleasure. Enjoy it while you can, catching glimpses to the left, through the trees, of the two summits, one treed, the other nude—West and East Peaks. Just short of reaching the AT lean-to, two miles from the trailhead, you come to a register sign-in board on the left side of the trail and then immediately afterward, on the right, a sign indicating the lean-to 200 yards beyond and reached by crossing a gully on a couple of planks. Unless you're giving up, don't go to the lean-to, but rather, take your last easy breath, fortify yourself with power snacks, and head straight ahead for the challenge—1000 feet of tough climbing in 0.8 mile.

More on the Angels of the AT

The next time you're out on the AT, remember those 104 AT Maintainers in Maine who volunteer to keep Maine's 281 miles of the 2175-mile Appalachian Trail as passable as possible. They're the ones who clear the trail of brush and blow-downs, paint the white blazes, and build water bars and bog bridges which protect the trail from the erosion that occurs when hikers construct their own trails around muddy sections. Altogether, some 20,000 hours of volunteer labor go into keeping Maine's AT in great shape, so if you see a work crew along the way, tell them thank you. We'd all have a lot more difficulty without them.

Shall we admit it? It took us an hour and eighteen minutes to reach the West Peak the last time we were out. So, feel proud, since you're probably going to beat us in terms of time. Even on the descent, we were only able to shave off a mere ten minutes, because knowing that accidents are much more likely to occur when going downhill, we took it slow and cautious on our now quaking legs.

But let's not forget your reward! When you arrive at the summit of West Peak, a sign will announce that you are at 3660 feet, and you'll be momentarily disappointed because there are no views. But continue on a bit further and you'll be in a pleasant alpine environment of stunted trees and fragile alpine plants, with super views opening up on your left.

And, if your experience is like our last one, you may well be joined by a pair of very friendly high-altitude birds, Canadian Jays, accustomed to getting handouts but polite enough to keep their distance if you do the right thing and refuse to feed them. They are handsome little guys, with black and white coloring, emitting an occasional loud chirp so that you know they are present. They'll often perch on a skinny tree trunk above you or even make so bold as to walk around at your feet. We hear that they will actually eat out of your hand, though our strong recommendation is that you not encourage that kind of friendliness.

But the views! If you carry on to East Peak, sitting opposite and at a distance of 0.9 mile, you will have 360-degree views, while those from West Peak are more limited but no less fine. On a fall day, when we had to stop at West because of shortened daylight hours, we were entranced by the patterns of late-afternoon sunlight falling on layer after layer of gold-burnished mountains. We had been apprehensive that a mostly leaden sky would not offer much reward, but just the contrary was true, and the effect was literally magical.

Reluctantly, we pulled on our daypacks to make the three-hour trek back down the trail to our car, a bit sorry to have had to forego East Peak because we had lost some time doing the lower loop, but in awe of the glorious views from West Peak, which even today remain luminous memories in our mind's eye.

Poundage and Resolutions

Since every extra pound we gain increases by several times the stress on knees, is it any wonder that during every ascent, the hiker is inclined to make a silent resolution to lose weight before the next hike, while on the actual descent s/he just tries to stay vertical on those wobbly legs? Actually, the ibuprofen trick works very well for counteracting debilitating stiffness following the hike and can even lessen other aches and pains during the hike. And then there is always Ben-Gay. Or perhaps the custom brew to which you will treat yourself, along with that scrumptious burger and fries, because, after all, you *did* finish the hike and deserve a tangible (read, food) reward—even if it means your body holds on to every one of those pounds.

Carlo-Goose Eye Loop (Mahoosucs)

On this hike, you'll be in two states, conquer two summits, and be wowed by views onto the mighty Mahoosucs, which straddle the Maine-New Hampshire border.

Driving directions: The trail is accessed from Success Pond Road, either from Maine or Berlin, New Hampshire. **1) Directions from Maine** (DeLorme 18, D-1): Traveling north on ME-26, which passes by the Grafton Notch trailheads for hikes such as the Baldpates and Old Speck, make a left turn 2.8 miles north of the Grafton Notch parking area, onto York Road, which will become Success Pond Road. This is a heavily used logging road that requires careful driving but is generally well maintained. Look for the Carlo Col/ Goose Eye trailhead at about 11.5 miles. The trail begins on the left. **2) Directions from New Hampshire:** From the Berlin Mills Bridge, proceed east for several blocks, turning left onto Hutchins Road. At 1.9 miles from the Bridge, take a right on an unnamed gravel road, which may carry a sign saying "Danger. Closed Road" (as a hiker, you can ignore the "closed" part). This is Success Pond Road. Follow it for about 8 miles, where, on the right, you will find a small parking area for a couple of cars. A grassy road leads up to the trailhead.
Total round-trip distance: 7.7 miles.
Vertical rise: 2170 ft.
Highest point: 3870 ft. at Goose Eye Mountain main summit.
Miscellaneous: No restroom or water at trailhead. Purify water you take from any mountain stream. At the Carlo Col campsite, 2.7 miles in, there is a privy and reliable water.
Map: AMC Maine, Map 7 Mahoosuc Range, B-C, 2.

Description of the hike. Walk straight up the grassy road from where you parked with an eye peeled for a trail sign, on the left, for the Carlo Col and Goose Eye trails. The two trails follow the same route for about 0.1 mile. Then the Goose Eye Trail diverges sharply left, while the Carlo Col trail continues straight up the grassy route, which narrows into a trail. This trail heads toward the Carlo Col Shelter, which is 2.7 miles from the trailhead and about 0.5 mile into Maine.

The challenge and the payoff. You're in the Mahoosucs, which should say to you three words: *steep, wild,* and *remote*. You might add the adverb "very" to all the preceding adjectives. More precisely: do note that the altitude gain is far more than it appears, since there are two summits to attain and both have very steep patches, sometimes accompanied by ladders. Add in a boulder scramble or two, which may require taking off your pack and pulling it up after you, and you get the idea. But, on the other hand, the start of the hike—and therefore the end—is through a relatively level and pleasant woods, especially in early summer, and you will definitely feel like you're on top of the world when you reach the summit at Goose Eye and look over the spread that surrounds you.

For the first 0.8 mile of the hike, there is only a modest gain in elevation. You will probably reach the Carlo Col campsite within an hour and a half, and will find that it is a very nice spot, especially in summer when the forest trees, warmed by the sun, exude a sweet scent and the woods are very quiet.

Upon leaving the shelter, the trail becomes considerably steeper, as it makes a 300 foot ascent in 0.4 mile up Mt. Carlo ((3565 ft.) and to the intersection with the AT. Having just climbed to the open summit, you will now immediately descend it, losing somewhat more feet than you just gained. In approximately 0.6 mile, you arrive at the bottom of the sag between Mt. Carlo and the West Peak. From here, you head west, on the AT, toward Goose Eye Mountain and its main (west) peak at 3790 feet. Note that you will be passing through a fragile alpine environment, so please stay on the trail. From the summit of Carlo to the Goose Eye Trail, you will be covering 1.8 miles. Toward the end, you'll have a difficult boulder scramble up a steep section, aided, in one part, by a ladder. On a summer day, when we came to this spot, we met a work team with picks and shovels, detailed to make improvements on the trail. On top of this rocky scramble, you will head west toward the main summit of Goose Eye where you are going to be able to claim some magnificent eye candy.

On top of the world at Goose Eye in the Mahoosucs

To begin the last part of the loop back to the trailhead, look for the Goose Eye Trail. It is located 0.1 mile west of the summit, and it will take you down, down, and down, 3.2 miles, to Success Pond Road. You will be dropping over 2100 feet, but given that the last mile or so back to Success Pond does not contain a great deal of gradient, the arithmetic tells you that a lot of that drop will occur in 2.4 miles. Toward the beginning of the descent, there is one particularly sharp drop—about 150 feet—over boulders that can be tricky to negotiate. But based on personal experience, we can assure you that we found it easier coming down than going up, when, on another occasion, we did an out-and-back 6.4-mile round trip hike using just the Goose Eye Trail.

On the return, do take it slow, because your leg muscles are surely stressed out. Pop an ibuprofen or a mint, eat a Power Bar, take a footbath in a creek, or just plain remove your boots and wriggle your toes. In other words, replenish your reserves, as you anticipate that soft and supportive seat in your car and revel in the fact that you will have achieved yet another strenuous feat!

A Walk on the Wild Side

In 2007, for the first time since 1987, a group of hardy souls, the ATC Boundary Crew, spent six weeks walking the corridor of the remote and rugged Mahoosucs. To "walk" any AT corridor is tough, but this one is more like an epic battle with nature, as crew members fought their way through almost impenetrable stands of spruce and fir trees, followed survey lines that go straight up one cliff and then drop off the next rock ledge. Their mission was to locate and uncover circular boundary markers (monuments), spaced 600 feet apart, sometimes covered with a foot of soil. Kudos to the team who participated in this "walk on the wild side" achieving success and fulfilling an important ATC assignment!

Gulf Hagas Trail
(Katahdin Ironworks/Brownville Junction)

Recognized in 1968 as a national Natural Landmark, Gulf Hagas offers the resolute hiker a one-of-a-kind experience in Maine, along the rim of a deep, three-mile long canyon with impressive views of the gorge and no fewer than five major waterfalls.

Driving directions (DeLorme 42, D-2 & E-4): On ME-11, drive 5.5 miles north of Brownville Junction, turning west (or left) on a gravel road marked by a sign for Katahdin Iron Works. Continue 6.8 miles to the gate, where you register, pay a use-fee, and get a map. Check your mileage before leaving the gatehouse; you'll be driving 7 miles to the trailhead on a rough road with lots of potholes and few direction signs. After crossing the West Branch of Pleasant River, take the first right. Subsequently you will cross a smaller bridge and pass Silver Lake on your right. Bear left at a fork in the road at 3.4 miles, continuing on past the West Branch of Pleasant River campsites 4 and 5 and then, after crossing a bridge, campsite 6. (Do *not* take the High Bridge turn to the right, as for the White Cap hike, although if you do so mistakenly, you can still get to the parking area by taking the Hay Brook turn, later on.) About 2.5 miles after campsite 6, you will see your parking area on the right.

Total round-trip distance: 8.2 miles for the Loop circuit, plus more for the spur trails to viewpoints.

Vertical rise: 500-600 ft. **NB:** Do not be misled by this modest number, since the quantity of rocky escarpments to ascend and descend substantially increases the actual gain.

Miscellaneous: At the parking area, there is space for about eight cars. There is a privy to the right of the parking area but no drinking water. **NB:** Please do not attempt to ford the river if the water is higher than knee-level, and we specifically recommend against making small children ford it, even at low water levels.

Map: Purchase a map at the entry gate. The map that comes with your entrance fee is insufficiently detailed for hiking.

The challenge and the payoff. The warning at the trailhead says that this is a strenuous trail and that the full circuit will take between 6 and 8 hours. That's no lie! First, you must ford the West Branch of the Pleasant River for 150 feet—half a football field—in icy water that is at least mid-calf, and often knee-to-thigh deep. Further challenges come on the Rim Trail with its often very rough and sometimes slippery footing, plus repeated rock escarpments to be ascended, descended, and re-ascended. Experienced hikers will, however, be well compensated by the opportunity to make a unique hike in an unusual canyon area with a rich geological and human history. If you're out on a gorgeous fall day in October, as we were on one occasion, you'll have a fabulous journey through the majestic Hermitage area with its tall white pine trees and in a forest ablaze in autumnal yellows, plus you'll have all those waterfalls and rim views that you can't get anywhere else in Maine.

Description of the hike. At the parking area, you are only 0.2 mile from the unbridged stream crossing, so you may as well begin by wearing the footgear you intend to use for fording the river. While quite a few people cross barefooted, this seems rather foolhardy to us, because you'll be making a 150-foot traverse over rocks, frequently slimy and slippery, and perhaps even sharp and in water that is *very* cold. So opt for tennis shoes and carry your hiking boots in a plastic sack or tied to your backpack. We've crossed the stream in late July and early October, when the water was not much above mid-calf, but at other times of the year, especially after heavy rain or in the spring, the crossing should be considered too dangerous to undertake. Also remember that for kids or short people, what is calf-deep for someone taller will be quite a bit deeper and scarier, especially with an undercurrent. As with any stream crossing, you can increase your confidence by using hiking poles to provide security and help with balance. If you don't have your own, grab one from the collection of wooden staffs that other hikers often leave behind, on either shore.

Once across the stream, you'll find several logs on which to perch to change your footgear before resuming the hike. The trail takes off behind you and to the right. In 0.2 mile from the stream crossing, you come to Map Point 1, corresponding to a purchased map that you can obtain from the gatehouse (note again that their free map is not adequate for hiking and just barely so for route-finding on the road). A left turn on the trail at this point launches you toward the Gulf Hagas trail, 1.1 miles further on, whereas a right turn will send you toward the AT and, ultimately, after 83.9 miles, to Katahdin. Assuming that you're here for Maine's famous canyon, take the left turn. You'll soon cross an easy brook and, at 1.2 miles from where you forded the West Branch, come to Map Point 2. The signpost announces the Circuit Loop Rim trail and return by Pleasant River Road for a total loop of 5.2 miles. (For AT hikers taking the trail to the right, their next destination will be the summit of White Cap, 9.5 miles away.)

The AT and Ridgerunners

√   FYI: The Gulf Hagas area is part of the Appalachian Trail corridor, which is federally owned and managed by the National Park Service (NPS) and the Appalachian Trail Conference (ATC).

√   From June to Columbus Day, AT Ridgerunners ply the trail to educate hikers about the leave-no-trace ethic, give trail information, and monitor trail usage. It's said that during a single season, Ridgerunners may talk to over 4000 people, which gives you an idea of the popularity of the remote Gulf Hagas Trail.

Gain access to the Loop trail by crossing Gulf Hagas Brook, either by fording—it's not too wide but can have a lot of water—or by using the log bridge: two logs strapped together and standing about 5 or 6 feet above the water with no handrail or cable. If you'd rather not put your powers of balance to the test, go by foot across the brook, using your hiking poles to step carefully from stone to stone. If the water is not too high and your boots are waterproof, you probably won't get your feet wet and will feel much safer. Or, of course, you can always change back to your soaking wet "tennies" from the previous crossing, but this also slows you down.

On the other side, you'll see a bronze monument that identifies Gulf Hagas as a national Natural Landmark. Now you have a choice between taking the Rim Trail to the left or the Pleasant River Road Trail, straight ahead. Don't underestimate the Rim Trail, which is considerably more difficult because of uneven terrain over roots and eroded sections of the trail, plus a large number of rock escarpments that will require scaling—nothing technical, but nothing really easy, either, and certainly not for small folk. Moreover, a number of the overlooks are placed precipitously above steep drop-offs, an added reason for avoiding this route with small children.

Waterfall at Gulf Hagas

The Pleasant River Road Trail, on the other hand, climbs moderately through a pleasant woods and has many bog bridges to ease your way over wet patches—of which, this being Maine, there are many! Naturally you can take the Pleasant River Road Trail in both directions, first up to the Head of the Gulf, and then adding on a segment or two of the Rim Trail to go to some of the overlooks and waterfalls. Without doing the overlooks, you'll be missing the real essence of Gulf Hagas, but your hike will be a lot easier. So make your choice. Do note that two "escape" routes from the Rim Trail have been cut to take you back to the faster and easier Pleasant River Road Trail, should you run short of time or energy. The "escape" routes are marked by signposts; one is in the area of Map Point 4, the other at Map Point 7.

Having been duly forewarned, let's assume that you are going for the challenge and take the Rim Trail, which means that you will turn left onto the trail toward Screw Auger Falls. Soon you'll see a sign, also on the left, pointing to the spur trail leading down to an overlook to the falls. Descend this path, which is steep and highly eroded, to an overlook onto the falls where you can get a fine picture. The especially hardy—and young—may want to descend further to the falls, but we knew better and saved our climbing strength and knees for the further challenges of the Rim Trail.

Maine History

When you stopped at the entry gate, you saw a part of old Maine history: a blast furnace and a charcoal kiln, remnants of the Katahdin Iron Works that operated between 1843 and 1890 and once included a village of two hundred homes. During the height of the operation in 1884, it is said that the fires of the blast furnace flamed nonstop, lighting up the night sky for miles around. While the presence of such an operation in the wilderness seems strange, it made sense, because everything that was needed was ready at hand: iron ore, fuel wood, and water power.

In the 1880s, the summer resort business flourished in this area, with period advertisements promoting the curative powers of Katahdin Mineral Springs at Iron Mountain. Folks stayed at Silver Lake Hotel (located on the lake you passed driving to KIW) and traveled to the springs by buckboard, horseback, or foot in order to take those restorative "waters." You may wish you could do likewise after this tough hike!

After Screw Auger, you will have at least eight more occasions to take spur paths to other overlooks, and nearly all of these paths are harder than the main trail—which is hard enough. Just so that you know what is forthcoming, here's the rundown:

- Lower Falls (a couple hundred yards off the main route)
- Hammond Street Pitch (0.8 mile beyond Screw Auger on a short, rough spur trail)
- The View of the Gulf (at 0.25 mile beyond Hammond, 200 feet down a narrow spur trail)
- The Jaws (another short spur trail, 0.5 mile from Hammond)
- Buttermilk Falls (0.6 mile beyond the Jaws)
- Stair Falls (0.6 mile beyond Buttermilk)
- Billings Falls (0.4 mile beyond Stair Falls)
- Head of the Gulf, a mere 0.1 mile further

In our view, not all the overlooks are worth the effort and loss of time, so we're inclined to recommend just Screw Auger and The View of the Gulf, the latter being a really quite nice, broad view up the Gulf. Other views are possible just by going out a few feet to the precipice of the escarpment that you are climbing. From points on the trail, you have a view of Buttermilk Falls, Stair Falls, and Billings, and the trail automatically leads you right out at the scenic Head of the Gulf before beginning the north stretch of the loop. Some people think that the Hammond Street Pitch is great, because you can peer down into a 400-foot deep gorge from a steep cliff. We saw two fearless young women seated together on a tiny outcropping over a 90-foot cliff, nonchalantly eating their sandwiches while enjoying whatever they could see, but as for us, we were more than happy to cede to them such a precarious perch. Prudence permitted us to judge the drama of the vertical drop from afar without risk of experiencing sudden vertigo. But each to his or her own . . . .

After the Hammond Street Pitch, which is 2.4 miles from the Head of the Gulf, and the first "escape" route at Map Point 4, just 0.6 mile before the Jaws, the Rim Trail gets more serious about making itself difficult. You face numerous rock escarpments that challenge you to figure out a route up, over, and down to the rough trail below, which merely leads you to more of the same. This is the part of the hike that you will find either wearying or weirdly fun, depending, doubtless, on your fitness level. When you do finally hit the Head of the Gulf, a delightful area where the water spreads out on either side of an island, cascading over step falls, you'll be in more "civilized" terrain. Take a breather here, and see if you can claim for yourself a very neat little rock ledge right by the water's edge, off the trail.

When you're ready for the return trip, the real work of the hike will have been completed, because the route down Pleasant River Road (yes, it was a road, formerly used by loggers and now overgrown) is easy treading, with plenty of bog bridges and no rock faces. Even if you return at a less than rapid pace, you'll find that the estimated 3.5 miles back to your car, even counting rest stops, stream crossings, and shoe changing, won't last more than two or two-and-a-half hours, and is, to boot, very pleasant.

Little Jackson Mountain (Weld)

This is a hike with two fine parts—forest and ledge—both of which keep you climbing, first through a birch-and-beech forest, and then around and up ledge with views of Lake Webb to the southeast and, to the west, Tumbledown Pond, a beautiful mountain tarn surrounded by high cliffs.

Driving directions (DeLorme 19, B-1 & 2): The hike is located in the northern section of Mount Blue State Park. From the town of Weld Corner, take ME-142 north to Byron Road for 2.1 miles. Just after a well-kept cemetery on the right, you will come to another dirt road, Morgan Road, which leads back to the trailhead. Take it for 0.8 miles and park off the road.
Total round-trip distance: approximately 7 miles.
Highest point: 3434 ft. at the summit of Little Jackson.
Vertical rise: 2300 ft.
Miscellaneous: No restrooms or water at the point where you leave your car.
Map: AMC, Maine, Map 6 Weld Region, D-2.

> **The challenge and the payoff.** You'll be climbing and descending 2300 feet at a rate of more than 650 feet a mile, first during a climb through a forest with stands of beautiful birch trees, and then up and over largely open ledges for the last mile or mile and-a-half, during which there are outstanding views. But while the vertical gain is substantial, it is divided over 3.5 miles, and your visual rewards are also nicely parceled out throughout the hike.

Description of the hike. You begin by climbing a grassy road and going up and down small dirt cliffs. Within minutes, the trail diverges: Parker Ridge trail to the left and Little Jackson and Pond Link (to Tumbledown Pond) to the right. Take a right to go to Little Jackson summit. You will continue a steady climb up a wide pathway with some rocks, none of which require clambering.

After about an hour and fifteen minutes (hiking at our pace), you will reach another trail intersection. On the left is the Pond Link Trail, should you decide that you want to go to Tumbledown Pond instead. On the right is the Little Jackson trail, which meanders less steeply for a while and is very pretty in the fall, with the white and silver bark of the birches and beeches set off amidst the fall leaves of rust, gold, and red. In the next hour of uphill hiking, and about 0.3 mile before the ledges begin, you will cross a pretty brook. Note that the last quarter-hour before you reach the first ledge is very steep.

The distance from the col to the summit is about one mile. You will now traverse and climb segment after segment of the ledge. At one juncture, there is a sign pointing to Big Jackson, though there is not an official trail up that mountain. The trail to Little Jackson is very well marked by blue blazes. You will have fine, open views all the way to your destination, as you continue to climb, sometimes descending into patches of short trees and vegetation, then climbing once again.

From Little Jackson to Lake Webb

At the summit, which spreads out across the open ledge and is marked by high alpine vegetation—clumps of grasses, mountain cranberry, and ash berry—there are excellent views. On the west, and some 560 feet down, is Tumbledown Pond, dramatically nestled between high cliffs, while beyond it are the summits of Tumbledown Mountain, the highest standing at 3068 feet. Do note, however, that despite the presence of rock cairns, there is no trail from the Little Jackson summit down to Tumbledown Pond. Many people have tried and have had to return to the summit of Little Jackson because of the danger they encounter.

So enjoy this summit and plan to go to Tumbledown another day. Now just retrace your route back to your car, following the well-marked blue blazes. By the time you re-pound your way back down those 2300 feet, you may feel that the hike *had* to be longer than seven miles, but we can promise you that you'll be glad you did it. Just take another ibuprofen.

Trail History

Until about 2004, the trailhead was also the site of a campground and shelter. But when the owner ascertained that the campground drew too many revelers who liked loud music and probably did not partake in much hiking, she razed the shelter and constructed earth barriers to the former campground. The result is a much more pleasant beginning and end to a wonderful hike that will give you a workout and rewards you with views that are various and impressive.

Puzzle Mountain, South Summit (Grafton Notch)

Climb through a pretty woods of showy ferns and a pine-needled forest floor, then steeply up to the South Summit of this unusually named mountain, for magnificent panoramic views of Old Speck and the New Hampshire Presidentials—and you will have earned your "cool one."

Driving directions (DeLorme 18, 3-E): From US-2 in Newry, take ME-26 approximately 4.7 miles north. Near the intersection with Eddy Road, but on the opposite side of the road, you will see a parking area large enough for several cars. Next to it is a gated private road and a sign for a planned new development of mountain luxury properties.
Total round-trip distance: 6.4 miles.
Vertical rise: 2360 ft.
Highest point: 3080 ft. at South Summit. The actual highest point at 3120 ft. is 0.4 mile beyond South Summit but without the same quality of views. On this hike, you go just to the South Summit, which is the best terminus point.
Miscellaneous: No restroom or water at parking area. Some seasonal creeks along the way if you have the equipment to purify.
Map: AMC, Maine, Map 7 Mahoosuc Range, E-3.

> **The challenge and the payoff**. You ascend nearly 2400 feet in 3.2 miles, which is pretty stiff, to say nothing of all those rock boulders that you must climb or clamber over as you approach the summit. But the views to Old Speck and the Presidentials from the broad summit are impressively rewarding, especially when you have the summit all to yourselves, as we did on a mid-week day in July. Moreover, should your energy flag, it is possible to end the hike a mile short of the summit, at the first overlook, which is pretty impressive itself. If you take that option, consider your hike to be a Boomer Rating Four.

Description of the hike. The trail sign at the parking area indicates that this is part of the Grafton Loop Trail. The GLT is of fairly recent construction; this particular trail was inaugurated in summer 2003. Maintained by the Maine Appalachian Trail Club (MATC)**,** the trail is marked by blue blazes and starts off on a bed of needles under a canopy of trees. In about ten minutes, you cross a road and then reenter the forest. Here you will cross several seasonal brooks. You begin climbing somewhat steeply into the forest, then seem to round one mountain and begin climbing another one. In a little over an hour, you cross a grassy logging road, and switchback your way upward.

The trail is of varying condition, sometimes with pine needles, sometimes gravel, and other times loose dirt; the ascent, however, is constant.

As we were changing film in a particularly pretty stretch with white-bark birches in beds of bright green ferns, we were surprised by the sound of barking, and were soon to meet Shelley from Iowa, a Bolivian-born pooch, accompanied by her owners, two Northern Iowa University professors who make an annual trip to Maine specifically to leave the flatland and climb mountains. On Puzzle, you get that opportunity in spades!

As you hit the 2.4-mile mark and stand by some house-sized boulders, the trail opens to good views of the Sunday River ski area, plus surrounding mountains.

Soon after, you arrive at the Overlook with truly excellent views. This would make a good turn-around spot, if you're really tired, because it constitutes a pretty substantial reward unto itself, with the views of Old Speck and the Presidentials. Apparently, this was more or less Shelley's thinking, because soon after, Bolivian-born or not, she found a bush where she collapsed, panting hard. Time to go down, Shelley's had enough, her owners told us, as we, panting just about as hard, came into view. To realize that we were actually outlasting a dog immediately gave us a renewed sense of energy, crazy as that may be.

After the Overlook, you turn back into the forest, and for the next mile, confront the hardest part of the hike—which means the steepest sections. Take it easy, breathe deeply, and know that the reward on top is worth it. As you continue the ascent, there are alternating patches of ledge and forest, and then, a quarter-hour before arriving at the ledgey summit, *a lot* of rock boulders to figure out how to negotiate. Some, fortunately, are placed as though they were stairs—very *steep* stairs, mind you. And then, finally, mercifully, there you are in the sky, at the summit, marked by a giant stack of rocks.

Rock cairn at the South Summit of Puzzle Mountain

A Neat Collaboration
Throughout this hike, you'll actually be on the private property of the families and timber companies who have kindly granted the public access to this great area. In fact, the story of Grafton Loop Trail (GLT) is one of exemplary collaboration between the visionary landowner of Puzzle Mountain, who wanted to see a major new trail cross his property, and then of the labor and goodwill of nearly two dozen partners—AMC, MATC, private landowners, nonprofits, private companies, and federal and state agencies.

After working so hard for the reward, we indulged ourselves and spent more than a half-hour at the broad summit, exhilarated by the view—and by our accomplishment—before starting back down. After close to an hour of negotiating the boulders, we gave ourselves another break at the first overlook, for purposes of sketching and photographing. Moreover, we've read that rest stops help the lactic-acid build-up to dissipate, and besides, if the truth be told, our legs were kind of jelly-like, at this point. About an hour-and-a-half later, we were back to the car and ready for that restorative visit to a nearby brewery.

Puzzling Nomenclature

How to explain the name of the mountain: "Puzzle"? Everyone we talked to was mystified. How can a mountain be a puzzle? Or is it that with three separate summits of nearly the same height, the namers couldn't decide which was the most important? Your guess is as good as ours. It remains a puzzlement.

Speck Pond Trail (Mahoosucs)

From the calm shoreside of beautiful, serene Speck Pond, surrounded by a deep green forest, you will have an unusual view over to a low V-shape indicating the infamous Mahoosuc Notch, far off on the opposite shore.

Driving directions: The trail can be accessed both from Maine (DeLorme 18, D-1) and from New Hampshire on Success Pond Road. The following description departs from Berlin, New Hampshire. Coming off the Berlin Mills Bridge, proceed east for several blocks, turning left onto Hutchins Road. You will go by paper mills and cross a railroad spur. At 1.9 miles from the Berlin Mills Bridge, you come to an *unnamed*, gravel road on the right, with a sign that reads, "Danger. Closed Road." This is Success Pond Road, which, despite the sign, you will take. It is an active logging road, generally very well maintained, leading both to several trailheads and to summer cabins on Success Lake. Take it for about 12.5 miles, avoiding a left fork for Success Lake and homes and cabins, until reaching, on the right, a white sign indicating the Speck Pond Trail. Park off the road, on either side.

Total round-trip distance: 7.0 miles.
Highest point: 3760 ft.
Vertical rise: 2013 ft., plus 300 ft. on the return up boulders from Speck Pond.
Map: AMC Maine, Map 7 Mahoosuc Range, C-3.

> **The challenge and the payoff.** Steep climbing, after the first 1.5 miles, on a typical Maine rocks-and-roots trail. The last 0.4 mile down to Speck Pond is a vertical and sometimes very awkward descent over rock ledge. But it's worth it for the lovely beauty of the mountain lake with its view of the far-off Mahoosuc Notch area and of Speck Mountain, Maine's third-highest peak at 4180 feet. When we did this hike in early August, there were yellow stand-up lilies in the pond, the air was crystal-clear, and the silence was nature-perfect. A great reward for the hauling we did to get there.

Description of the hike. This is a blue-blaze trail, so you start out crossing Sucker Brook three times, watching carefully for those blazes. The first mile is easy. After about an hour, you pull away from the creek and climb more stiffly over rocks and roots. In a few minutes, you reach a number of cut-away sections or former logging drag roads descending the mountainside. From this vantage point—you've now gained about 950 feet—you can look down on Success Pond with its many houses and cabins. Take a breather, then continue hiking and climbing on the flank of the mountain.

Trail makers literally had to trench and dig down to ledge to make the trail. Sometimes they give extra help, as with a log ladder up one particularly steep section of ledge. Throughout the hike, we marveled at the brightness of the green moss growing on logs and on just about everything, for, like a typical Maine forest, this one is relatively wet. Note that the closer to the top, the more rugged the trail becomes.

From Speck Pond toward the Mahoosuc Notch

After literally pulling ourselves up one portion of the trail by arm power, we reached the May Cut-off, 3.1 miles from the trailhead and, for us, three hours after starting (including a fifteen or twenty-minute rest and snack break). Here, you can look back over your left shoulder and glimpse a silvery bit of the tip of Success Pond. You've now gained 2013 feet. But don't give up! The best is still to come, though it does involve descending a very steep 300 feet, over a lot of rock and ledge to get to Speck Pond. The forest is so thick on either side of the boulder chute that there are just a couple spots where you can barely glimpse Speck Pond. You must continue down the chute to the Pond level for your real reward.

It took us twenty-five minutes to get to the bottom of the boulder chute and be shoreside. We noted that the Speck Pond campsite is 0.1 mile further, but since we weren't planning on spending the night, we were more than satisfied to stop here and revel in the beauty of the lake on a perfect, humidity-free day with temperatures in the low 60s. We lingered by the shore for a half-hour, exchanging a few words with a fisherman and his son, who complained that the fish weren't biting, before setting out for the return. Curiously, we found the boulder ascent easier than the descent. On the rest of the return, we made a single rest stop after the steepest downhill section to rest our wobbly knees, and shaved off time from the three-and-a-half hours it had taken us to reach the Pond. We arrived back at the car tired but delighted to have found this gem in the Mahoosucs.

The Notch, the Edge, and the Pond

From the shore of Speck Pond, you have an extremely benign view of the famously infamous mile-long Mahoosuc Notch, which many AT thru-hikers consider the worst mile on the entire 2175-mile Appalachian Trail.

According to thru-hiker Jan D. Curran (*Onward to Katahdin*, Rainbow Books, 1999), the experience of going over the scary Knife Edge in Baxter State Park is tough, but the Notch is *"several times more demanding."*

In comparison, your hike to Speck Pond is child's play, even though it's plenty demanding. But at least with our hike, you won't be risking life and limb!

White Cap Mountain
(Katahdin Ironworks, Hundred-Mile Wilderness)

An adventurous trip in the famed Hundred-Mile Wilderness, requiring a rugged drive back into a remote area and a hike up an exceedingly steep trail over rocks. But for the views—considered to be some of the best in the state—you will be amply rewarded!

Driving directions (DeLorme 42, E-4, D-2 & 3, C-2 & 3): From ME-11, go west on the dirt Park Road for about 10 miles to Katahdin Irons Works. After registering and paying a day-use fee at the KIW visitors center, check your mileage counter and follow exactly the mileages indicated. First, drive across the bridge over the West Branch of the Pleasant River. Take a right fork, and cross a smaller bridge, passing Silver Lake on your right. Ignore a right turn 2.3 miles from the gate at KIW. At 5.9 miles cross High Bridge over White Brook. On your left is campsite 2, down toward the brook. Pass it, continuing straight, and ignore a left turn to Hay Brook and the Hermitage. You will need to drive carefully, because the road is rutted and rocky and often littered with branches and bark from logging operations. At roughly 8.7 miles, go past a road uphill to the left, instead continuing on the main road, which becomes increasingly overgrown. Take care to avoid rocks possibly hidden in the grassy center strip. Note that there are not many areas where you can easily leave a car, unless your vehicle has high enough clearance to get you all the way to the gravel pit area. A typical passenger car can be parked 8.9 miles from the KIW visitor center, off the road in the grasses.

Total round-trip distance: 7.5 miles if you leave your car at 8.9 miles from the KIW visitor center; 5 miles if you can get to the gravel pit area.

Highest point: 3644 ft., summit of White Cap.

Vertical rise: 2078 ft.

Miscellaneous: Since you are leaving your car off a logging road, there are, of course, neither water nor restroom facilities. Use the privy at the entrance station when you pay your day-use fee. Note that if you're a Maine resident and over age seventy, you hike for free. Yeah, Post-Boomers!

Map: Purchase a map at the entry gate. The map that comes with your entrance fee lacks sufficient detail for hiking in the backcountry.

> **The challenge and the payoff.** The mile-long White Brook trail to the intersection with the AT is a very rough and demanding climb up (and, of course, down) 1086 feet in a mile or less. Even on a mild day, let alone a humid or wet one, you'll work up a sweat. And you will need to be very careful about not slipping on the rocks. Remember you are in the Hundred-Mile Wilderness, far from quick help. Yet, at the same time, such remoteness gives a special sense of adventure to the hike. That, plus the relative shortness of the climb, are real positives, to say nothing of the impressive and even "thrilling" views from the bare summit. Just make sure that for the effort you will exert, you go on a clear day.

Description of the hike. After parking, begin hiking up the road. Your destination is the unsigned White Brook trailhead off the logging road, marked by some small boulders. In fifteen or twenty minutes of modest uphill walking on the road, about 1.25 miles, you will come to a gravel pit and a wide turn-around for logging trucks. Continue on, crossing three seasonal streambeds far too steep for a vehicle to negotiate. Depending on the season, you may go through marshy areas, but keep to the old logging road, which is sometimes very overgrown. Keep looking for the blue blazes on rocks or boulders. About 1.75 miles from your car, you will see a cairn of piled stones (but no sign) on the left indicating the entrance to White Brook Trail and soon verified by blue blazes on rocks and trees. You will have climbed roughly 500 feet at this point in pleasant fashion. Now the work begins.

The first part of the trail climbs through a former cutover area, with uncertain footing and often in knee-high grasses, until your route narrows and rises more steeply for about 0.5 mile to the headwaters of White Brook. There you have a very pretty glen, where you can splash your face with cold water before crossing on the wet rocks and ledge. Do be careful here, since the moss and wet ledge can be extremely slippery.

One Hundred Wild Miles

The Hundred-Mile Wilderness is a 100-mile section of the AT between Monson, Maine, and Baxter State Park and its Katahdin Peak, which marks the northern terminus of a trail that started some 2175 miles back at Springer Mountain in Georgia.

Hikers entering the trail outside Monson, see an AT sign that seeks to send a warning chill down their spine, saying that they're about to enter a multi-day trek that "crosses no road and offers no re-supply point along the trail." It's clear that the idea is to warn the long-distance hiker about the potential danger of not being prepared, but even we day hikers may get a shiver from the cautionary language.

In point of fact, there are ways of leaving the Wilderness area, but none of them is short or easy. To leave the AT from the White Cap area requires a hard hike out and scant chance of being able to summon help until you get to the KIW visitor center. Vehicle traffic on the rough logging road is sparse to nonexistent. You can't count on finding a party of campers in any of the High Bridge campsites—we've never seen any, even in high summer. Nor have we ever shared the logging road with any other vehicle. If something goes wrong, it's a long haul out, at least to the Silver Lake area where there are cabins, or beyond, to the KIW visitor center, which closes at 9:00 PM.

All of which means is that in this part of the Hundred-Mile Wilderness, you are pretty much on your own—which is precisely one of the reasons for doing the hike.

About 80 yards further steeply uphill (at 2088 ft.), you will come to a fork in the White Brook Trail. To the left, you can go another steep 0.4 mile to the intersection with the Appalachian Trail, which will deposit you 1.1 miles and 636 feet from the summit. Or you can shorten the ascent by taking the just-as-steep branch to the right, and a shorter 0.4 mile stretch on the AT to the summit. Given that both are hard but that one will ultimately be shorter, we prefer the trail to the right up a rough creek bed. Note that on most maps the east (right) fork is marked as less important. Having done both, we can testify that the east fork is no harder and maybe just a tiny bit easier than the west fork. Most importantly, it is ultimately shorter. We surmise that the west fork is primarily used by northbound hikers who wish to exit the AT and head for Katahdin Iron Works, some 10.75 miles from the two forks.

The hike up the White Brook Trail to the AT is by far the toughest part of this hike, since you climb almost 1100 ft. in a mile. About two-thirds of the way up, you will find that some thoughtful person has built a seat on a tree log that has fallen over the trail. The seat even has a backrest, so take advantage of it to catch your breath before continuing constantly up, up, and up! About five or six minutes before the junction with the AT, the trail flattens and there are fewer rocks. At the intersection with the AT, turn right for—at last!—a relatively easy 0.4 mile to the summit.

When you emerge from the woods, you will be on a broad, rocky area studded with stunted alpine trees and offering layer upon layer of mountain and lake views. There is also another side with views, indicated by an arrow painted on the ground with the word "View." Take this short path to the north side of the summit, where you'll have a super view onto Katahdin, surrounding peaks, and lakes. You'll probably be whipped by wind on this side but will find it exhilarating. For AT thru-hikers, it's good news to reach the summit of White Cap, because now Mt. Katahdin, their ultimate destination, is only a further 72.8 miles. For us, it was also good news, because it had taken us three attempts to finally reach the White Cap summit.

The first time we started the hike too late in the day, and the second time, the threat of lightning made it too risky to continue to the bare summit. The third time, on a superb, sunny day in the low 60s, with nary a cloud and no humidity, we finally made it! In terms of hiking time, we spent three hours and ten minutes on the trip out, including time for rest breaks and lunch; and two hours and forty-two minutes, with breaks, on the return.

For a long time we remained perplexed as to why we seemed to proceed so slowly on our second attempt, until we recalled the energy-depleting heat and humidity of the day and that we had to put on and take off rain gear several times during the return and even wait out some of the heavier showers while descending the rocky brook bed. (Trekking poles were absolutely necessary both for safety and to save knees.) Our hats off to the three AT thru-hikers

234

we saw that day who were not deterred by inclement weather even though, given the misty conditions of the day, they were not going to get the reward of great views from the summit.

For Photo Buffs

As you walk from your car up the logging road, be sure to shoot the view onto White Cap so that you can remind yourself later how benign the mountain looks. On the trail itself there is relatively little to record, although one time on the west fork of the White Brook Trail, in a pretty area of birches and ferns, we did see a neat pile of moose bones, tibia and skull, all picked clean! At the summit you'll have multiple layers of mountains to capture. Just make sure to have a polarizer to help deflect the haze and to enhance the sky. And, after the hike, as you exit the Park Road, stop at Silver Lake to shoot over the reeds growing in the lake to the far-off range of mountains, one of which you just conquered.

Moose bones on the White Cap trail, Hundred-Mile Wilderness

Wright-Goose Eye Loop (Mahoosucs)

From high up on Goose Eye Summit, there are magnificent views over the Mahoosuc Range, your reward for making the tough climb up the Wright Trail to where it intersects with the AT, and then down, down, down back to Goose Eye Brook.

Driving directions (DeLorme 10, A-2 and 3): On US-2, at 2.8 miles north of Bethel, turn onto Sunday River Road and set your odometer. You will be going 9.5 miles to the parking area. At 2.2 miles, Sunday River Road forks to the right (on the left is Skiway Road, which leads to the Sunday River ski complex). At 3.8 miles, you will see, on the left, the picturesque Artist's Covered Bridge. At 5.6 miles, you pass the Outward Bound Newry Mountain Center. The road turns to hard-packed dirt and gravel at 6.5 miles. At 7.8 miles, turn left across two closely spaced steel bridges, then immediately make the first right, passing by two old camps (cabins) close to the road. At 9.3 miles, cross Goose Eye Brook on a wooden bridge. In another two-tenths of a mile, you will see, on the left, the trailhead. The parking area is ahead on the right.
Total round-trip distance: 8.7 miles to East Peak of Goose Eye; 9.3 miles including West Peak.
Vertical rise: 2500-2586 ft.
Highest point: 3790 ft. to East Peak of Goose Eye Mountain; 3870 ft. to West Peak of Goose Eye Mountain.
Miscellaneous: No restroom or water at trailhead.
Map: AMC Maine, Map 7 Mahoosuc Range, C & D-2.

Description of the hike. As noted in our description for the Lower Wright Trail to the North-South Junction (Boomer Rating Three), the beginning of this trail was re-routed in 2008. Now when you enter the woods at the trailhead, you have two choices. The left choice leads to the water and some very pretty scenes with the waters of Goose Eye Brook spilling shallowly over a broad swath of ledge. This former route was often hard to follow, which may be one of the reasons why the trail was re-routed. The hike we describe takes the now-official path to the right.

The challenge and the payoff. Rated as one of the most strenuous trails in Maine, the Wright-Goose Eye Loop offers all the usual Maine impediments plus a frequently eroded trail that is all up or all down, all the time! When you add on rotting bog bridges and sometimes inadequate blazing, plus a vertical rise of 2500-plus feet, the challenge is yet more increased. But the lower trail is delightful along Goose Eye Brook, the tough sections are "genuine Maine," and the views from on high, looking in all directions to surrounding mountains—with far-off hikers on trails snaking up and down the open heaths—are really quite superb.

You will be above the Brook on a former road that has been trenched to allow runoff water from rain and melting snow to flow downhill. As you will shortly see, and as we have experienced, water on the trail ahead has created conditions leading to some serious erosion in places and may at times (after heavy rains) slow down your progress here and on the upper trail. Until the entire route to the Junction is improved, expect occasionally to find rotted bog bridges, broken boards sitting in mud, and a highly eroded footpath. Under dry conditions, you won't be unduly impeded, although you will still need to keep your head down to watch your footing, since the trail is often uneven and small stumps, hidden under fallen leaves, may be waiting to trip you.

About twenty minutes into the hike, you will see a blue blaze on the left and will turn down into the woods, descending some stone steps to a creek. Shortly, you will find a second set of stone steps to climb and a second creek crossing, and within a half-hour, a third crossing of the brook, followed by some wooden steps leading up.

After 2.5 miles of hiking, you will arrive at a tent site on the right, and shortly thereafter at the North-South Junction. This is an especially nice spot to take a breather or have a power snack, because there are a couple of well-placed logs on which to sit, and from your perch you have a nice view of the rocky glen, with water moving over moss-covered ledge and a small waterfall tumbling into the shallow pool.

It's after this point that the heavy lifting begins—meaning the substantial climbing challenge. You now have a choice between two branches of the Wright Trail leading to the Mahoosuc Trail and the two peaks of Goose Eye Mountain. The South Branch, on the left, is 1.9 miles long, while the shorter and steeper 1.5-mile North Branch departs from the right. We've done them both and can attest that both of them are hard. There is just no way around the fact that you're going to deal with all those many tightly packed topographical contour lines as you make the ascent. What's more, the footpath is often rough, wet, and encumbered by roots and rocks and is sometimes even overgrown in summer.

Looking back, we see that we have usually opted to begin by the South Fork, probably because there is a tough pitch at the top of the North Branch for a short person. We've often lost a lot of time at that pitch, trying to figure out how to negotiate it, and have usually had to skirt the rise of rock on a steeply slanted slope tightly packed with bushy Maine "hedgerow" in order to reach the top.

Oh, Those Names

Why is it called Goose Eye? Because there are two summits, an east and west peak, hence two eyes? Or because, as the mountain is viewed from Success Pond Road, the protruding nubble on the top may kinda look like a bulging eye?

Accordingly, we'll describe the South Fork route and return by North Branch. Going left from the Junction, cross Goose Eye Brook and begin your ascent. The first 0.6 mile proceeds from a gradual to a moderate climb by switchbacks, with tough patches and wooden steps, leading to the ridge crest. The next 0.3 mile makes for a rough ascent, coming to an open spot and then descending slightly into the woods. This is followed by 0.2 mile of stiff ascent on the ledges to an open knob with great views. There are several tough rocky areas to ascend. In the next 0.8 mile, you will be along the ridge, with open areas, and descents to cross sags before climbing moderately to the Mahoosuc Trail in the small gap between East and West peaks of Goose Eye. Follow the Mahoosuc Trail westward for 0.3 mile to access the main summit.

When you've reached the highest point at 3790 feet, you may be, as we were, wiped out, so kick back and enjoy the marvelous views—you've earned them! On a beautiful sunny day in the low 70s, we could hardly believe our luck at having the mountain, or rather, mountains, all to ourselves. In the far distance, we could make out the tiny figures of hikers along both the Mahoosuc and the Goose Eye trails, and earlier we had met a group of Outward Bounders who were ending their overnight outing after having been caught in thunder and rain the night before. But our day at the summit was just perfect.

To return by the North Branch of the Wright trail, you will descend the sag for 0.3 mile, then, in the col, turn northeast (left) on the Mahoosuc Trail for another 0.3 mile and some steep rock ascents, leading to East peak. As you descend the area of East peak, you will re-access the north branch of the Wright Trail, which cuts off from the Mahoosuc Trail in an eastward direction. You now have 1.5 steep miles to descend, so take it easy on your shaky legs. In many places, the rock ledge goes straight down, but in recent years improvements have resulted in the construction of rock steps, chiseled footholds on ledge, and wooden ladders. One particular "beauty spot" about halfway down to the Junction is a wide ledge with running water and beautiful views across the forest to far-off mountains. Subsequently, there are many spots where the trail is badly eroded. Note particularly that, when wet, both ledge and roots are slippery so you'll be using your leg muscles to brake more often.

By the time you reach the North-South Junction, you will probably need to take a real rest before completing the remaining 2.5 miles back to your car. Typically, it's taken us eight-and-a-half hours to complete the loop—in other words, a pretty long day of hiking—though it has taken as much as an hour longer when the trail is wet. Which means that if you can't get an early start, you may not have time to finish the hike, because you certainly don't want to have to do this one by headlamp! Our "time" is about two hours longer than what another source suggests the trip should take, but of course ours includes lunch, rest stops, photographing, and *enjoyment.*

Different Access

There is another way of doing the Goose Eye Trail from Success Pond Road, accessed either from Maine (see driving directions for Success Mountain hike) or from Berlin, New Hampshire (see driving directions for Speck Pond hike). It can be done as an out-and-back of 6.4 miles, or can be part of the 7.7 mile loop for Carlo Col and Mt. Carlo (3565 ft.) to the west peak of Goose Eye Mountain (3790 ft.). For the latter, see Featured Hike, Carlo-Goose Eye Loop, in this section.

Other Hikes
Boomer Rating Five

Barren Mountain, Hundred-Mile Wilderness (DeLorme 41, D-5)
The last peak in the Hundred-Mile Wilderness, Barren Mountain makes for an unusual hike, beginning with a ford across Long Pond Stream using an overhead rope. Roll up your trousers at least to knee-level, because the rapid water is deep and has both slippery rocks and a couple of foot-deep sink holes. Don't try this barefoot; you need shoes on your feet to cross safely. Also, only one person at a time should be on the rope, since the second person might wobble the first off his or her footing. When you emerge from the stream on the other side, you'll be climbing through a nice forest. In about 3.25 miles (depending on where you had to leave your car) and a vertical rise of nearly 1500 feet, you'll arrive at the Barren Ledges with great views across Onawa Lake over to Borestone Mountain. If time is short, this is an appropriate turn-around point. Of course, you can also continue for 1.8 miles to the summit of Barren (2671 ft.), first doing about 0.5 mile of flattish walking, followed by a steep ascent, over boulders, of nearly 670 feet in 1.3 miles.
Round-trip distance: 6.5 miles to Barren Ledge; 10.1 miles to Barren summit.
Vertical rise: 1375 ft., Barren Ledges; 2046 ft., Barren summit.
Map: AT in Maine, Map 3 West Branch of the Pleasant River to Monson (Barren-Chairback Range, Wilson Valley Area).

NB: To get to the trailhead requires a twelve-mile drive on a rutted and often flooded road. Take care, because it's hard to know how deep the water is, or whether it hides rocks that could damage the underside of your car. We ourselves got our car stuck in the mud one October day, and were rescued by an unlikely pair: a couple of can-do Tennesseans, flying the Confederate flag at their backwoods cabin, who chained up our Honda Civic to their truck and literally sucked it out of the mud stew. Sheepishly, we gratefully had to recognize that sometimes politics isn't everything.

View onto Onawa Lake from Barren Ledges

Fire Wardens Trail, Bigelows (DeLorme 29, C-4)
While the Fire Wardens Trail is a ridiculously steep ascent up an excessively rugged stretch of 1.2 miles that rises 1500 feet, it will definitely prove that you still "have it." Plus, it is the shortest, if most super-demanding, way up to some excellent views from West and Avery peaks. Just don't add to the challenge by choosing a sticky, humid day!

You can easily be beguiled at the start of this hike, because you'll be coming from the beautiful Stratton Brook Pond outlet area (see the Featured Hike, Horns Pond, in Boomer Rating Four), 0.4 mile from where you left your car and then a pleasant 1.7 miles to the cut-off. Here you go left for access to the Horns and to West and Avery peaks by the Horns Pond Trail, but for the Fire Warden's trail, stay straight for the Avery/Bigelow Col, which is a tough 2.3 miles further. In a little over two miles, you'll be climbing 2200 feet, with the hardest part coming after the Moose Falls tent site (located 1.3 miles from the junction). To get to the tent site, you will have climbed about 700 feet, but there are still 1500 feet to go in the last mile or so before you reach the Col. The extreme steepness begins soon after you pass the campsite's privy, when the broad path narrows to an overgrown rut and the trail rises, often over boulders, in an intensely rugged and steep ascent before junctioning with the AT trail at 3900 feet. And they call this "hiking"??? One-third of a mile to the west, you hit West Peak (4145 ft.) and one-quarter mile to the east is Avery (4088 ft.). If you do this hike, you deserve major kudos!

Round-trip: approximately 8.8 miles to the Col, plus 1.4 miles to and from both peaks.

Vertical rise: 2445 ft., much of it concentrated in a two-mile stretch.

Map: AMC Maine, Map 2 Rangeley/Stratton Region, B-3.

Climbing Katahdin on the Hunt Spur

Katahdin, by the Hunt Trail, Baxter State Park (DeLorme, 50, D-5) You can't live in Maine without hiking Katahdin at least once, for there is nothing in the state to compare with the climb up this mile-high mountain. The further you ascend, the more impressive become the views of the expansive and pristine wilderness of 204,733-acre Baxter State Park. At the end of the 5.2-mile climb to the summit, you'll likely be in the company of dozens of others, many of whom are AT thru-hikers celebrating their achievement of having walked 2175 miles from Springer, Georgia. In comparison, our "celebration" was more like grateful if temporary relief for our overtaxed nervous systems, severely challenged by the nearly mile-long Hunt Spur. Some will tell you that a "spur" is "a minor summit projecting from a larger one," a very anodyne definition, which to acrophobes like us doesn't even begin to capture the real experience of dealing with this very, very scary geologic phenomenon.

"Is this hiking or rock climbing?" Hunt Spur, Katahdin

We could go on and on about how unforgettable our experience was but will confine ourselves to giving you the hike in a nutshell.

From Katahdin Stream Campground, the trail goes one mile before hitting, on the left, the junction for the Owl Trail, which you ignore. At 1.1 mile, a bridge crosses beautiful Katahdin Stream. Continue climbing another 1.7 miles (you are now 2.8 miles from the campground) to reach the treeline at the base of the boulders on the Spur. For the next 0.8 mile, you ascend the section called the Boulders, sometimes with the help of iron rungs that leave you spread-eagled in order to get the "purchase" to vault yourself up several more scary feet. Acrophobes will be battling their fear until they reach the top, called the Gateway—finally, terra firma—1.6 miles from the summit. You'll hike past Thoreau Spring through the Tableland, a virtual piece of cake, considering what you've just been through. At the summit, 5267 feet up, you'll gulp at the view of the Knife Edge to the southeast and mix with the thru-hikers to jostle for a spot next to the summit sign for the requisite picture-taking. Then, hoist your backpack and face the trek back through the Spur, knowing that your acrophobic authors, at least, found the descent marginally less frightening—and that, on a clear-weather day, everyone will come off the mountain with the most amazing photographs and memories for a lifetime.

Round-trip: 10.4 miles.
Vertical rise: 4168 ft.
Map: AMC Maine, Map 1 Baxter State Park/Katahdin, D-2.

Old Speck, Grafton Notch (DeLorme 18, E-1).
If you haven't had your fill of challenge, you can always do Old Speck out in the marvelous Mahoosucs, where "steep" is the rule for all trails. Though we've done it, we personally prefer to gaze upon Old Speck from other trails, including the Speck Pond trail (see our Featured Hike) and the Mahoosuc Arm (plenty hard in its own right), but if you want to boast having wrestled with the mountain on its own terms, you can access the Old Speck trail from ME-26 (the same parking lot as for Featured Hike, The Eyebrow).

Since Old Speck is Maine's third highest mountain at 4180 feet (edged out by Sugarloaf at 4237 ft.), and since the trail you'll be following is the former Fire Warden's, you know what that means: *straight up*. Accordingly, you'll be achieving another notch on your hiking belt. But do be forewarned that the views from the summit, unless you climb the fire tower, are not really fantastic, and that the relentlessly steep downward trail will jelly your legs for sure. Still, the woods are great, and if you use those hiking poles that we recommend, you'll be greatly aided in moving—or hobbling—down the mountain.

Round-trip mileage: 7.75 miles.
Vertical rise: 2730 ft.
Map: AMC Maine, Map 7 Mahoosuc Range, C-3.

Saddleback, Rangeley (DeLorme 19, A-1 & 29, E-1 & 2)
This is a great classic Maine hike of tremendous variety to a summit standing at 4116 feet, which seems intent on fooling you with a large number of "false" summits as you climb ledge after ledge. But know, too, that it's worth it!

You begin from the same point as for our Featured Hike to Piazza Rock. After the 1.8 mile trek to Piazza Rock campsite, you will carry on for 3.9 miles more, passing first Ethel Pond and then Eddy Pond, on a trail with rocks and roots but also sometimes a level footpath of pine needles. After crossing an ATV road, the hike becomes more demanding, although in recent years, trail maintainers have made a number of improvements, with iron rungs set into the ledge so that you no longer have to pull yourself up by tree limbs. Follow rock cairns along the beautiful, mile-long, open crest to the summit—not the place to be during inclement weather, but glorious on a clear, sunny day in the low 70s. This hike is definitely an all-day affair and you'll feel it in your bones, for sure, but it's also splendid.
Round-trip mileage: 11.4 miles.
Vertical rise: 2900 ft.
Map: AMC Maine, Map 2 Rangeley/Stratton Region, D & E-2.

Sugarloaf, Carrabassett Valley (DeLorme 29, D-4)
Downhill skiers want the thrill of a steep mountain, something that Sugarloaf (4250 ft.) amply provides. What this means to hikers is pretty obvious to you by this time. But we'd also like to tell you that this is a very nice hike over a surprising variety of terrains. On a sunny, humidity-free day, like we had one summer day, you'll find the hike to Sugarloaf a rewarding outing, both in terms of cardiovascular workout and in the variety of scenery and number of peaks viewed from the summit.

From the directions below, you will be taking the AT westward, from the left side of the road. You will quickly come to the south branch of the Carrabassett River, which you will cross (sometimes dangerously high, at other times no more than a brook), then encounter steepness, boulders to climb over and through, and finally a stretch of nice ridge-walking with great views. After 2.3 miles, you come to a junction with the Sugarloaf summit side trail. Turn left into the forest, leaving the AT, which continues to the right or southward. Follow the blue-blazed side trail for the last 0.5 mile of considerable steepness alongside a chair-lift, to arrive at the summit with its microwave tower. Since you will be ascending nearly 2500 feet in three miles, the steepness is a constant, but the variety of views makes it worthwhile. So do try it. We think you'll like it!

Round-trip: 6 miles.
Vertical rise: nearly 2500 ft.
Map: AMC Maine, Map 2 Rangeley/Stratton Region, C-3.
Directions to trailhead: Traveling westward on ME-16/27, almost a mile past the main entrance road to the Sugarloaf ski area, turn left onto the dirt-surfaced Caribou Valley Road. (This intersection bears the place-name, "Bigelow," on DeLorme 29.) Follow this road for about 4.5 miles to its crossing with the AT. There are a limited number of parking spaces.

West and Avery, Bigelows (DeLorme 29, C-4)
This is a wonderful hike in the beautiful Bigelow Preserve, a favorite area of ours. You start out in the same way as for several other hikes in this book, including featured ones to Horns Pond (Boomer Rating Four) and to Cranberry Pond (Boomer Rating Three) as well as the infamous Fire Warden's Trail (see above).

After crossing the Stratton Brook Pond outlet, follow the lower Fire Warden's trail 1.7 miles to the cutoff for the Horns Pond Trail. Turn left and climb 2.5 miles to the Horns campground where you will pick up the AT route eastward to West and Avery peaks. West, which is 0.8 mile from the campground, stands at 4150 feet, while Avery, at 4088 feet, is 0.3 mile further. The views from both onto the long expanses of Flagstaff Lake and the surrounding area are truly superb. On one of our hikes, on a very windy and troubled mid-October day at the summits, we were struck by how the late-afternoon sun cast glistening rays through the clouds like star rays from a camera's lens. Together with the wind that threatened to whip us off our feet, it was a real study in a high-drama landscape.

For the return—but only if you have better knees than we do—you can descend by the Fire Warden's trail for three miles back to the Horns Pond Trail cut-off, but you're going to have to deal with a stretch that drops a terrible 1500 feet in 1.2 miles.—Which is why we recommend returning the same way you came for a less rugged conclusion to a beautiful hike.

Round-trip mileage: 11 miles.
Vertical rise: 2850 ft.
Map: AMC Maine, Map 2 Rangeley/Stratton Region, A-3.

From West to Avery in the Bigelow range

Bonus
Good Places for Snowshoe Jaunts

While we know that some people snowshoe just about anywhere they can walk or climb, unless you're particularly daring, you probably will prefer snowshoeing in areas where there is not much vertical rise. With this in mind, we suggest the following places, nearly all of which figure in this book as regular hikes or walks.

Bald Mountain, Lincolnville
Cranberry Pond, Bigelows
Fernald's Neck, Camden
Deer Hill (lower portion), Evans Notch
Gott Pasture Preserve, Wayne
Jamies Pond, Hallowell/Manchester
Monument Hill, Leeds
"The Mountain," Rome
Northern Headwaters Trail, Freedom, Sheepscot Wellspring
Porter Pond Preserve, Fayette
Sabbath Day Pond/Shelter (entering from ME-17, south of AT Sabbath Day Trail)
Sanders Hill, Kennebec Highlands
Schoodic Peninsula
South Baldface, White Mountains
Spruce Mountain, Georges Highland Path
Vaughan Woods, Hallowell

Lower Deer Hill area, Evans Notch

Appendices

Map Recommendations

1. Two of our favorite maps for Maine trails are published by the Appalachian Mountain Club. Excellent maps, they show contour lines and mileages by trail segment, which we find extremely helpful. Each 18" x 24" map folds into a handy pocket size and is printed on both sides. One map gives you sub-maps for Baxter and Katahdin on one side, and Rangeley/Stratton and Gulf Hagas on the other side. The second folding map is divided into five areas, with sub-maps for Camden Hills, Pleasant Mountain, and the Weld Region on one side; and Evans Notch and the Mahoosuc Range on the reverse side. We strongly recommend obtaining both these maps with their eight sub-maps, which cover a large number of the hikes described in this volume.

Appalachian Mountain Club: Maine
Map 1: Baxter State Park/Katahdin
Map 2: Rangeley/Stratton Region
Map 3: Gulf Hagas
Map 4: Camden Hills
Map 5: Pleasant Mountain
Map 6: Weld Region
Map 7: Mahoosuc Range
Map 8: Evans Notch

Example of listing: **AMC Maine, Map 6 Weld Region, C-3** (for instance, for Blueberry Mountain hike)

NB: In this book, we identify a recommended map for each *Featured Hike* at the end of the initial section that starts with "Driving directions." In the section, *Other Hikes* for Boomer Ratings Three, Four, and Five, the recommended map is given below the description of the hike.

2. Another useful map put out by the **Appalachian Mountain Club** combines Evans Notch and the Mahoosucs in one, two-sided map, again with detailed and easy-to-read trail information:

Map 5: Carter Range - Evans Notch
Map 6: North Country - Mahoosuc
Listed as: **AMC White Mtns. NH & Maine, Map 6 C-13** (for instance, for Wright/Goose Eye hike)

3. The **Appalachian Trail in Maine series** of seven maps, the "bible" of AT thru-hikers, gives topographic and profile maps on one side and trail descriptions and mileage between points, on the other. For the non-thru-hiker, it's the profile map that is particularly eye-popping, since it shows oh-so-graphically how steep a trail is.
Listed as: **AT in Maine, Map 6, Maine Highway 27 to Maine Highway 17** (for instance, for Sabbath Day Pond hike)

4. For Acadia National Park, the single map we strongly recommend is a large format (19" x 27") map that folds to 4" x 9" called "Acadia National Park: Trails, Carriage Roads, Hiking, Biking," published by Map Adventures LLC, www.mapadventures.com and available in Park stores. It's wonderfully legible and includes contour lines and trail segments marked by mileage. One side includes the trails for West Side Acadia and the other East Side Acadia. Definitely get it, since on occasion you may have to detour off a trail where protected birds are nesting, or (like us) you didn't pay sufficient attention and end up taking a wrong turn away from your intended trail.
Listed as: **Acadia NP, West Side, H & I-7** (for Acadia and St Sauveur hike)

5. As a last resort, we sometimes list USGS quad maps when the above do not include a trail, as, for instance, with Big Moose Mountain.
Listed as: **USGS 15' Greenville**

6. Miscellaneous other maps, for land trusts and so forth, are often available at the trailhead or perhaps at the Land Trust Web site.

A Caveat about Trail Signs and Hiking Guidebooks

√   Sometimes you will note that your sources do not agree on how long a trail is or on the length of its constituent parts. Usually, the differences are within a few tenths of a mile, but sometimes there are more significant mistakes. So have your own map from a reliable source to verify things for yourself. And carry and know how to use a compass.

√   Another reason for a map: on occasion you may inadvertently wander away from your intended trail, or miss a turn, or become confused by the presence of too many cairns, as can be the case in Acadia National Park. In those cases, it will save you a great deal of grief if you have a map of the *larger area* in your pocket to ascertain where you are and how best to get back to your car. Our rule of thumb: don't leave the car without a trail map of the *broader* area!

A Lighthearted Glossary

AT - The reference is to the 2175-mile Appalachian Trail, extending from Katahdin (5267 ft.) in Maine's Baxter State Park to Georgia's Springer Mountain (3782 ft.).

baby boomer - An elastic term, generally referring to people born between 1946 and 1964.

blaze - Painted slashes on trees: white for AT trails, blue for many Maine trails. A double blaze means "Pay Attention!" because the trail is about to change direction.

boundary monitor (AT) - A volunteer with the AT who hikes the boundary of the trail to make sure that no illegal incursions have occurred. Same thing as *corridor monitor*.

bushwhack - Hiking off-trail through bushes, brambles, grasses, and fallen timber and using a compass and GPS readings to find your way.

cairn - That pile of stones indicating the trail's route. Please don't remove or make your own!

caretaker (AT) - The person charged with overseeing a portion of the trail or camping site, such as at Horns Pond, who lives for weeks in the summer in a platform tent.

cirque - Upper end of the valley with a half-bowl shape. There's a great example on the Wright-Goose Eye Loop, on the Wright side, North Branch trail.

col - When you read *col*, understand that what it means in "real time" is that you'll go down before having to go up again. It's the low point between two mountains.

corridor monitor (AT) - See *boundary monitor*.

environmental monitor (AT) - Person charged with measuring air and water quality on the trail and recording and monitoring evidence of wildlife.

flip-flopper (AT) - Not a politician, but an Appalachian section-hiker who does portions of the trail out of sequence.

flume - For one of us, it sounds like a dessert, but it's actually a narrow gorge with a stream running through it.

gaiters - Not the Florida reptile kind (spelled with an "o" and without the "i"), but the 12-inch low leggings that slip over your boots and keep the mud and grit out of your shoes.

GPS - Global Positioning System, available in a variety of sizes and prices. A GPS unit has the virtue of letting you gauge your location, within a small margin of error, when using appropriate maps. It can provide a "bread-crumb trail" and give your altitude but may not work very well in a thick forest.

heritage monitor (AT) - The person charged with monitoring and protecting the many historic cultural sites along the Trail.

hiking poles - We're still occasionally asked why we hike with "ski poles" and if they really help. The answer is that they are not the skier's poles, but, rather, spring-loaded, adjustable length *hiking* pole and they *do* help. Some folks use walking sticks, despite the fact that they are neither spring-loaded nor adjustable, but we swear by our Leki poles. Also known as *trekking poles*.

ibuprofen - The tiny pill that packs a wallop, reducing inflammation of the joints.

krummholz - It ought to be a cookie but in fact refers to the stunted trees that grow just above the timberline.

land trust - Land purchased by individuals who form a trust to protect and conserve the natural environment and provide use of it to the public.

lean-to - A simple, three-sided dwelling, found in the woods. *Not* an outhouse, which is usually four-sided, with a hook-latching door. In the Maine woods, an example of the latter even has a name: "Your Move."

leave-no-trace ethic - The philosophy that comes down to: "Bring it in, take it out," whether *it* be gum wrappers, tab openers, toilet paper, used matches, or whatever!

ledge - Although for many people, ledge means a shelf of rock, in the Northeast hiking community, *ledge* refers to any large area of flat or sloping rock.

long-distance hiker - Those who are out for the long haul over days or weeks or months. Thru-hikers on the AT are long-distance hikers, as are those who take the Pacific Crest Trail and the Continental Divide Trail.

loop hike - You don't retrace your steps on this hike, so get double the views. A loop hike is sometimes shorter than an out-and-back hike.

maintainer (AT) - These volunteers cut the brush, wield saws, and paint the blazes. We couldn't do without them!

MATC - Acronym for Maine Appalachian Trail Club.

multi-use land - A new concept in land use, with varying consequences. Private landowners grant rights to hikers but also to loggers, hunters, and trappers.

out-and-back hike - In contra-distinction to a loop hike, on this kind, you come back by the same route as for your out-trip.

personal locator beacon (PLB) - This instrument costs a bundle, but can be a lifesaver because it radioes your exact location. It should be used only when a person in distress is incommunicado with normal emergency services, like 911. Aaron Ralston, the guy hiking in Utah who cut off his hand in order to free himself from a boulder that wouldn't budge, wished he'd had one of these.

potable - This means drinkable water, of which you won't find any in nature, these days. Use a purifier or iodine (drops or tablets) when you collect water from creeks or streams, no matter how clear the water looks.

ridgerunner (AT) - Similar to a roadrunner of the American Southwest, but 1) is not a bird, and 2) runs ridges and not the road. Seriously, it's a person who hikes along high-use trails to educate hikers about using the outdoors with minimum impact. In short, the roadrunner belongs to the cuckoo family, while the ridgerunner is a human biped who loves the outdoors.

saddle - From a distance, this flattish, low ridge that connects two mountains looks like the thing you put on horse. Think, Saddleback Mountain ("Other Hikes," Boomer Rating Five).

scrub - A noun, not a verb, and of the plant variety, referring to low trees near the treeline.

segment hiker (AT) - Thru-hikers who don't have a stretch of four to nine months to devote to hiking the entire AT, so opt for completing it, segment by segment, sometimes over several years.

spur trail - Trails off the main trail, sometimes leading to a view point, but always adding more length. Our recommendation is to do them on the return trip because you may need to conserve energy for the summit.

switchback - Think of them like zigzags up a mountain, intended to make the vertical ascent more gradual. The down-side is that since it's not the shortest way between two points, they'll make your hike longer. Trails in the American West usually incorporate switchbacks, while most in the East get their "kicks" out of sending you straight up a mountain.

tarn - From the Scandinavian, referring to a small mountain lake or pool. Generally means "beautiful."

technical climb - To scale especially steep sections, climbers use ropes, carabiners, and other specialized equipment. We don't describe any of these!

tent platform - A raised, wooden "stage" on which to plant your tent; intended to protect the ground beneath from erosion.

thru-hiker (AT) - Admirable beings. Same thing as long-distance hiker.

trailhead - Where the trail begins, and what you're dying to get back to after an arduous hike.

trail register - A sign-in, useful to maintainers charged with knowing how many people are using a given trail.

treeline - No more trees; they can't make it beyond this altitude.

trekking poles - Just a fancy way of referring to hiking poles. See above.

wagbags - Not yet adopted in Maine, these human waste management bags (WAG for Waste Alleviation and Gelling) are required out West in the John Muir Wilderness and at Mt. Whitney and the Grand Canyon. A part of the leave-no-trace and pack-it-out ethic, the wagbag is a double plastic bag with a powder that turns into a gel and encapsulates anything in the bag when water is added.

Hike Locator

For page references to each hike, check the Table of Contents according to the Boomer Rating marked in parentheses below. Note that some of the hikes may be listed in the "Other Hikes" section of the appropriate rating.

Acadia National Park, West Side
Acadia and St. Sauveur Loop (BR4)
Bernard Mountain by Great Pond (BR4)
Great Pond to Great Notch (BR3)
Little Harbor Brook (BR3)
Valley Trail to Beech Mountain (BR3)

Acadia National Park, East Side
Acadia Gardens (BR1)
The Bowl and Champlain (BR4)
Cadillac by South Ridge (BR 3)
Sargent and Penobscot (BR4)
Thuya Gardens to Jordan Pond House (BR3)

Schoodic Peninsula hikes on the mainland one hour from Bar Harbor (BR3)

Northeast of Acadia National Park and east of Ellsworth in East Franklin
Schoodic Mountain (BR3)

Baxter State Park
Doubletop (BR4)
Katahdin (BR5)
Little and Big Niagara Falls (BR3)
Sentinel Mountain (BR3)

Bigelow Mountain Range
Cranberry Pond (BR3)
Fire Wardens Trail (BR5)
Horns Pond (BR4)
Piazza Rock (BR2)
Sabbath Day Pond (BR3)
Saddleback Mountain (BR5)
West and Avery (BR5)

Central Maine
Bog Brook Trail (BR2)
French Mountain (BR2)
Frye Mountain (BR3)
Gott Pasture Preserve Loop (BR1)
Hogback Mountain (BR3)
Jamies Pond (BR2)
Monument Hill (BR1)
"The Mountain," (BR1)
Northern Headwaters (BR3)
Parker Pond Headland Preserve (BR1)
Round Top (BR2)
Sanders Hill (BR2)
Spruce Mountain (BR2)
Vaughan Woods (BR1)

Coastal Maine
Bald Rock, Lincolnville (BR3)
Fernald's Neck Preserve, Camden (BR2)
Ovens Mouth Preserve Trails, Boothbay Region Land Trust (BR2)
Porter Preserve, Barters Island, Boothbay Harbor (BR1)

Greenville Area
B-52 Crash Site, Elephant Mountain (BR1)
Big Moose Mountain (BR4)

Hundred-Mile Wilderness
Barren Mountain (BR5)
Borestone Mountain (BR3)
Chairback (BR4)
Little Wilson Falls (BR3)
White Cap Mountain (BR5)

Katahdin Ironworks Area
Chairback (BR4)
Gulf Hagas (BR5)
White Cap (BR5)

Western Maine
Andover:
Surplus Pond (BR3)

Evans Notch:
Caribou Mountain (BR4)
Oxford Hills/Evan Notch: Bald and Speckled Mountains (BR4)

Fryeburg: Jockey Cap (BR1)

Grafton Notch:
Baldpate Peaks (BR5)
Eyebrow (BR4)
Old Speck (BR5)
Puzzle Mountain (BR5)
Table Rock (BR3)

Mahoosuc Mountain Range:
Baldpate Peaks (BR5)
Carlo-Goose Eye Loop (BR5)
Dunn Notch and Falls (BR2)
Lower Wright Trail to North-South Junction (BR3)
Mahoosuc Notch (feeder trail to Notch) (BR3)
Speck Pond (BR5)
Success Mountain (BR4)
Wright-Goose Eye Loop (BR5)

Phillips/Andover:
Lone Mountain (BR4)
Lower Lone Mountain (BR3)
Surplus Pond (BR3)

Rangeley area:
Bemis Mountain (BR4)
Sabbath Day Pond (BR3)

Rumford Center:
Rumford Whitecap (BR4)

Stratton area:
Cranberry Pond (BR3)
Fire Wardens Trail (BR5)
Horns Pond (BR4)
North Crocker Mountain (BR4)
Piazza Rock (BR2)
Saddleback Mountain (BR5)

Sugarloaf area:
Burnt Mountain (BR4)
Sugarloaf Mountain (BR4)

Weld:
Blueberry Mountain (BR4)
Little Jackson (BR5)
Tumbledown Mountain (BR4)

York Pond Road/Success Pond Road:
Carlo-Goose Eye Loop (BR5)
Mahoosuc Notch feeder trail (BR3)
Speck Pond (BR4)
Success Mountain (BR4)

About the Authors

Suellen Diaconoff's roots in Maine go back to the eighteenth century and a great-great-great grandfather who was one of the founders of China, Maine. After growing up in Oregon and living throughout the States and abroad, she had a twenty-year teaching career at Colby College in Maine. As a Boomer (post-Boomer, really), she discovered hiking on the rugged trails of Maine, against which she compares all others. She holds a Ph.D. in French from Indiana University and has published several books and many articles on literature, as well as an essay on hiking in Morocco.

Peter Diaconoff also claims New England ties, having been born in New Hampshire. He grew up in California. His love of nature and commitment to Maine trails have been demonstrated by his volunteer activity as both a Maintainer and a Corridor Monitor of the Appalachian Trail and participation in grant development initiatives for the AT. His professional activities in Maine included newspaper journalist and editor, teacher, and technical writer, as well as employment with L.L. Bean. Peter holds a Ph.D. in political science from Indiana University.

Since discovering their passion for hiking during their twenty-year residence in Maine and in their Boomer years, the authors have backpacked and hiked in nearly all the national parks of the American West and Southwest, as well as in Canada, Europe, and North Africa. Upon retirement, they moved to Santa Fe to learn about the challenges of hiking in the high desert. Their hearts, however, remain on Maine trails.

The Authors at Katahdin summit